CRITICAL ESSAYS ON GEORGE ELIOT

CONTRIBUTORS

Derek and Sybil Oldfield, University of Sussex.

John Goode, University of Reading.

Barbara Hardy, Professor of English, Royal Holloway College, University of London.

Lilian Haddakin, University College, London.

George Levine, Professor of English, University of Indiana.

Arnold Kettle, University of Leeds.

Isobel Armstrong, University College, London.

Graham Martin, Bedford College, London.

W. J. Harvey, formerly Professor of English, Queen's University of Belfast.

John Bayley, New College, Oxford.

CRITICAL ESSAYS
ON
GEORGE ELIOT

Edited by

BARBARA HARDY

NEW YORK
BARNES & NOBLE, INC.

First published in Great Britain 1970
Published in the United States of America 1970
by Barnes & Noble, Inc., New York, N.Y. 10003
© *Routledge & Kegan Paul Ltd. 1970*
SBN 389–01085–5

Printed in Great Britain

CONTENTS

INTRODUCTION *Barbara Hardy*   *page vii*

I   'SCENES OF CLERICAL LIFE': THE DIAGRAM AND THE PICTURE
    Derek and Sybil Oldfield   I

II   'ADAM BEDE' *John Goode*   19

III   'THE MILL ON THE FLOSS' *Barbara Hardy*   42

IV   'SILAS MARNER' *Lilian Haddakin*   59

V   'ROMOLA' AS FABLE *George Levine*   78

VI   'FELIX HOLT THE RADICAL' *Arnold Kettle*   99

VII   'MIDDLEMARCH': A NOTE ON GEORGE ELIOT'S 'WISDOM'
    Isobel Armstrong   116

VIII   'DANIEL DERONDA': GEORGE ELIOT AND POLITICAL CHANGE
    Graham Martin   133

IX   IDEA AND IMAGE IN THE NOVELS OF GEORGE ELIOT
    W. J. Harvey   151

X   THE PASTORAL OF INTELLECT *John Bayley*   199

INDEX   215

INTRODUCTION
Barbara Hardy

THIS IS a collection of fresh evaluations of George Eliot's novels by a group of critics with some knowledge of one another's work and a special interest in George Eliot, in the Victorian period, and in the aesthetics of fiction. The book consists of essays on the individual tales and novels, with two general essays by W. J. Harvey and John Bayley which discuss the novels as a whole and cut across the individual works.

I had not originally thought of the book as so consistently concerned with evaluation, but there is perhaps a greater significance in a unified image which has not, so to speak, been commissioned, and there is no doubt that these essays might have composed a mere miscellany, but are in the event unified by the common pursuit of judgment. And the wisdom of hindsight is quick to see the inevitability of what it never foresaw. It is indeed tempting, and I think true, to say that a prime characteristic of this moment in the criticism of fiction – taking 'moment' rather lavishly, to cover several years – is a free, searching, and fundamental process of evaluation. This is not to say that evaluation of George Eliot has been hard to seek. From contemporary reviews up to F. R. Leavis's *The Great Tradition*, critics have canvassed and discussed the merits and defects of this great novelist. But since *The Great Tradition*, critics of George Eliot have been rather more occupied with doing something else. They have given their minds to an analysis of her art as a novelist, for the very good reason that such analysis had not really been very prominent before the mid-fifties, though Dr. Leavis must be excepted from this generalization, since his discussion, though not exactly what I should call sustained in practical criticism, did have much to say about details of craft, language, and notation, and grounded its judgment on examined details of evidence as well as on assumptions about the maturity and externalizing powers of the highest art.

But technical and aesthetic criticism of George Eliot had been very much less in evidence than, say, in the criticism of Dickens or Henry James or Conrad. During the last ten years or so critics have worked hard to make up for this neglect, and we have seen a thorough – some would say an excessive – elucidation and description of her themes and their forms. I would not want to suggest that such analysis and elucidation is now complete, nor would I agree that it has been excessively reductive and abstract. The New Criticism has been tempted into more excesses of over-interpretation and abstraction in the case of Dickens than in the case of George Eliot, and I hope I shall not be misunderstood when I point out that George Eliot criticism lacks both its Edmund Wilson and its Hillis Miller. Her art is at once too realistically humane and too intellectually analytic to make it good material for the creative activity of interpretative critics, whether their interests are psychological, philosophical, or technical.

W. J. Harvey's essay is evidence that there is still more to say about the forms and expression of the novels, and it is typically marked by a questioning scrutiny of current interest both in imagery and ideas, and typically concerned, too, with the relation between criticism and scholarship of a narrower and more factual kind. In all the essays there is a good deal of concern with the novelist's art, and, picking almost at random, I would instance the concern with character which runs through the collection, and which is usually raising both the questions made conspicuous by Dr. Leavis – questions of concrete reality and felt life – and questions of necessary stylization and historical realism. Lilian Haddakin – briefly but firmly – makes an interesting new defence of the 'cosiness' and sweetness of *Silas Marner*, and her account of this story has implications for other Victorian novels as well as for the other works of George Eliot. Isobel Armstrong makes a new defence of the wisdom of the author's voice in *Middlemarch*, which is totally free from the dramatic fallacy which has blurred so much discussion, it seems to me, of the undramatic elements in fiction. John Goode's analysis of the historical naïvety of *Adam Bede* makes its points through a very close analysis of psychology, action, and language.

However, technical criticism is throughout subordinated to a concern with judgment. I might go further and say that this concern, though using technical analysis, is inseparable from a concern with content. It is the quality of statement, of vision, of argument, of subject which is our interest here, and we have been freed to make it our concern by the formal preoccupations of critics of the past decade. No one doubted that George Eliot was a 'great novelist' and the neglect of her art, joined with a rational assumption of her greatness, allowed us in the past to examine the novels with a pretty concentrated interest in form, in language, and in the technical means towards the humane ends. Now we may move back to see what the limits of her greatness are, what the purpose and end of the technical brilliance was and is, what she has to say to us across a century of change and developing historical and psychological consciousness.

Derek and Sybil Oldfield, in their revaluation of *Scenes of Clerical Life*, are interested in the unique use of the Feuerbach source, never again to appear so simply and singly, but are also driven to perceive a tension between her stated meliorism – the moderate faith that things have a potential capacity for improvement – and her bleakly dramatized conclusions. The tales take a long look at the worst, and where that look falters, as with the uncomfortable and inappropriate idealizing of Milly Barton or the sleight-of-hand about Gilfil's fabled unattractiveness, judgment is passed, as by now it should be, without too much reference to the 'literary convention', which can and has been allowed to cover a multitude of sins, but with a demand for openness and honesty. With this essay may perhaps be bracketed my own commentary on *The Mill on the Floss*, which I see as a novel reversing the balance of honest realism and meliorism in the *Scenes*, but showing the same tension between the novelist's desire to tell the whole truth about life and the novelist's ability to tell consoling lies. The realism is narrowed into a falsifying reconciliation which, to repeat, can be explained away by reference to literary history and convention, but which, I suggest, should be rigorously examined in the light of the novel's own eloquence on behalf of undrugged existence. Incidentally, one of the pleasures both of editing and reading this kind of collection must lie in seeing the clashes and disagreements: neither John Bayley nor W. J. Harvey would entirely agree with me about Maggie's end.

There are disagreements too within a group of essays more plainly concerned with the novel as history, but these are less important than the direction of judgment. Academic criticism has the 'academic' qualities of historical research, close analysis, and a study of internal and external evidence of belief, but if it is to have anything vital to say about the novel's powers and limits, anything vital to say about being a member of society, or, come to that, about being alive, it has to ask its own contemporary questions. It must justify its interest in history by asking mid-twentieth-century questions of the mid-nineteenth-century novelist. John Goode, Arnold Kettle, Graham Martin, and John Bayley all conclude, out of their differing insights and methods in judgment, that this mid-nineteenth-century novelist communicates not the controlled and articulate criticism of her society which she thought she was communicating, but the limitations and confusions which artists, as well as political thinkers, so often try to break through, and are broken by. John Goode concludes that her historical sense is much vaguer and more uncertain than Mrs. Gaskell's, and that her criticism of society and her sense of morality are weakened, though for reasons that become interestingly clear, in *Adam Bede*. Arnold Kettle, convincingly arguing that he is judging *Felix Holt* by its own premises, concludes that the novel does not keep faith with itself, and fails to establish a contrast between the politics of expediency, which may take on a radical colour, and that true radicalism which believes in the possibility of changing society as well as hearts. His essay shows very clearly why John Blackwood was able to say approvingly, with the conservative complacency which is more irritating than its cynicism, that he was a radical of Felix's kind. This kind of analysis of George Eliot's attempts to write political novels which ultimately fail to face political reality is continued in Graham Martin's study of *Daniel Deronda*, the novel which is her most historically up-to-date and yet the most remote of all from the situation of England 100 years ago. And, interestingly, what was remote 100 years ago is remote now: nowhere is the myth of artistic universality overtly discussed in this book, but what seems unmistakably to emerge from the questioning of past by present is the equation of contemporary historical sense with a lasting historical interest. Because George Eliot's organicism or her lack of profound radicalism makes her social criticism confused, her evasions and confusions make her less, not more, interesting to other creatures of

x

time reading her 100 years later. This implication emerges too from George Levine's more technical essay on *Romola*, where a split between realism and romance is inextricably bound up with her distrust of politics and ability to evade – not marvellously and timelessly transcend, please – that exploration of history which she keeps telling us is her subject and her form. John Bayley, in the last essay, sees the limitations of her art of historical pastoral as perfect of its kind, but trapped, again explicably, in its own illustrativeness, and his discussion is both historical and formal.

Like the essay on *Romola*, the discussions of *Silas Marner*, *The Mill on the Floss*, and *Middlemarch* are also not as disconnected in interest from this historical concern as might at first appear, concerned as they are to place the novel, as an inevitably personal and imperfect creation, in the context of George Eliot's life, reading, and developing art, and concerned as they are with the content of the fiction. Certain technical distinctions which crop up over and over again between fable and realistic novel, between realism and romance, or realism and fantasy, and between picture and diagram should be seen in the context of this interest in what the novel has to say. Ultimately, of course, a concern with content must involve form: if we simplify, or idealize, or omit, or more blatantly tell lies or make mistakes in works of art, we involve ourselves not straightforwardly in saying the thing that is not, but in certain convenient forms of expression and organization. Lawrence said that we needed the critic to help us to trust the tale rather than the artist. The artist we dare not trust does not always remain external to the tale, as the reader of Lawrence must know just as much as the reader of George Eliot, and the critic must be on his guard, and put us on ours. I do not want to suggest or imply that criticism is simply concerned with content, but that it can no longer be simply concerned with form. It must consider form as the means whereby a certain impression, false, true, or, most usually, mixed, is created. It is with this relation between form and content that these essays are directly or indirectly concerned.

I

'SCENES OF CLERICAL LIFE': THE DIAGRAM AND THE PICTURE

Derek and Sybil Oldfield

...THAT DEAR, old, brown, crumbling, picturesque inefficiency is everywhere giving place to spick-and-span new-painted, new-varnished efficiency, which will yield endless diagrams, plans, elevations, and sections, but alas! no picture.

(Amos Barton, ch. 1)

The *Scenes of Clerical Life* resemble *Lyrical Ballads*, of which Hazlitt said, 'Fools have laughed at, wise men scarcely understand them'.[1] These stories, so often dismissed as mere sentimental apprentice-work, grew out of many years' wide-ranging study and emotional experience, and, faulty as they are, they nevertheless contain real insights into personal and social relationships and the connections between them.

The *Scenes* have also been criticized for their excessive explicitness, whilst the precise nature of their moral aim, other than that it focuses on the necessity for sympathy, has not always been so clear. What, for instance, are we to make of the much-quoted author statement from the *Sad Fortunes of Rev. Amos Barton*:

Depend upon it, you would gain unspeakably if you would learn with me to see some of the poetry and the pathos, the tragedy and the comedy, lying in the experience of a human soul that looks out through dull grey eyes, and that speaks in a voice of quite ordinary tones.

(ch. 5)

I

What exactly is the nature of this unspeakable gain? It is clear, certainly, that there are a great many dull grey eyes around; and it is also suggested that dullness may conceal real quondam brightness as in Maynard Gilfil, or even future nobility as in Janet Dempster. But what if the spiritual dullness is real, and so great that to read about it must be to register its human inadequacy? Given an Amos Barton who lacks both emotional imagination and the ability to express the degree of love he can feel, the reader is shown nevertheless that after a terrible crisis even Amos can grow emotionally, and if we are imagining truly, we must identify even with him, though not just with him at his moment-of-truth best. Is the unspeakable gain, then, the insight that we too are as limited as Amos, but that if he can grow, there is hope for us? Or is it that, even if the individual is sadly limited, human nature never becomes contemptible?

To understand the structure of thought behind the *Scenes*, and in particular George Eliot's insistence on the paradox of individual finitude within the magnificent potential of human nature as a whole, it is helpful to ask what was the dominant philosophical influence on her when she began to write fiction. The answer would clearly seem to be the writings of Ludwig Feuerbach, whose *Essence of Christianity* she had translated in 1854, saying to a friend: 'with the ideas of Feuerbach I everywhere agree'.[2] And for the strong personal rapport George Eliot felt for Feuerbach's highminded humanism we get ample corroborative evidence from her own letters written in the early 1850s.

Why, after all, should George Eliot have decided to begin her writing of fiction with scenes of *clerical* life, if not to give herself the best focus for discussing the *essence* of Christianity? Feuerbach gives a totally humanistic interpretation of Christian theology, and it is interesting that G. H. Lewes should have written to Blackwood concerning the *Scenes*: 'It will consist of tales and sketches illustrative of the actual life of our country clergy about a quarter of a century ago; but solely in its *human* and *not at all* in its *theological* aspect'.[3] For Feuerbach, theology was anthropology; his whole treatise on the nature of the Christian revelation of God hymns his discovery of the revelation of the nature of man. 'God is for the man the commonplace book where he registers his highest feelings and thoughts, the genealogical album into which he enters the names of the things most dear and sacred to him' (*Essence of Christianity*, ch. 5). These things comprise the *human* capacity for love, wisdom, and justice. The core of the Christian religion, the mystery of the suffering God, means that our feeling for others and capacity for self-sacrifice are divine:

> ...out of the heart, out of the inward impulse to do good, to live and die for man, out of the divine instinct of benevolence which desires to make all happy, and exclude none, not even the most abandoned and abject, out of the moral duty of benevolence, in the highest sense, as having become an inward necessity, i.e. a movement of the heart, – out of the human nature, therefore, as it reveals itself through the heart, has sprung what is best, what is true in Christianity.
>
> (*Essence of Christianity*, ch. 5)

Similarly, George Eliot's letters at this period register her supreme value of loving and reverencing her fellows. Whilst nursing her dying father, she wrote: 'Strange to say I feel that these will ever be the happiest days of my life to me. The one deep strong love I have ever known has now its highest exercise.'[4] Six years later she wrote to Bray: 'If the discipline of years has taught me anything, it has taught me to be reverent to all good in others....'[5] And a little later to his wife: 'It is not healthy to dwell on one's own feelings and conduct, but only to try and live more faithfully and lovingly every fresh day.'[6]

Tempering Feuerbach's optimistic emphasis on the best in human nature is his realistic awareness of the finite individual man. To exist is to be limited: 'All real existence is qualitative, determinative existence' (*Essence of Christianity*, ch. 1). With George Eliot this acknowledgement of limitation tends to be self-critical: her letters are movingly aware of her own mistakes and failures in relationships:

> I think not one of the endless words and deed of kindness and forbearance you have ever shewn me has vanished from my memory. I recall them often, and feel, as about everything else in the past, how deficient I have been in almost every relation of my life. But this deficiency is irrevocable and I can find no strength or comfort except in pressing forward towards the things that are before, and trying to make the present better than the past.[7]

And to another friend:

> *Now* on looking back to the days we have passed together, and the conversations in which you have told me something of your thoughts,

3

or of your griefs, I feel what a poor narrow cup I held out to receive all that, and how often I wounded when I might have helped you, if I had only had a larger and more reverent heart.[8]

It is important to remember that the great spiritual demands George Eliot makes on her characters, she made first on herself. Yet the finitude of the individual personality has its positive aspect — 'for to know oneself is to distinguish oneself from another', being finite is the condition for living in a world of other finite but unique human beings —

> Consciousness of the world is consciousness of my limitations: ... the first stone against which the pride of egoism stumbles is the *thou*, and *alter ego*. .... Without other men, the world would be for me not only dead and empty, but meaningless. Only through his fellow does man become clear to himself and self-conscious; but only when I am clear to myself does the world become clear to me.
>
> (ch. 8)

Hence comes the 'categorical imperative' to relate ourselves to our fellows: 'The ego then, attains to consciousness of the world through consciousness of the thou.' The essence of man exists

> only in community, it is found only in the unity of man with man — a unity that is supported only by the reality of the difference between I and Thou.... Man with man — the unity of I and Thou — is God.[9]

The highest form of unity is, of course, love, but 'Love does not exist without sympathy, sympathy does not exist without suffering in common' (*Essence of Christianity*, ch. 4). Love is the recognition of our human brotherhood: 'it is nothing else than the realization of the unity of the species through the medium of the moral sentiment' (ch. 26).

This emphasis on the necessity for sympathy rooted in suffering and for seeing ourselves as insignificant parts of a wonderful whole also reappears in the letters:

> I begin to feel for other people's wants and sorrows a little more than I used to do. Heaven help us! said the old religious — the one, from its very lack of that faith, will teach us all the more to help one another.[10]

In July 1852 she wrote to John Chapman:

> ... if you believe as I do, that the thought which is to mould the Future has for its roots a belief in necessity, that a nobler presentation of humanity has yet to be given in resignation to individual nothingness,

than could ever be shewn of a being who believes in the phantasma-
goria of hope unsustained by reason. . . .[11]

And in May 1854 to Cara Bray:

> We are all islands . . . and this seclusion is sometimes the most intensely
> felt at the very moment your friend is caressing you or consoling you.
> But this gradually becomes a source of satisfaction instead of repining.
> When we are young we think our troubles a mighty business – that the
> world is spread out expressly as a stage for the particular drama of our
> lives and that we have a right to rant and foam at the mouth if we are
> crossed. I have done enough of that in my time. But we begin at last
> to understand that these things are important only to one's own con-
> sciousness, which is but as a globule of dew on a rose leaf that at mid-
> day there will be no trace of.[12]

Are we now in a position to see more fully all that George Eliot
implied with her 'gain unspeakably if you would learn with me to
see some of the poetry and the pathos, the tragedy and the comedy,
lying in the experience of a human soul that looks out through dull
grey eyes . . .'? What we gain through being forced to feel real
kinship with someone to whom we had first felt aloof and superior
should be nothing less than a revelation of our essential, shared
human nature at once pitiful and sublime, when Amos at last cries,
'Milly, Milly, dost thou hear me? I didn't love thee enough – I
wasn't tender enough to thee – but I think of it all now.' This is
not to suggest that George Eliot actually achieved in the *Scenes*
anything comparable to Lear on the heath, but simply that George
Eliot came to write her first stories in a spirit of high seriousness,
anxious to transmit the truths she felt she had learned from Feuerbach and, of course, her own life.

Feuerbach's humanist interpretation of Christianity and of life
pervades all three stories. Despite the characters' natural references
to faith, Heaven, sin, grace, and God in *Scenes of Clerical Life*, the
ethic that emerges is as secular and man-centred as Feuerbach could
have wished. The point is worth making if only because when the
Scenes were first published, Marian Evans was so notorious for her
free-thinking and apparently free-loving relationship with Lewes,
that to Crabb Robinson, for one, in *Janet's Repentance* 'there is what
I cannot think to be other than cant. . . . It is so very Evangelical in
its tone that it is quite unpleasant thinking of it as the writing of
Miss Evans.'[13] In fact, of course, the uncritical Evangelicalism is
dramatic statement by some of the characters, none of whom is

treated uncritically by the author, whereas the real guts of the story concerns how we behave within our families and to our neighbours here and now. 'Attempting to be more than man we become less', says Blake, and Amos Barton, for example, is coldly inhuman as he plays out his rôle of spiritual mentor to the poor devils in the work-house:

> Mrs. Brick's eyes twinkled with the visionary hope that the parson might be intending to replenish her box, at least mediately, through the present of a small copper.
>
> Ah, well! you'll soon be going where there is no more snuff. You'll be in need of mercy then. You must remember that you may have to seek for mercy and not find it, just as you're seeking for snuff.
>
> (ch. 2)

Or to Master Fodge, aged seven and in trouble with the master of the workhouse, Mr. Spratt:

> 'If you are naughty, God will be angry as well as Mr. Spratt; and God can burn you for ever.'
>
> (*loc. cit.*)

Only when Amos is broken by his own anguish at Milly's death does he come to be seen as a fellow human being by his neighbours, who then minister to him in a more real way than ever he could to them: 'Amos failed to touch the spring of goodness by his sermons, but he touched it effectually by his sorrows; and there was now a real bond between him and his flock.'

At what point does the reader at last stop merely observing Amos and come to be totally implicated in his experience? For us this happens just before the end, as Amos visits the grave:

> He stood a few minutes reading over and over again the words on the tombstone, as if to assure himself that all the happy and unhappy past was a reality. For love is frightened at the intervals of insensibility and callousness that encroach little by little on the dominion of grief, and it makes efforts to recall the keenness of the first anguish.
>
> (ch. 10)

That is the voice of universal human experience – not just applicable to the inadequate Amos – and once we have put ourselves completely on a level with him we are fit for the 'unspeakable gain', which is not, in Willey's terms, a synthesis of head and heart,[14] but the more complex, bifurcated vision of both head and heart perform-

6

ing their distinct functions simultaneously. We still know all Amos's mediocre human qualities, we have not forgotten his few and worse-for-wear teeth, but our imagination has at last been struck by a probing reminder of the transient nature of all grief, including our own superior brand. What Feuerbach calls 'sympathy for finiteness' and George Eliot 'our dim and narrow existence' is inseparable from wonder at 'the glorious possibilities of that human nature which [we] share' as Amos breaks down 'kissing the cold turf'.

It is impossible to discuss *Mr. Gilfil's Love-Story* with anything like the same seriousness, the central narrative, for all its pace, amounting to little more than a sentimental melodrama. There is just one moment of real moral insight, for which the whole story seems to have been written, when Maynard reassures Tina that she could never, in fact, have committed a murder:

'But when I meant to do it,' was the next thing she whispered, 'it was as bad as if I had done it.'

'No, my Tina,' answered Maynard slowly, waiting a little between each sentence; 'we mean to do wicked things that we never could do just as we mean to do good or clever things that we never could do. Our thoughts are often worse than we are, just as they are often better than we are. And God sees us as we are altogether, not in separate feelings or actions, as our fellow-men see us. We are always doing each other injustice, and think better or worse of each other than we deserve, because we only hear and see separate words and actions. We don't see each other's whole nature. But God sees that you could not have committed that crime.'

(ch. 19)

This focus on 'the whole personality' is shared by Feuerbach in his emphasis on the total nature of man – not just mind or will, but heart and stomach as well: ' I differ *toto coelo* from those philosophers who pluck out their eyes that they may see better' (*Essence of Christianity*, Preface). Feuerbach goes on to say that this whole man only exists in relationship with another: 'Where there is no *thou*, there is no *I*' (ch. 9). And it is interesting to note that although Maynard says that God alone can see Tina whole, he has already shown her that through love he himself knows and responds to her as a whole person, and in doing so he salvages her sanity, and, for a little while, her life. Tina's very 'I' is dependent on her being Maynard's 'Thou'. Humanism is implicitly asserted in the same

7

breath as being explicity denied. But Tina, alas, is never *there*, as Forster's Stewart Ansell would say; and no words of wisdom about her can atone for lack of fictional life.

The influence of Christian teaching on the quality of life in a provincial town is the background subject of *Janet's Repentance*, and George Eliot makes it clear in a letter to Blackwood, June 1857, that for her, conduct *is* religion: 'I thought I had made it apparent in my sketch of Milby's feelings on the advent of Mr. Tryan that the conflict lay between immorality and morality – irreligion and religion.'[15] That Mr. Tryan happens to be an Evangelical is much less important than the kind of human being he is. Human relationships are all-important in the story, Tryan himself says:

> No sense of pardon for myself could do away with the pain I had in thinking what I had helped to bring to another. My friend used to urge upon me that my sin against God was greater than my sin against her; but – it may be from want of deeper spiritual feeling – that has remained to this hour the sin which causes me the bitterest pang. I could never rescue Lucy; but by God's blessing I might rescue other weak and falling souls; and that was why I entered the Church.
>
> (ch. 18)

Tryan's good influence on Milby is entirely owing to his sympathetic character as a man, and his influence on Janet stems from her overhearing his admission to the consumptive Sally Martin:

> 'It is one of my worst weaknesses to shrink from bodily pain.' Janet then thinks: 'Mr. Tryan, too, like herself, knew what it was to tremble at a foreseen trial – to shudder at an impending burden, heavier than he felt able to bear.'

The most brilliant deed of virtue could not have inclined Janet's goodwill towards Mr. Tryan so much as this fellowship in suffering (ch. 12). At the moment of crisis Tryan saves Janet from her 'sin' of self-despair, which is a sin in the Feuerbach sense of 'a contradiction of [her] personality with [her] fundamental nature' (*Essence of Christianity*, ch. 1), by offering her the knowledge of his own former despair. As George Eliot says: 'it is because sympathy is but a living again through our own past in a new form, that confession often prompts a response of confession' (*Janet's Repentance*, ch. 18). And Feuerbach:

> Love does not exist without sympathy, sympathy does not exist without suffering in common. . . . I feel only for that which has feeling, only

8

for that which partakes of my nature, for that in which I feel myself, whose suffering I myself suffer. Sympathy presupposes a like nature.

(ch. 4)

And through the catalyst of the author's power of sympathy for his characters, the reader ought to grow in sympathy as he reads.[16] In one of the most telling author-statements in the book, George Eliot declares her own hand as she rejects the 'objective' assessment of Tryan by a detached historian. She begins:

... anyone looking at him with the bird's-eye glance of a critic might perhaps say that he made the mistake of identifying Christianity with a too narrow doctrinal system; that he saw God's work too exclusively in antagonism to the world, the flesh, and the devil; that his intellectual culture was too limited – and so on; making Mr. Tryan the text for a wise discourse on the characteristics of the Evangelical school in his day.

But I am not poised at that lofty height. I am on the level and in the press with him. . . .

'One of the Evangelical clergy, a disciple of Venn,' says the critic from his bird's-eye station. 'Not a remarkable specimen; the anatomy and habits of his species have been determined long ago.'

Yet surely, surely the only true knowledge of our fellow-man is that which enables us to feel with him – which gives us a fine ear for the heart-pulses that are beating under the mere clothes of circumstance and opinion. Our subtlest analysis of schools and sects must miss the essential truth, unless it be lit up by the love that sees in all forms of human thought and work, the life and death struggles of separate human beings.

(ch. 10)

Here we have again the bifurcated vision of head and heart, with the heart uppermost, and this time 'the whole', alias 'all forms of human thought and work', gains from the pathos of its finite part, the limited, 'separate' human being.

'Love', says Feuerbach, 'is the middle term, the substantial bond, the principle of reconciliation between the perfect and the imperfect, the sinless and the sinful being, the universal and the individual, the divine and the human.'

(ch. 8)

So far we have been concerned to indicate that behind *Scenes of Clerical Life* there is the scaffolding of a coherent humanist philosophy. But before discussing other positive aspects of this early work its basic vitiating flaw of sentimentality must be squarely faced.

9

It has been argued that George Eliot sins much less under this head than do her contemporaries, but the very fact that she aimed at and often achieved a much greater degree of realism in the *Scenes* than was achieved by Mrs. Gaskell in *Ruth*[17] or Mrs. Craik in *John Halifax, Gentleman,* or Charlotte Yonge in *The Heir of Redclyffe* means that even minor traces of sentimentality immediately jar and are disproportionately important. But there are more than minor traces of sentimentality in every scene. In *Amos Barton,* the whole conception of the character of Milly is surely out of place in a story so concerned to emphasize the prosaic nature of most tragedy. It is as though the author were compensating herself for her thoroughly unattractive hero by pulling all the stops out in creating his wife:

> She was a lovely woman...a large, fair, gentle Madonna.... Soothing, unspeakable charm of gentle womanhood! which supersedes all acquisitions, all accomplishments...let the sweet woman go to make sunshine and a soft pillow for the poor devil whose legs are not models, whose efforts are often blunders, and who in general gets more kicks than halfpence. She – the sweet woman – will like it as well; for her sublime capacity of loving will have all the more scope; and I venture to say, Mrs. Barton's nature would never have grown half so angelic if she had married the man you would perhaps have had in your eye for her....
>
> (ch. 2)

Milly never has a selfish thought or utters an irritable word or does an impatient thing. She wakes herself at half-past five to finish the darning, and when she has to endure social ostracism and near-penury through the prolonged visit of the equivocal Countess, 'She was only vexed that her husband should be vexed – only wounded because he was misconceived. . . . A loving woman's world lies within the four walls of her own home' (ch. 7). But the sad fact is that such paragons of wife-and-motherhood are only to be found in fiction, and in what Lewes called the school of 'Falsism' at that. Milly could not be more blatantly a case of over-compensation on George Eliot's part for her own refusal to fulfil the Victorian ideal of Angel in the House.

But mother-love is always a fatal subject for George Eliot in the *Scenes.* Apropos of Tina's prospective motherhood, we are told, 'A mother dreads no memories – those shadows have all melted away in the dawn of baby's smile', which is simply untrue. Of Janet's childlessness we read:

If she had had babes to rock to sleep – little ones to kneel in their night-dress and say their prayers at her knees – sweet boys and girls to put their young arms round her neck and kiss away her tears, her poor hungry heart would have been fed with strong love, and might never have needed that fiery poison to still its cravings. Mighty is the force of motherhood! ...

Yes! if Janet had been a mother, she might have been saved from much sin, and therefore from much of her sorrow.

(ch. 13)

There is no attempt to imagine concretely what it would have been like to have had children in the Dempster household, witnessing the father beat the mother, or being beaten themselves. Even more unconvincing is the treatment of Dempster's mother, 'Mamsey', as his good angel. The statement 'the drunken tyrant of a dreary midnight home, was the first-born darling son of a fair little mother' (ch. 7) is meant as a surprising paradox, rather than possible cause and effect. Of course, it would be foolish to ascribe the sadistic bullying nature of Dempster simply to the blindly doting Mamsey, but the fact remains that Dempster is the only evil-natured character in the *Scenes* and there is no attempt at explanation for the origin of this evil, at least as important a subject, one might think, as the origin and nature of good, on which George Eliot is unsurpassed. Karl Barth finally rejects Feuerbach on this very point – his nineteenth-century innocence of evil – 'anyone who knew that we men are evil from head to foot ... would recognize it to be the most illusory of all illusions to suppose that the essence of God is the essence of man'.[18]

Sentimentality about motherhood naturally means sentimentality about children, and the children in *Scenes of Clerical Life* are awful. They speak with an adenoidal lisp: 'Dit id my noo fock. I put it on tod you wad toming' (ch. 8). With the exception of the Confirmation Class in *Janet's Repentance* and Dicky at Mrs. Barton's funeral,[19] the children are all idealized, and near-caricatures of that inarticulateness which George Eliot was so concerned to show in Amos.

The sentimentality in *Mr. Gilfil's Love-Story* is of two different kinds. There is the romantic sentimentality of the 'first and only love' (Epilogue), which all readers of Jane Austen know to be against nature; and there is the sentimental cheating about Mr. Gilfil's old age. A great deal is made of Mr. Gilfil drinking a little gin-and-water of an evening, and growing ever more parsimonious in his own habits in order to leave a good legacy for his nephew, and the reader is supposed to be a little alienated by these two 'weaknesses'. Then follows the flashback of the pathetic love-story, and in the Epilogue we are told: 'Many an irritating fault, many an unlovely oddity, has come of a hard sorrow.' The implication is that we needed to know of Maynard's earlier grief in order to tolerate him better in his old age. But in fact, of course, he is a dear old man, with no irritating faults or unlovely oddities at all. George Eliot has a real point about our need for imagination and knowledge of the past in order to love most old people who *are* unattractive, but she has only pretended to make the point through Maynard.

We have already noted the sentimental narrator's tone exalting Milly. The narrator's voice is even more fatally prominent in Mr. Gilfil's love-story, not only in the obtrusive 'little bird' imagery noted by Barbara Hardy,[20] but also in breathless, cliché-ridden exclamations trying to force our pity for Tina:

> With this tempest pent up in her bosom, the poor child went up to her room every night, and there it all burst forth. . . .
>
> (ch. 10)
>
> Poor child! Poor child! she who used to cry to have the fish put back into the water – who never willingly killed the smallest living thing – dreams now, in the madness of her passion, that she can kill the man whose very voice unnerves her.
>
> (ch. 13)

The author is leaving no breathing-space for the reader. Even what should have been an effective crisis in the action of *Janet's Repentance* when the drunken husband locks Janet out in the winter night (think, for example, of the Morels) is ruined by 'over-writing':

> The stony street, the bitter north-east wind and darkness – and in the midst of them a tender woman thrust out from her husband's home in her thin night-dress, the harsh wind cutting her naked feet and driving her long hair away from her half-clad bosom, where the poor heart is crushed with anguish and despair.
>
> (ch. 15)

George Eliot's narrative tone in the *Scenes* can also be cloyingly familiar: she does here what she is to do ever less frequently in her more mature work – she keeps reminding us of our separate identities with references to 'I' and 'you' instead of the vaguer 'we'. By the time she comes to write *Middlemarch*, if she asks the reader a question, she will often answer it through a third person, a hypothetical looker-on, such as the 'wary man' considering Dorothea as a marriage-proposition in chapter 1. This is much less embarrassing, and the reader is much less conscious of being manipulated than in such passages as:

> Reader! *did* you ever taste such a cup of tea as Miss Gibbs is this moment handing to Mr. Pilgrim? ... No – most likely you are a miserable town-bred reader....
>
> *(Amos Barton*, ch. 1)

Or the unnecessary question and answer form in:

> Mr. Gilfil was a bachelor then?
> That is the conclusion to which you would probably have come.
>
> (ch. 1)

In *Amos Barton* George Eliot is even more ill at ease with what is necessarily the author's godlike rôle, and keeps interrupting the narrative to explain just why she is going to follow one character back to his home rather than another:

> We will not accompany him to the Clerical Meeting today, because we shall probably want to go thither some day when he will be absent. And just now I am bent on introducing you to Mr. Bridmain....
>
> (ch. 2)

Or else she will highlight the fact of our having to eavesdrop:

> Here Mrs. Barton reached the note from the mantelpiece, and gave it to her husband. We will look over his shoulder while he reads it.
>
> (ch. 2)

Such awkwardness is never to be found in her dialogue. It was of *Amos Barton* already that Lewes wrote to Blackwood, November 1856, delighted to point out its 'exhibiting in a high degree that faculty which I find to be the rarest of all, viz. the dramatic ventriloquism'.[21] But she is less happy in recording her character's thoughts. She fails to get inside Tina's mind as she thinks of killing Wybrow. It is essential that Tina should not seem capable of a circumstantially premeditated murder. Therefore George Eliot does not dramatize her thoughts directly; she does not write:

> He will be here – he will be here before me in a moment. He will come towards me with that false smile, thinking I do not know his baseness – I will plunge this dagger into his heart.

She writes:

> He will be there – he will be before her in a moment. He will come towards her with that false smile, thinking she does not know his base-ness – she will plunge that dagger into his heart.
>
> (ch. 13)

But this use of the third person future simple is misleading; in fact Tina will not plunge her dagger, and we are still made to think Tina too explicitly determined on the act. In George Eliot's mature work we think this passage would have been changed into *erlebte Rede*, which always merges the distinction between writer and reader as it approaches the character's consciousness whilst he entertains, pre-verbally, *a possible* line of action:

> He would be there – he would be before her in a moment. He would come towards her with that false smile, thinking she did not know his baseness – she would plunge that dagger into his heart.

It has been necessary to indicate the blemishes in the *Scenes*, but it should be clear that these are faults very much to be expected from a first work likely to be influenced by contemporary conventions, whether these relate to the sanctity of motherhood or addresses to the reader, and that they should obtrude as inorganic elements. But these faults do not invalidate the strong humanist ethic mentioned earlier or the successful 'novelizing' of this ethic in psychological and social terms. The *Scenes* have many profoundly perceptive insights, which owe nothing to her reading of German philosophy and everything to her own intensely-experienced past, as well as to her observing of those around her. These psychological bull's-eyes often take the form of narrator's comments either on human nature as a whole or on one character in particular. We think of:

> ... what mortal is there of us, who would find his satisfaction enhanced by an opportunity of comparing the picture he presents to himself of his own doings, with the picture they make on the mental retina of his neighbours? ... The very capacity for good would go out of us ... the greater part of the worker's faith in himself is made up of the faith that others believe in him. ...
>
> Let me discover that the lovely Phoebe thinks my squint intolerable, and I shall never be able to fix her blandly with my disengaged eye again.
>
> Thank heaven, then, that a little illusion is left to us, to enable us to be useful and agreeable ... we are able to dream that we are doing much good – and we do a little.

Or:

> For though Amos thought himself strong, he did not *feel* himself
> strong. Nature had given him the opinion, but not the sensation.
>
> (ch. 2)

There are egoists like the Countess 'feeling she was really behaving
charmingly' (ch. 7), or Wybrow 'rarely led into any conduct of
which he could not give a plausible account of himself' (ch. 4), or
Mrs. Hackit, 'whose good-nature began to act now that it was a
little in contradiction with the dominant tone of the conversation'
(ch. 1), or the contrast between Mr. Gilfil, able 'to approximate his
accent and mode of speech' (ch. 1) to the farmers in his parish, and
Captain Wybrow, whose perceptions were 'not acute enough for
him to notice the difference of a semitone' (ch. 5). In *Janet's
Repentance* there is the very telling perception about the special
horror in the *intervals* of suffering. After Janet, happy for once, has
left:

> The mother leaned back in her chair when Janet was gone, and sank
> into a painful reverie. When our life is a continuous trial, the moments
> of respite seem only to substitute the heaviness of dread for the heavi-
> ness of actual suffering; the curtain of cloud seems parted an instant
> only that we may measure all its horror as it hangs low, black, and
> imminent, in contrast with the transient brightness.
>
> (ch. 5)

Other critics have been embarrassed that Tryan should come to
love Janet, but it is made so clear that she is the outstanding human
being in the first place, and her looks and plight had so struck Tryan
from the beginning, that it would seem far more unnatural and
forced if Tryan had maintained his rôle of merely spiritual guide
to the last. There is real pathos in his final, struggling reluctance to
die, and in the painful reticence of his implied love:

> There was no-one else in the room, and his eyes followed her as she
> moved with the firm grace natural to her, while the bright fire every
> now and then lit up her face, and gave an unusual glow to its dark
> beauty. . . .
>   'Janet,' he said presently, in his faint voice – he always called her
> Janet now. In a moment she was close to him, bending over him. He
> opened his hand as he looked up at her, and she placed hers within
> it . . . 'you will not feel the need of me as you have done. . . . Let us
> kiss each other before we part'.
>
> (ch. 27)

There are many splendid comic touches – best of all old Mrs. Linnet:

> Mrs. Linnet had become a reader of religious books since Mr. Tryan's advent, and as she was in the habit of confining her perusal to the purely secular portions, which bore a very small proportion to the whole, she could make rapid progress through a large number of volumes. On taking up the biography of a celebrated preacher, she immediately turned to the end to see what disease he died of; and if his legs swelled, as her own occasionally did, she felt a stronger interest in ascertaining any earlier facts in the history of the dropsical divine – whether he had ever fallen off a stage-coach, whether he had married more than one wife, and, in general, any adventures or repartees recorded of him previous to the epoch of his conversion. She then glanced over the letters and diary, and wherever there was a predominance of Zion, the River of Life, and notes of exclamation, she turned over to the next page; but any passage in which she saw such promising nouns as 'small-pox', 'pony', or 'boots and shoes', at once arrested her.
>
> (ch. 3)

When we read such a passage we are at once in the world of Audrey and Justice Shallow, and Mr. Woodhouse and Flora Finching and Mr. F.'s Aunt. Once there, we realize that we too belong to the forked-radish brigade; we too would be much more gripped by an account of a divine's pre-conversion marriage than by one of his later piety. Deeply serious though she is, George Eliot can yet make us laugh at our inadequate attempts to be serious, reminding us that we are each of us Moth playing Hercules. And far from diminishing her serious impact, this comedy deepens it and even possibly enables it to exist. Totally unintellectual as Mrs. Linnet is, it is to the presence of people like her and Mr. Lowme, that elderly Lothario leaning against Mr. Gruby's doorpost, that we owe our willing suspension of disbelief in Milby, which then leaves the way open for seeing all that 'Milby' stands for. The diagram depends on the picture.

Another important aspect of this fictional 'picture' is the creation of two social worlds. The interlinking circles within Shepperton and Milby are brought to life by talk. We think of the neighbour's gossiping in Mrs. Patten's farmhouse; or the Monthly Clerical Meetings at Milby Vicarage; or the ladies' bookbinding session in the Linnets' parlour; or the boorish exchanges in Dempster's pub, the Red Lion. The organic interaction of every class in the community and the influence that neighbours do have upon each other's lives are stressed at every opportunity. It is Mrs. Hackit's hampers which help to keep the Curate's family going; it is the maid Nanny who finally saves the Bartons from the Countess; it is social snobbery which is largely responsible for the prejudice against Tryan, and the material self-interest of different professional groups which at first unites to persecute him. This penetrating social coverage is deepened by ironic analysis and judicious affection. (One needs to quote the whole splendid second chapter on Milby. Theodore Noble gives a particularly helpful account of the social study in *Janet's Repentance, op. cit.*, pp. 153 foll.).

Added to her grasp of sociology is George Eliot's grasp of history, which is her real debt to Scott. Milby is shown us at a particular moment in its social and intellectual history as it finally allows itself to be influenced by the Evangelical Movement – Mr. Tryan is an historically significant 'type' as well as what is still more important to George Eliot, his unique self. And the final, balanced verdict on the moral benefit brought to Milby, and by implication to England, by Evangelicalism, in Chapter 10, is a brilliant piece of historical summing-up, alive with imaginative particularity.

Thus George Eliot's three great strengths, her permanent undercurrent of ethical concern, her wealth of psychological insight both comic and tragic, and her ability to re-create a whole past society which is at once its unique 'historical' self and also universally human – these are all already to be found in *Scenes of Clerical Life. Amos Barton* begins with the juxtaposed images of Shepperton Church as it is now and as it used to be, the 'restored' version belonging in spirit to the unsentimental, Radical spirit of reform with its 'endless diagrams, plans, elevations, and sections, but alas! no picture'. 'Diagram' and 'picture' are both present in this first work, but George Eliot is never again to have so homogeneous an intellectual substructure, nor one so dominated by just one thinker, Feuerbach, nor will her 'picture' ever again be so liable to blurring through false sentiment or narrative clumsiness.

The real subtlety in the *Scenes* pertains not at all to technique and less to thought than to feeling. The final impression we are left with is a tension between what Carlyle called 'the Everlasting Yea and Nay' – between, in George Eliot's words, a faith in 'the glorious possibilities of that human nature which [we] share, whether revealed in Amos or in provincial Milby, and a strongly

17

pessimistic sense that life is not going to turn out ideally for any of us. Milly dies, Amos has to leave Shepperton, Mr. Gilfil never has children of his own. Janet and Tryan cannot marry. George Eliot has described herself as a meliorist, but she insists that we, as well as her characters, should live without the opiate of false optimism. Human wishes are not vain, but neither will they be fulfilled.

NOTES

1. William Hazlitt, *Spirit of the Age*, 'Mr. Wordsworth', 1818.
2. *The George Eliot Letters*, ed. Gordon S. Haight (Yale U.P. and Oxford U.P., 1954), ii. 153.
3. *ibid.*, ii. 274.
4. *ibid.*, i. 283.
5. *ibid.*, ii. 199.
6. *ibid.*, ii. 216.
7. *ibid.*, ii. 215.
8. *ibid.*, ii. 278.
9. L. Feuerbach, *Die Philosophie der Zukunft*; quoted by Karl Barth in his Introduction to *Essence of Christianity* (Harper Torchbook Ed., 1957), p. xiii.
10. *Letters*, ii. 82.
11. *ibid.*, ii. 49.
12. *ibid.*, ii. 156.
13. H. Crabb Robinson, *Diary*, ed. D. Hudson (Oxford U.P., 1967), p. 303.
14. Basil Willey, *Nineteenth Century Studies* (Chatto & Windus, 1949).
15. *Letters*, ii. 347.
16. For other discussions of the doctrine of sympathy in *Scenes of Clerical Life*, see Barbara Hardy, *The Novels of George Eliot* (Athlone Press, 1957), ch. 1, and Theodore Noble, *George Eliot: Scenes of Clerical Life* (Yale U.P., 1965), pp. 55 ff.
17. *Letters*, ii. 86, where George Eliot herself says of Mrs. Gaskell's *Ruth*: 'She is not contented with the subdued colouring – the half tints of real life.'
18. Introduction to L. Feuerbach, *Essence of Christianity* (Harper Torchbook Ed.), p. 28.
19. Cf. P. Coveney, *The Image of Childhood* (Penguin, 1967); first published as *Poor Monkey* (Barrie & Rockliff, 1957).
20. *Novels of George Eliot*, pp. 202–4.
21. *Letters*, ii. 274.

II

'ADAM BEDE'
John Goode

I

Adam Bede can be described as the first major exercise in programmatic literary realism in English literature. Yet most of the essays which approach it as a totality are content to treat it as a dramatic poem.[1] It is not difficult to see why this has happened. As Ian Gregor has argued, there is, despite the precision of dates, very little sense of the historical actuality of the vast upheavals in rural life which typify the 1790s.[2] The suggestions of historical change are marginal. If the Poysers are threatened by squirearchic tyranny, this is only to show their resilience. If Loamshire is ominously juxtaposed with Stonyshire, the relationship is merely symbolic and there is no sense of the new world really impinging on the old. Methodism is brought in only to show how unimportant it is as a social force in a rural community, and ultimately it serves merely as the particular 'clothing' of Dinah's humanitarianism. Time itself, in fact, is primarily a cyclical presence (naturally, Loamshire is bound up with the seasons), and it only has a linear existence in the context of purely personal histories. Loamshire is protected from time by the hills that surround it, for they are 'wooed from day to day by the changing hours, but responding with no change in themselves' (ch. 2). Thus the historical specificity seems merely decorative, a matter of giving the symbolic patterns a local habitation.

However, Ian Gregor has equally shown that an approach to the novel in terms of its symbolic patterns necessarily makes it incoherent: it is both pastoral, a celebration of the idealized past, and moral fable, looking forward to the great interior dramas of George Eliot's later work. I have no intention of resolving the duality that he perceives, because it is certainly there. What needs to be shown is that it grows out of an inner coherence which can only be fully defined by approaching the novel in terms of its explicit programme and the problems that it raises.

The most obvious rehearsal of the social reality of *Adam Bede* is in George Eliot's review of Riehl's *The Natural History of German Life*,[3] in which she describes, with details that are repeated in the novel, what she regards as the English equivalent of the German peasantry: 'we must remember what the tenant farmers and small proprietors were in England half a century ago'. The context of the passage is extremely important. George Eliot begins with a didactic rationale of realism in art: 'Art is the nearest thing to life; it is a mode of amplifying experience and extending our contact with our fellow men'. Riehl achieves this, though he is not an artist, through his descriptions of the peasantry. The essay concludes with a statement of George Eliot's '*social—political—conservatism*'. Approvingly, she summarizes Riehl's views: 'He sees in European society *incarnate history*, and any attempt to disengage it from its historical elements must, he believes, be simply destructive of social vitality. What has grown up historically can only die out historically by the gradual operation of necessary laws'.

'History' in this passage has a very specialized meaning which would be better covered by 'tradition' which *pervades* history. George Eliot focuses on the German peasantry and its English equivalent because 'it is among the peasantry that we must look for the historical type of the national physique', thus on an essence which transcends specific historical conditions, but which is more or less disguised by them. The German peasantry, then, approximates more nearly to the laboratory conditions necessary for the study of 'the popular character', because it is less prone to historical mutation than more sophisticated groups. Thus it serves more readily for the extension of sympathies with the populace because its portrayal is the nearest thing to a *natural* history of 'life'. Moreover, it is good evidence of the need for 'the vital connection' with the past which nourishes progress and makes it natural or organic (incarnate, in fact):

> The nature of European men has its roots intertwined with the past, and can only be developed by allowing those roots to remain undis-

turbed while the process of development is going on, until that perfect ripeness of the seed which carries with it a life independent of the root. This vital connection with the past is much more vividly felt on the Continent than in England, where we have to recall it by an effort of memory and reflection; for though our English life is in its core intensely traditional, Protestantism and commerce have modernized the face of the land and the aspects of society in a far greater degree than in any continental country. . . .

This makes it clear why, if George Eliot is to write a natural history of English life both to effect a real extension of sympathies and to illustrate a process of development which is organically related to the past, she has to choose an epoch in which 'the core' is still visible in 'the face of the land'. She has to choose an historical reality that she can dehistoricize, and which is not modernized by the Industrial Revolution.

There are two reasons why she should choose the 1790s and not an earlier period. Firstly, she mentions that Protestantism as well as commerce has 'modernized' the face of the land. Unless she is going to write a medieval novel, she therefore has to choose a phase in which Protestantism has ceased to be protesting. In *Adam Bede* Anglicanism has become socially catholic, an integral part of a whole community and neither exclusive nor proselytizing. Moreover, it is morally organic: it no longer focuses on specialized activities (prayer, worship), but takes in the whole of man's activity. It is the nearest modern equivalent to the religion of Carlyle's Abbey of St. Edmund, which is explicitly contrasted, in *Past and Present*, with Methodism. Thus, by choosing an era of 'catholic' Anglicanism which post-dates the Methodist Movement, George Eliot is able to emphasize its rootedness by contrast.

This leads to the second reason, which is that the choice of 1799 is a defiant one. The 'modernizing' influences of history are there in the novel. Arthur Donnithorne returns from Ireland full of plans for 'drainage and enclosure'. His grandfather tries to make the Poysers specialize as dairy-farmers, and, of course, Methodism is a force which sets Will Maskery against Irwine, which separates Seth Bede from his work, and which creates incipient hysteria in Hayslope. But none of these threats is realized, because George Eliot is concerned to demonstrate the intensity of tradition and the resilience of the core even in years of acute crisis. Against the factitious historical changes, too, there will be, in the presentation

of Adam himself, a demonstration of the true, evolutionary process
of development in which ripeness rather than severance creates a life
independent of the root.

This defiant dehistoricization is borne out by the novel's technique. The early parts of the book show a persistent tendency to
resolve the narrative into pictures. We begin with the static vision
of the workshop, and when the men begin to talk it is as though
a painting were to begin to move. Later, Dinah 'stood with her
left hand towards the descending sun' (ch. 2), and our first view of
Adam's home is equally pictorial: 'The door of the house is open,
and an elderly woman is looking out; but she is not placidly con-
templating the evening sunshine' (ch. 4). The whole community
moves, in Book II, towards the stasis of the church scene: 'I be-
seech you to imagine Mr. Irwine looking round on this scene. . . .
And over all streamed the delicious June sunshine through the old
windows...' (ch. 18). The comparison to Dutch genre painting
is thus more than a plea for humble and rustic life: it really defines
the procedure of fixing the core through the arrested moment. Hence
the important emphasis on sunlight; E. H. Gombrich has said that
Vermeer, through the use of light, gives his animate portrayals the
stability of the still life, and George Eliot does the same – she
fixes the world she describes through the creation of representative
scenes. Thus the novel has the air of an anthropologist's notebook:
'Have you ever seen a real English rustic perform a solo dance? . . .
Wiry Ben never smiled; he looked as serious as a dancing monkey
. . .' (ch. 25). Even Mrs. Poyser is to be read as an 'original':
'Sharp! yes, her tongue is like a new-set razor. She's quite original
in her talks too; *one of those* untaught wits that help to stock a
country with proverbs' (ch. 33 – my italics). The 'pastoral' structure of the novel, with its fixed, cyclical rhythms and its illustrative
'types', is there not to idealize a past and to provide criteria for
judging the present so much as to create a medium for the 'natural'
historian. And if the medium is fixed, it is still part of a *process*.
The animal imagery which is so prevalent in the novel is not merely
serving an aesthetic function; it also establishes an evolutionary
scale. And it is on this scale that human change bases itself. Thus
the pupils of Bartle Massey: 'It was almost as if three rough
animals were making humble efforts to learn how they might
become human' (ch. 21).

We shall see that this evolutionary process, the struggle of the individual to adapt to the given medium, is precisely the basis of the moral fable. In the contrasting stories of Hetty and Adam we have an evolutionary drama of alienation and individuation which can only take place on a 'pastoral' stage. We shall see too that this involves an important transformation: social convention becomes natural law.

II

This transformation is enacted within the novel, and it only becomes clear with the wisdom of hindsight. Initially we have the sense of an appearance of stability ironically underscored by its historical limitations. Thus, though Hall Farm has the order and integrity of pastoral, its temporality is implied in our first view of it as though it were a manor 'in the early stage of a chancery suit'; however rooted the Poysers think themselves, the farm has a history to which they do not belong, so that they are themselves the instruments of change. The structure of the first three books as a whole moves ominously towards crisis. The first book moves spatially through the social totality to give a precise delineation of social distinction; the second, through the focus of the church service, brings together the society as an organic community. Both books have undertones of change (Methodism and the death of Thias Bede), but predominantly they establish the everyday life of the community. This prepares us for the unique, and therefore historical event of Arthur's birthday feast in the third book. Here the separate orders of society confront one another, so that from class-distinction we turn to class-relationship. Both the comedy of the arrangements, carefully organized so as to include the whole community and to preserve the social distinctions, and the satire of the upper-class incomprehension and intolerance of the lower orders (Lydia Donnithorne and Chad's Bess) illustrate the paternalist basis of human relationships. Irwine sets the tone when he says: 'In this sort of thing people are constantly confounding liberality with riot and disorder' (ch. 22), and Arthur dramatizes the paternalist ideal (liberality and order) in the feudal ceremony of Adam's promotion. At the same time we are conscious that the order is being destroyed by the hierarchic relationships it supports. The tributes of Poyser and Adam to Arthur are the central ironies of the book: we know that the class-gap is being closed by exploitation: the public liberality which goes with order is undermined by the private liberality, the locket and earrings that will disrupt that order. Book II opens with the Poysers making their way to church, a unified group which is a microcosm of the integrity of the community; Book III also opens with the Poysers' journey, but preluded by Hetty's secret, so that we have a sense of the group riding to its destruction.

That this should emerge in the very section which highlights the social structure through its special celebration emphasizes how much, in one perspective, the disruptive change grows out of the existing order. Arthur's feeling for Hetty is intensified by Mrs. Irwine's consciously class-based remark: 'What a pity such beauty as that should be thrown away among the farmers, when it's wanted so terribly among the good families' (ch. 25). Arthur's disruptive egoism grows directly out of his social situation. This is insisted on from his first appearance: 'If you want to know more particularly how he looked, call to your remembrance some tawny-whiskered, brown-locked, clear-complexioned young Englishman whom you have met with in a foreign town, and been proud of as a fellow-countryman' – the compliment depends on the Grand Tour. Everything about him suggests the paternalist psychology: he is keen on enclosure and admires Arthur Young; if he reads the *Lyrical Ballads* it is for *The Ancient Mariner*, not for the scenes of humble, rustic life, which he dismisses as 'twaddle stuff' (so that he is incapable of learning from *The Thorn*, for example). His evasion of moral responsibility recalls the explicit doctrine of *Tom Jones*: 'There was a sort of implicit confidence in him that he was really such a good fellow at bottom, Providence would not treat him harshly' (ch. 29), and when he is arranging his conscience to cope with his dishonesty by marrying Hetty off to Adam, he resorts to a note of aristocratic cosmic optimism which might come from the *Essay on Man*: 'So good comes out of evil. Such is the beautiful arrangement of things' (ch. 29). And, obviously, it is a class-psychology which allows him to destroy Hetty. The sin becomes a peccadillo because the gentleman can always compensate. Compensation creates a safe distance between offender and victim because it easily merges into another class notion, 'liberality'. The process is made explicit in Arthur's childhood: he kicks over an old man's broth in a fit of temper and repents by giving him a favourite pencil-case. He makes retribution for an offence against human relations with a *thing*; the thing has not relevance to the old man's needs, and its value is defined entirely by Arthur. The liberality and the solipsism are equally part of the same habitual process of reducing human relationships to a reflection of the social hierarchy. By the same class-psychology, he has to limit his relationship to Hetty to exploitation: 'No gentleman, out of a ballad, could marry a farmer's niece' (ch. 13). Thus the potential of social tragedy is certainly laid in the opening books of the novel: the order which seems pastoral, is threatened by its own basis in class-deference.

In one sense, this potential is realized. In his clash with Arthur, Adam momentarily crosses from deferential humility to egalitarian defiance: 'I don't forget what's owing to you as a gentleman, but in this thing we're man and man, and I can't give up' (ch. 28). Arthur tries to assert his class-privilege, but has to recognize his defeat and hide behind it afterwards: 'Even the presence of Pym, waiting on him with the usual deference, was a reassurance to him after the scenes of yesterday' (ch. 29). Nor is the private conflict merely a parable of possible social unheaval. The old Squire's threat to turn out the Poysers is, it is true, never fully realized, but this is precisely because structurally it is highly ironic. It is the new Squire, with his millennial promise, who is destroying the basis of the Poysers' world, and, immediately after the old man's threat has dissolved in gentle comedy, Hetty discovers her pregnancy and sets off to Windsor.

But, of course, in the end this does not mean disruption. The social group merely loses an unassimilable fragment, and the only result is that Adam joins the Poyser family, not on the false basis of marriage with the niece who doesn't love him, but on the basis of marriage with the sincere niece. The ending of the novel demands a different perspective on the total structure, and this means that we are conscious of a narrowing-down process which finally undermines the novel's potential for social tragedy. At the beginning the massively established world of Hayslope is threatened by three major possibilities of change, Methodism, the death of Thias Bede, and the affair between Arthur and Hetty, suggesting religious upheaval for Hayslope as a whole, familial disruption for the Bedes, and social exploitation of the Poysers. By Book IV the novel has been reduced to the last of these, which is also the most private. Dinah and Lisbeth appear at this stage of the story only as background, and the Poysers recede increasingly into the background (the structural gratuitousness of the chapter called 'The Bitter Waters Spread' is obvious). The seduction theme is severed from the social portrayal, so that, in so far as it has any social implication at all, Hetty's story is simply that of the outcast.

This change in perspective is implicit from the beginning in the ideological shaping of the social realism. Even Arthur, who is the most socially defined character in the novel, is also a moral case. His decision to conceal the truth about Hetty from Adam is partly a patronizing egoism (note the tone of chivalry in 'his first duty was to guard her'), but is also an immoral attempt to mitigate the law of consequences through the principle of expediency ('duty was become a question of tactics'). This is precisely the basis of Herbert Spencer's attack on the Utilitarians.[4] For him, the law of right is a law of perfection, and, though imperfect man is unable to fulfil it, to substitute an interim law of expediency is disastrous. Men have 'to give up their own power of judging what *seems* best' and act according to 'the belief that that only *is* best which is abstractedly right'. In Spencer's terms, Arthur is a moral infidel who doubts the efficiency and foresight of the Divine arrangements, and 'with infinite presumption' supposes a human judgment less fallible. This is the basis of Spencer's argument against ameliorative legislation: 'all interposing between humanity and the conditions of its existence, cushioning-off consequences by poor laws and the like – serves but to neutralize the remedy and prolong the evil'. Arthur is to be condemned not only on the grounds of his own egoism, but because he wants, by exercising his social discretion, to mitigate the consequences for Hetty of her folly.

The important phrase is 'conditions of existence'. It suggests both natural conditions and social environment. For Spencer there is no real difference. Although man's evolution is from pre-social egoism to social altruism (or, rather, enlightened self-interest), this is merely the exchange of one fixed medium for another. Progress is a matter of man's adaptation to the fixed laws of the social state: 'The social state is a necessity. The conditions of greatest happiness under that state are fixed. *Our characters are the only things not fixed*. They, then, must be moulded into fitness for conditions'. Thus, although Spencer would have agreed with George Eliot that the imperfections of society are 'the manifestation of the inherited internal conditions in the human beings who compose it', and that therefore it is folly to attempt to change society by legislation, he also argues that the individual must perfect himself by bending to the social law. The apparent contradiction is resolved by a belief in 'the operation of natural laws' and in particular the law of natural selection: 'He on whom his own stupidity, or vice, or idleness, entails loss of life, must, in the generalizations of philosophy, be classed with the victims of weak viscera or malformed limbs'. Society, then, is a natural law. He who fulfils its demands will inevitably contribute to its improvement. He who fails will also contribute, but by being expelled.

In Spencerian terms, Hetty is obviously a case of a 'fatal non-adaptation'. But this is not a simple 'example'. Mimetically, Hetty is a brilliant study in alienation. She has to mediate her relationship with her social reality by living in a dream of the luxurious future in which she escapes the present. We can put it this way because in two respects George Eliot remains dispassionately descriptive. Firstly, her dream world is given psychological definition: 'Young souls, in such pleasant delirium as hers, are as unsympathetic as butterflies sipping nectar; they are isolated from all appeals by a barrier of dreams' (ch. 9). If 'unsympathetic' is rigorously judging, its context, 'delirium' and 'barrier', qualifies the sense of responsibility. Secondly, the alienation has a social basis. Hetty's performance in front of the mirror (ch. 15) is primarily intended to show how she inhabits a world of appearances (she is, of course, a moral Duessa), but it is also clearly a response to a concrete reality insisted on by the blindless windows and the blotchy mirror with its tarnished gilding which, like Hall Farm itself, belongs to a world of faded gentility. The Poysers inhabit a middle-class no-man's-land which glimpses at, but never achieves luxury. There are moments when we feel that Hetty's is a sympathetic rebellion. 'Hetty would have been glad to hear that she should never see a child again' is supposed to be shocking, but surely only on the basis of a sentimental stock response. Totty *is* unbearable, and the pampering she gets from her mother doesn't suggest human love so much as lower-middle-class stupidity. Again, in a later episode, Adam gives Hetty a rose, which Hetty puts in her hair. Immediately 'the tender admiration in Adam's face was slightly shadowed by reluctant disapproval' (ch. 20), and he rebukes her for aspiring to the finery of the great ladies of the hall. The gesture is flippant, but it is hardly worthy of an instant sermon, and when, after this, Hetty dresses up as Dinah, we feel that it is a judgment on the ponderous morality

27

of the Hayslope world as well as on Hetty. Later, in *Far From the Madding Crowd*, Hardy will see the vanity of woman as part of the indirect language with which she has to communicate her independence to a world of men, but in *Adam Bede* it means only isolation, and the isolated is a moral invalid.

For the fully realized alienation is subjected to an ideological framework. When we are told that 'Hetty would have cast all her past life behind her and never cared to be reminded of it again' (ch. 15), we have to see it as a biological deformity: she cannot shape herself to the medium she finds herself in. And in this respect, the authorial commentary has to work very hard. The evolutionary scale established in the descriptions of Massey's pupils and Wiry Ben becomes, in Hetty's case, overwhelmingly important. The lower orders are animals making efforts to become human. The Poysers are higher up the social, and therefore the evolutionary, scale, and thus the demands their environment makes are more sophisticated (the crucial test, as Creeger has pointed out, is the altruistic love of children). Hetty is, however, less than human. The animal imagery is bewildering but ideologically definitive: she is, at different times, a kitten, a duck, a lamb, a calf (all these on her first appearance), a butterfly, a pigeon, a canary, and a Brazilian monkey. She is also a rose-petal, a blossom, and a downy peach. At her most human she is a toddler like Totty. Obviously George Eliot is imitating the reifying language of men about women, but there is no attempt to distinguish between the language and the reality. Mrs. Poyser, who is shrewd, calls her a peacock, and Adam, who feels noble love for her, thinks of her in the same terms: 'he only felt a sort of amused pity, as if he had seen a kitten setting up its back, or a little bird with its feathers ruffled' (ch. 23). Hetty can hardly be other than an animal, but, of course, she has 'a woman's destiny', and thus, in the process of responding to its demands, she is necessarily destroyed.

The ideological pattern is coherent enough, but it is noticeable that, in working it out, George Eliot, like Spencer, dehumanizes social convention. For it is not nature that Hetty offends against (like Tess, she is 'a pure woman'), but the moral propriety which men have made. She murders her child because she fears social shame, and again *mimetically* George Eliot allows for the distinction. When Hetty at night finds straw to lie on she instinctively feels a return to life: she 'kissed her arms with the passionate love of life' (ch. 37). With daylight, she confronts social judgment ('that man's hard, wondering look at her') and life becomes 'as full of dread as death'. There is a bitterly ironic contrast between the interior presentation of Hetty's flight and the dry externality of the Court testimonies. Through this we achieve sympathy, but it is a sympathy which is halted before it questions social justice. Adam, naturally enough, wants Arthur to take the blame for what has happened: he sees her momentarily as the victim of social exploitation. Irwine, who is obviously George Eliot's spokesman, argues with him:

> you have no right to say that the guilt of her crime lies with him, and that he ought to bear the punishment. It is not for us men to apportion the shares of moral guilt and retribution. We find it impossible to avoid mistakes even in determining who has committed a single criminal act, and the problem of how far a man is to be held responsible for the unforeseen consequences of his own deed, is one that might well make us tremble to look into it. The evil consequences that may lie folded in a single act of selfish indulgence, is a thought so awful that it ought surely to awaken some feeling less presumptuous than a rash desire to punish.

(ch. 41)

Reading this is to have the sense of a loss of focus. Who is apportioning Hetty's share of guilt if it is not 'us men'? Of course, the key word is 'moral', and the advice is against the 'rash' desire for punishment on the part of the individual. Arthur may have caused a crime; Hetty committed it. But it shows quite clearly how the ideological pattern of the novel prevents us from carrying the limits of moral enquiry beyond the merely individual to the social. Society's conditions, like nature's, are inexorable. And if our sympathy can go beyond that of the Court and see that Hetty is not a *cold-blooded* murderer, it cannot question the right of a society in which, in Hardy's resonant phrase, 'the woman pays', to exact its due. Such sympathy would deny incarnate history.

The moral doctrine is, however, less important than the terms of the vision which it embodies. In Mrs. Gaskell's *Ruth*, the voice of convention is personalized in the figure of Mr. Bradshaw, and thus the dramatic formation of social law becomes clear as the dominating Christian gives way, under the pressure of revelation about Ruth, to obscene hysteria. Though this leads Mrs. Gaskell into dissolving social problems in terms of individual reform, it also enables her to portray the psychological basis of class relations. The basis of George Eliot's realism is an acceptance of the abstract nature of convention because she is concerned with the individual *in* society rather than the individuals who make it. Society thus becomes a brown pond, separate from the cygnets and ducks within it, and inexorably fixed. The story of Hetty shows us the reification of society in process as the social tragedy becomes a biological parable.

III

Most critics accept what George Eliot instructs us to understand in the presentation of Adam – that through the suffering caused to him by Arthur and Hetty, he moves towards a 'higher feeling' of sympathy with those less morally gifted than himself. The trouble is that the language in which Adam's suffering is realized is so often inadequate. The first major reassessment in Adam's coming to self-knowledge, for example, is his meditation during the service after his father's burial:

> 'Ah! I always was too hard,' Adam said to himself. 'It's a sore fault in me as I'm so hot and out o' patience with people when they do wrong, and my heart gets shut up against 'em, so as I can't bring myself to forgive 'em. I see clear enough there's more pride nor love in my soul, for I could sooner make a thousand strokes with th' hammer for my father than bring myself to say a kind word to him. And there went plenty o' pride and temper to the strokes, as the devil *will* be having his finger in what we call our duties as well as our sins. Mayhap the best thing I ever did in my life was only doing what was easiest for myself. It's allays been easier for me to work nor to sit still, but the real tough job for me 'ud be to master my own will. . . . It seems to me now, if I was to find father at home tonight, I should behave different; but there's no knowing – perhaps nothing 'ud be a lesson to us if it didn't come too late. It's well we should feel as life's a reckoning we can't make twice over; there's no real making amends in this world, any more nor you can mend a wrong subtraction by doing your addition right.'

(ch. 18)

In the presentation of Arthur and, to a large extent, of Hetty, George Eliot's normal mode of narration is to trace the dramatic curve of consciousness within a framework of moral judgment. In the case of Adam, however, it is more frequently this kind of

30

interior soliloquy, because, in fact, he doesn't need authorial commentary – he can provide his own judgment. And this means that
the language has a striking lack of urgency. The specific situation is
immediately generalized: 'people when they do wrong' reduces his
father to one of a series, and, at the same time, despite the 'humility'
of the speech, carefully maintains Adam's moral superiority. Despite
the dialect, the whole speech has a logic and an eloquence ('What
we call our duties', 'It seems to me now', 'It's well we should feel')
which would be effective from the pulpit. And this is borne out by
the movement of pronouns from 'I' to the generalized 'we' to the
impersonal 'you'. Indeed, the final aphorism is a moral more applicable to Arthur and Hetty than to Adam. Later in the novel, when
the emotional pressure is much stronger and George Eliot has to
show us Adam incoherent with suffering, she is forced to be melo-
dramatic and theatrical:

'No – O God, no!' Adam groaned out, sinking on his chair again; 'but
then that's the deepest curse of all ... that's what makes the blackness
of it ... *it can never be undone*. My poor Hetty ... she can never be
my sweet Hetty again ... the prettiest thing God had made – smiling
up at me ... I thought she loved me ... and was good.'

(ch. 41)

The vocabulary is stagey ('curse', 'blackness', 'my sweet Hetty ...
smiling up at me') and the incoherence is engrafted – in fact, there
is a clear enough progression of thoughts ('but then', 'that's what').
It is clear that George Eliot finds it consistently difficult to realize
'poor Adam's maddening passions'. In the chapters following
Adam's discovery of Arthur and Hetty in the wood, it is significant
that we learn very little of the 'scorching light' which comes to
Adam and move quickly to the much more assured dramatization
of Arthur's consciousness.

The contrast in quality suggests that George Eliot's failure to be
convincing is more than a technical ineptitude. Adam is, in the first
place, always on the margin of suffering. The repentance of his intolerance of Thias's wrongdoing seems gratuitous when it is set
against Lisbeth's finely realized misery. Her *whole world* is shattered by the destruction of its central relationship: the only way out
of her despair, as the careful attention to the corpse and the satisfaction she feels in the tribute of the Church service bitterly demonstrate, is through the embalming of the past. Beyond that she is

merely an obstruction: 'I'm no good to nobody now' is an objective summary of her predicament, and, shortly after, we see Adam pushing her away: ' "Well, well; goodbye, mother," said Adam, kissing her and hurrying away. He saw there was no other means of putting an end to the dialogue' (ch. 20). As this indicates, Adam does have a future beyond his father's death; he is, in fact, released by it – 'the heaviest part of his burden' has gone. Not only is he on the margin of Lisbeth's grief, but the suffering is marginal to him. The same is true of his relationship with Hetty: 'it was the supreme moment of his suffering: Hetty was guilty' (ch. 43). Something *outside* him has failed, and this too is ultimately a lucky break – he is spared marriage to Hetty by her 'guilt'. What Adam really has to learn is not to marry beneath him.

George Eliot is clearly embarrassed by the possibility of this reading, and she makes Bartle Massey its spokesman in order that we should see Adam angrily refuting it (ch. 46). But the events of the novel justify Massey's optimism, and she has to intervene directly, in a highly abstruse passage, to draw a distinction between benefits gained from one's 'own personal suffering' and the cynicism of supposing that one person's misery can be justified by another's resultant happiness. The speciousness of such moral economics, especially in a novel which insists on the communal interaction of guilt and sorrow, is obvious.

However, it would be wrong to suggest that, by being spared marriage with Hetty, Adam is spared the consequences of his own folly in loving her. Adam's love has a clear moral function; in order to ascend to the higher feeling of sympathy which is the basis of man's perfectibility, he has to have 'his heart strings bound round the weak and erring, so that he must share not only the outward consequence of their error, but also their inward suffering' (ch. 19). His love is *not* folly – it comes 'out of the very strength of his nature' (ch. 33). This clearly creates a problem, however, since Hetty is a deceptive appearance behind which is the reality of Dinah. (After his father's death, Adam dreams of Hetty and wakes to find Dinah; Hetty dresses up as Dinah.)

But Adam's love is a version of the Feuerbachian transformation: as the love of God is a sublimation of the love of humanity, so the love of beauty is a mistaken individuation. 'Beauty', we are told, 'has an expression beyond and far above the one woman's soul that it clothes . . . it is more than a woman's love moves us in a

32

woman's eyes – it seems to be a far-off mighty love that has come
near to us. . . . The noblest nature sees the most of this *impersonal*
expression in beauty' (ch. 33; George Eliot's italics). Although
George Eliot mocks the horseman for judging Dinah by her phy-
siognomy (ch. 2), she herself discriminates by physical appearances.
Adam's strength is distinguished from Seth's passive mildness by a
contrast of Seth's pale eyes with Adam's dark, penetrating glance.
The clue is heredity. Adam, we can see, is a perfect blend of Celt
and Saxon. Hetty's beauty is correspondent with a reality, but, because of heredity, the correspondence is indirect. Her eyelashes express 'the disposition of the fair one's grandmother' (ch. 15), and if
we should think this ironic, the theory is stated less coyly later:
'There are faces which nature charges with a meaning and pathos
not belonging to the single human soul that flutters beneath them,
but speaking the joys and sorrows of foregone generations' (ch. 26).
Hetty, in short, is a moral fossil. Thus evolutionary doctrine gives
the mystery of Adam's refining love a scientific basis.[5]

It is important to insist on this because the novel celebrates the
superior evolutionary adaptability in Adam by showing that he is
capable of an objective 'sympathy' which, through the punishment
and destruction of Hetty, becomes rightly focused. But, as in the
case of George Eliot's presentation of Hetty, it is necessary to discriminate between the mimesis and the ideology which frames it:
the concrete realization defines the social basis of the idealization.
We have already seen that Adam reifies Hetty. She is 'the prettiest
thing God made' and his own explanation of the mystery of love is
sexually impersonal – it is like 'the sprouting of the seed' (ch. 11).
At the same time, it is carefully contained within his social awareness of duty: 'She's more nor everything else to me, all but my conscience and my good name' (ch. 28). This is more than moral
limitation: his happiest reveries about Hetty are bound up with his
vision of 'an opening into a broadening path of *prosperous* work',
and he makes it clear to Arthur that she is something to be worked
for: 'And I never kissed her i' my life – but I'd ha' worked hard for
years for the right to kiss her' (ch. 27). The combination of reified
sexual attraction and social advancement creates a very precise impression of the basis of the envisaged marriage which is borne out
later when Adam confronts the future without Hetty: 'but now
there was no *margin of dreams* for him beyond this daylight reality,
no *holiday time* in the working-day world: no moment in the

distance when duty would take off her iron glove and breast plate and clasp him gently into rest' (ch. 50). Woman is thus marginal, an escape from, the immediate reward of self-fulfilling work. It is a basis for marriage similar to that of Philip Hepburn and Sylvia in *Sylvia's Lovers*, but in Mrs. Gaskell's novel it is seen as class-based and thus it is an institutionalized and repressive love which crushes the woman's being. *Sylvia's Lovers* is also about the 1790s, but it is a truly historical novel. The marriage between Philip and Sylvia comes into being as the result of the riot which leads to her Radical father's death. Philip, the draper, is a new man, the *bourgeois* who integrates and therefore survives. The terms of the marriage grow out of the concrete historical situation.

Because George Eliot doesn't see the historical and human basis of institutions, she incorporates Adam's love in a metaphysical scheme justified by natural law. In these terms, there is no essential difference between Adam's relation with Hetty and that higher feeling for Dinah: the epilogue shows us Dinah's 'more matronly figure' in what has become Adam's timber-yard. She has given up Snowfield and accepted Conference's decision to ban women preachers (that this is *her* choice is emphasized by the fact that Seth hasn't accepted it, but has joined a break-away group). She is the model *bourgeois* wife, shaping her destiny through her prosperous husband's work. Ian Gregor suggests that if the love between Arthur and Hetty is delusively Arcadian, Adam's love also looks back to a Golden Age. But they are different ideals, socially as well as morally, and they correspond differently to reality. The reality of Arthur and Hetty's relationship is aristocratic exploitation, and thus the Arcadian dream is directly antithetic to it, since Arthur and Hetty are neither children nor gods. Adam's love is based on the *bourgeois* mode of integration through work, and his love for Hetty is only delusive in so far as it is badly focused: socially and biologically, it adapts properly to the prevailing realities once beauty and soul correspond in the object.

I say *bourgeois* because I think that the doctrine of work as it emerges in the novel is related to the notion of the self-made man, the fittest survivor. This, of course, is far from explicit. Indeed, the concept of work is primarily integrative and it looks back to an ideal close to that celebrated in *Past and Present*. This is clear from the first chapter in the contrast with Seth. Seth is apparently more amiable but he is also ineffectual: he forgets the door-panels, he is unable to comfort his mother, he is unable to bring Dinah into direct relation with material reality. More importantly, he looks forward to the dreamers who are to precipitate the disasters of the novel – Hetty and Arthur. Thus Adam's materialism comes to seem a more truly religious activity, because through work he transforms egoism into creativity: 'All passion becomes strength when it has an outlet from the narrow limits of our personal lot in the labour of our right arm' (ch. 19). Work communicates with reality: it also communicates with other men: Adam tells Dinah that he likes to go to work through hilly country so that he can survey the land from a height, because 'it makes you feel the world's a big place, and there's other men working in it with their heads and hands besides yourself' (ch. 11). Physical integration with the universe, social integration with the community, and, besides these, self-integration through the provision of a moral absolute. At the height of his despair, when work has become momentarily meaningless, Adam says to himself, 'But tomorrow . . . I'll go to work again. I shall learn to like it again some time, maybe; and it's right whether I like it or not' (ch. 48). In all this, he closely resembles Carlyle's Abbot Samson (who has 'a terrible flash of anger' at wrongdoing), and is thus a nostalgic figure in whom the true religion, as opposed to the 'diseased introspections' of Methodism, contrasts with the 'present' world of mammonism and dilettantism.

But work is much more than the expression of the community: 'a man perfects himself by working' – finds, that is, his individual destiny. The great individualists, the heroes, Wren and Columbus, are praised too, and Carlyle looks forward as well as back to the captains of industry and the aristocracy of talent. Mammonism is better than dilettantism and all it needs is a soul. In *Adam Bede* this forward-looking movement is present in the individuating process which ties up with the integrative one. Adam is not only defined by the moral contrast with Seth in the first chapter, but by the social contrast with the clock-watching workmen. Wiry Ben says to him, 'Ye may like work better nor play, but I like play better nor work; that'll 'commodate ye – it laves ye the more to do.' Although we are meant to despise Ben for this, he has a point. Adam is already a foreman, and however much he talks of pleasure and pride in work, he is paid to stop clock-watchers. Moreover, he already has his eye on a partnership, and, as Ben says, his success depends on being accommodated by the lesser mortals who work only for *immediate gain*. It is more than incidental that Adam's axiom, 'God helps them that helps themselves', is from Franklin's Preface to *Poor Richard's Almanack* entitled 'The Way to Make Money Plentiful in Every Man's Pocket'. Combined with the sense of community is a loyalty to the great individualists – Franklin and Arkwright.[6] And it is significant that Adam makes no fundamental distinction between Capital and Labour:

> 'For I believe he's one of those gentlemen as wishes to do the right thing, and to leave the world a bit better than he found it, which it's my belief that every man may do, whether he's gentle or simple, whether he sets a good bit o' work going and finds the money, or whether he does the work with his own hands.'
>
> (ch. 25)

Because of this, the clash between Adam and Arthur can never fully become a class issue, for the individualism is integrative, a matter of adaptation. 'Th' natur' o' things doesn't change, though it seems as if one's own life was nothing but change' (ch. 11). We are back to Herbert Spencer and the fixed social laws. Adam may be an idealization, but this is because he is a new man *unhistorically* realized as a more perfect man who moves up the evolutionary scale because adaptation is the double movement of individuation and integration: 'the ultimate man will be one whose private requirements coincide with the public ones'. Thus if his decision not to leave Hayslope is stoicism: 'It's all I've got to think of now – to do my work well, and make the world a bit better place for them as can enjoy it' (ch. 48) – it is also a good evolutionary policy: the unfallen Adam gets Dinah and a timber-yard.

IV

To see the novel as a process of transforming historical realities into ideological fable is not to underestimate its impressiveness. I am not arguing that *Adam Bede* is a fictional version of Herbert Spencer, but that the concrete realization of the empirical vision exists in tension with the historically specific ideology which shapes it. To use Belinsky's formula, art is necessarily a convex mirror – only a subjective distortion can enable it to reflect a totality. We should recognize, as criticism has tended not to do, that the convexity of George Eliot's art is more specific than a vaguely defined and classless humanism. Herbert Spencer is useful as well as relevant because it is more obvious in his work than in, for example, that of Comte or Feuerbach, that his ethic springs from class-interest: he moves towards the pervasive formula of 'man versus state'. The difference between him and George Eliot is that his work does not confront empirical reality at all in a direct way – he is all system. But it still remains true that George Eliot's realism does not escape its historical context, and the context emerges, naturally, most clearly in her first novel. Moreover, I am not merely concerned to establish limitations – the convexity is a positively important feature of George Eliot's realism. In particular, the reified and dehistoricized vision of the social law is a major premise of the 'original psychological notation' of *Middlemarch* and *Daniel Deronda*: the great interior dramas of Dorothea and Gwendolen depend on George Eliot's subjective participation in the appearance of the structure of the relationship between the individual and society to them as *bourgeois* consciences. And if, as I have implied, *bourgeois* abstractions play a more active rôle in George Eliot's realism than in Mrs. Gaskell's, this is not because Mrs. Gaskell's realism is more objective or less *bourgeois*, it is because George Eliot has a firmer grasp of a later, more alienated phase of development, in which the *bourgeois* vision has ceased to appear historical. And if this means the loss of a certain kind of objectivity, it also means that for George Eliot there is no escape into sentimental solutions through the 'one human heart'. Paradoxically, the apparent dehistoricization of social reality in George Eliot's work means that there is no escape from history.

Adam Bede, however, does witness an attempt to escape through the portrayal of historical forces as 'natural' history, and I have tried to suggest that George Eliot is too great a realist for this to be successful: in future the reifications will appear as reifications; individuation will be separation, not integration; the virtues of Adam will be divided between Caleb Garth, who is on the fringe of society, and Lydgate, who is in collision with it. Even within *Adam Bede* there is a radical questioning of the ideological pattern, though in a way which so fully probes the social basis of alienation that it is never fully repeated in the later work. This emerges in the portrayal of the relationship between Dinah and Hetty.

Most critics see Dinah as a wearyingly theoretical character. She is George Eliot's tribute to Feuerbach, the higher nature who sublimates her love of human beings through Methodism. Her sympathy, in the Spencerian formulas I have been suggesting, gives her a great potential for adaptability which is realized through her material participation in reality when she marries the integrated individualist, Adam. But, I think, George Eliot goes beyond Feuerbach in her portrayal of Dinah and undermines the adaptational pattern in her relationship with Hetty.

Marx's most obvious criticism of Feuerbach is that in dissolving the religious world into its secular basis, he fails to explain the detachment of the religious world in terms of the 'self-cleavage and self-contradictoriness of this secular basis' (*Fourth Thesis on Feuerbach*). This is precisely what George Eliot does achieve, through the precise delimiting of Dinah's religious emotion in the superbly structured sermon. Dinah begins in social actuality: Christianity has a special relationship to poverty, and she returns again and again to the conditions of poverty. Combined with this is the personal concreteness of her story about seeing Wesley. The initial affirmation thus grows out of actuality – God looks after the poor and ignorant and provides their daily sustenance. Out of this grows, however, an encounter with doubt: 'It doesn't cost him much to give us our little handful of victual and bit of clothing; but how do we know he cares for us any more than we care for the worms and things in the garden, so as we rear our carrots and onions? . . . For our life is full of trouble, and if God sends us good, he seems to send bad too.' With an effective candour, Dinah thus begins by registering the despair of poverty, and the sermon moves towards a far-reaching question: 'What shall we do if he is not our friend?' There is no other friend of the poor, but can we depend even on him?

At this point the narration changes from direct speech to *oratio obliqua*. This creates an obvious distance, for Dinah withdraws from her own question: 'Then Dinah told how the good news was brought.' Actuality is exchanged for story: the present is met with the past. Jesus *once* helped the poor. The move back to the present is achieved by a change from the historical to the suppositive: 'Ah! wouldn't you love such a man if you saw him?' The basis of Jesus's transcendence is thus wish-fulfilment. Again there is a change from direct speech to narrative as we move from wish-fulfilment to the nightmare of sin. This is not to *oratio obliqua*, but to description of Dinah and the change that comes over her as she says, 'Lost-sinners'. The religion of fear is a matter not of speech, but of dramatic projection which moves towards hallucination – 'see where our blessed Lord stands and weeps'. After the morbid details of the

38

Passion, she wrestles with Bessy Cranage's soul. She thus returns to reality, but not to preach so much as to set up a real-life melodrama. The return is mediated by the series of transitions which has moved towards hysteria: reality, doubt, narrative, supposition, desire, fear, hallucination, reality. This is more than just brilliantly accurate: it brings out fully the connection between social alienation and its resultant dreams – desire and fear. There is no attempt to sentimentalize Methodism's ruthless exploitation of social injustice. Later, Dinah tells Irwine: 'I think maybe it is because the promise is sweeter when this life is so dark and weary, and the soul gets more hungry when the body is ill at ease' (ch. 8).

Thus, although Dinah is a sympathetic character, it is surely intended that she should be, as Barbara Hardy has described her, 'charmless'. What is sympathetic is the sense of human misery which is the basis of her Methodism, not the language in which that sense sublimates itself. But the radical limitation has a much more far-reaching effect. Dinah is a dreamer, and, as we have seen, the dream is a limited response to a concrete reality. Thus, the continual juxtaposition of her altruism in contrast with Hetty's egoism enforces as well a parallel between them in that both are alienated dreamers. If the primary function of the 'Two Bed-Chambers' scene is to underline the difference between them, it is also true that both are looking for a world beyond that in which they find themselves. The instinctive movement towards Hetty doesn't seem to me sentimental, because, in the first place, it grows out of a common withdrawal ('her imagination had created a thorny thicket of sin and sorrow'), and in the second, the communication between them is painfully limited by the inadequacy of Dinah's language: 'I desire for you, that while you are young you should seek for strength from your Heavenly Father, that you may have a support which will not fail you in the evil day' (ch. 15). Given the rigid formality and the lack of specific reference of this, it is not surprising that it merely creates a 'chill fear' which makes Hetty drive Dinah away. Nevertheless, beneath the failure, there is a communication which emerges in the prison scene much later. Irwine dismisses Hetty with a complacent insensitivity: 'some fatal influence seems to have shut up her heart against her fellow creatures' (ch. 41). We have already seen that Irwine, with his automatic acceptance of convention, is unqualified to communicate with Hetty (that 'some' is extraordinary – he has forgotten that Hetty has been shut up literally because of his mother's godson). Yet as soon as Dinah appears, we learn of Hetty that 'it was the human contact she clung to'. In Hetty's confession, it becomes clear that she sees Dinah as separate from the world of convention:

> 'I daredn't go back home again – I couldn't bear it. I couldn't have bore to look at anybody for they'd have scorned me. I thought o' you sometimes, and thought I'd come to you, for I didn't think you'd be cross with me, and cry shame on me: I thought I could tell you. But then the other folks 'ud come to know it at last. . . .'
>
> (ch. 45)

It is a revealing moment, for we know how justified Hetty is – the reactions of Martin Poyser and Bartle Massey define a communal attitude. But, more than this, Adam, we have seen, suffers because she is not 'good'. From the moment he says to Arthur, 'tell me she can never be my wife' (ch. 28) he declares the limits of his sympathy. Only Dinah, with her limited and alienated way of coping with the world, is able to offer *human* contact. Both Hetty and Dinah live in a dream which questions the justice of the secular world, and it is a bitterly ironic commentary on the secular ideology which the novel celebrates that it is Dinah who humanizes Hetty, because, in the enforced confrontation with reality, she can offer another, more resilient dream to replace the one which has been destroyed.

Thus, though through the destruction of Hetty and the self-fulfilment of Adam, George Eliot insists on the natural basis of the social law and so reifies the social vision of the novel, she also realizes through Dinah the 'validity' of a religion which escapes the apparently unchanging secular world, and thus reveals its 'cleavage' by showing that reification is a psychological response to a particular situation. In Stoniton Gaol the fixed 'medium' of Hayslope is momentarily given an historical identity.

NOTES

1. See for example: D. Van Ghent, *The English Novel Form and Function* (Holt, Rinehart & Winston, 1953); J. Arthos, 'George Eliot – The Art of Vision', *Rivista de Letterature Moderne* (1954); M. Hussey, 'Structure and Imagery in *Adam Bede*', *Nineteenth Century Fiction* (1955); W. M. Jones, 'From Abstract to Concrete in *Adam Bede*',

College English (1955); C. Creeger, 'An Interpretation of *Adam Bede*', *English Literary History* (1956).

2. I. Gregor and B. Nicholas, *The Moral and the Story* (Faber & Faber, 1962), p. 16.

3. First published in the *Westminster Review* (July 1856), pp. 51–79. Quotations here are taken from *The Essays of George Eliot*, ed. T. T. Pinney (Routledge & Kegan Paul, 1963), pp. 266–99.

4. This and subsequent quotations from Spencer are from *Social Statics* (1851). Lewes said of this book: 'We remember no work on ethics since that of Spinoza to be compared with it' (*Letters*, i. 364).

5. Herbert Spencer, *On Physical Beauty* (1853), makes these points about beauty and heredity.

6. It is worth noting that, in her journal in 1857, George Eliot describes Samuel Smiles' *Life of George Stephenson* as 'a real profit and a pleasure' (*Letters*, ii. 369).

III

'THE MILL ON THE FLOSS'
Barbara Hardy

I TAKE IT that *The Mill on the Floss* is the novel most visibly close to George Eliot's life. As in many novels loosely classed as auto-biographical, this closeness to life has advantages and disadvantages, and shows itself in various ways. It creates the loving and seemingly accurate chronicle of actual events; the successfully externalized conscious and unconscious disguise and transformation; and the glib, inventive fantasy of dreaming and wishing. I am separating these processes for the purpose of announcing my analysis, but the novel blurs the edges and blends the kinds. It is a novel where the author is recalling the landscape and feelings of her childhood, in ways both gratifyingly indulgent and rationally analytic. As she dwells on the relationship between a brother and a sister we can discern an understandable and undisfiguring nostalgia; a need to explain and justify in concretely imagined terms; and the falsifying pressures of a wish-fulfilling reconciliation. Where she modifies experience, in order to hide or reveal, we can find resemblance with difference: she brings out order and meaning, discovers and argues her case, by summoning variety and antithesis, by trying out her particular conclusions and experience in the generalizing process of ordered invention, which accumulates and patterns fresh particulars. The submission to pressures of wishing and dreaming shows itself in a failure to particularize, in a movement away from the scrupulous testing process into simplifications of symbol and plot. *The Mill on the Floss* is especially interesting as a novel because it sets up an expressive form which betrays itself, and because in so doing reveals the varying relationships between the work of art and the materials of life.

The uneven and complex relations between the work of art and its sources – which we can usually only guess at – is perhaps most clearly introduced by taking a look at some similar cases in the art of fiction. Like *The Mill on the Floss*, Charlotte Brontë's *Jane Eyre* and Dickens's *David Copperfield* also combine a strongly contrasted particularity with an uncontrolled submission to fantasy. Not surprisingly, all three novels sharply betray this submissiveness in the testing-ground where the novelist solves his problems and reaches his conclusions – at the end of the story. At the end of novels of education the novelist stands back and defines the nature and meaning of the process, the development, the *Bildung*. His conclusion is a conclusion in both senses: an end and an arrival at meaning. Behind such problem-solving lies the more or less invisible pressure of the artist's personal problems, and it is characteristic of such mid-Victorian novels that they should arrive at conclusions which are affirmative, reconciliatory, and final. Charlotte Brontë, Dickens, and George Eliot do not exactly create simple fables for their time, but achieve affirmation and finality by crushing a complex experience into narrow simplifications of plot and symbolism. The endings of all three novels are religious or quasi-religious, and are marked by a strong emotional crescendo which betrays the uncontrolled urge to reach an end. They make an under-distanced appeal which can command the assent of tears or the dissent of stony recognition – or both. Charlotte Brontë kills off Rochester's mad wife, and brings him through the fire, mutilated and penitent, to Jane's arms: there is the triumphant reconciliation after all that pain, and the triumphant discovery of meaning. Dickens kills off David's child-wife, Dora, and brings him through visionary experience in the high and lonely Alps to Agnes's arms: there is the triumphant reconciliation after all that pain, and the triumphant discovery of meaning. George Eliot kills off Tom and Maggie, bringing them through the waters of the flood into each other's arms: there is the triumphant feeling after all that pain, and the triumphant discovery of meaning. Each novel ends with a double Eureka feeling: the final embrace of the loved-one and the final vision of meaning. The blinded Rochester now sees the pattern in his life and Jane's; David ceases to be metaphorically 'blind, blind, blind'; and Tom Tulliver at last sees (and Maggie sees that he sees) 'the depths in life, that had lain beyond his vision which he had fancied so keen and clear'. The imagery of blindness and good vision is there in each novel.

In *Jane Eyre* and *David Copperfield* the fantasy runs as a vivid unreal thread through the novel, and is particularly associated with Rochester and Agnes. In both novels there is an increase in authorial magic at the end, but the wish-fulfilment also shapes a kind of character who will make for that end, fantastically idealized and simplified. In *The Mill on the Floss* there is no such character – not even Maggie – and the drop, or rise, into the heights of the false Sublime and a false catharsis is therefore especially violent. All three novels show a controlled and controlling particularity *and* an abrupt movement into unparticularized consolations and conclusions. Whether we see the novel as an imitation of reality or as an expressive form creating virtual experience, it seems right to speak of partial failure. Each novel seems to fail for a good reason: the solutions and conclusions are so visibly needed by the artist, not by the tale. Each novel is an instance of technique acting, not as discovery, but as obscuring fantasy.

Perhaps all we can really say about autobiographical novels is that they are novels which reveal this connection between the life-need and the completed form. Novels which seem more objectified are often novels which we simply cannot check against biographical data. The weakness in Coleridge's distinction between the Shakespearian or Spinozan imagination which becomes all things and the Miltonic imagination which brings all things into itself, or in Keats's distinction between the chameleon poet and the Wordsworthian or egotistical Sublime, is their reliance on the distinction between an artist's life about which little is known and an artist's life about which a great deal is known. We happen to be in a position to say that Charlotte's sexual and social experiences may well explain her need for a sexual and religious solution like the one provided by the conclusion to *Jane Eyre*, to see that Dickens's marriage encouraged fantasy, and to see that George Eliot's break with family and society shaped the form and content of her solution. The actual prayers of Jane, David, and Maggie all correspond closely with the needs of their authors, and the needs produce the facile sublimity of the answers. But we do not find that the novel is totally falsified, wholly shaped by the fantasy of wishing and dreaming: each novel challenges the notion of an evenly objectified and totally realized work of art.

Each novel happens not only to betray wish-fulfilment, but to discuss it. If there is the self-indulgence of fantasy here, it is not the gross indulgence of ignorant artists, but the fine indulgence of intelligent artists, alive to the nature and dangers of romantic fantasy. Dickens creates a comic inflation and deflation of the fantasy and romantic imagery of David's immature loves. Charlotte Brontë has an intense analysis of the nature and the origin of fantasy in Jane's deprivation and ennui before she meets Rochester. George Eliot discusses and dramatizes Maggie's needs for various opiates – in daydreams, literature, religion, and personal relationships. The existence of this discussion of fantasy could mean no more than the unsurprising combination of rational insight with irrational blindness, but it happens also to be accompanied by a very strenuous effort to shape experience, to distinguish between dreaming and waking, and to break with the simplifications and stereotypes of fantasy.

The Mill on the Floss explores the realities of character and event by exposing human beings to life without opiate, but in the end it succumbs itself, as a work of art, to the kind of unreality it has been criticizing. The process by which it succumbs is not a simple one. I do not see the novel in terms of a polarity of soft dream and hard, daylight experience. There is a toughness and openness, a kind of pragmatism which shows itself especially in a movement away from heavy plotting and shaping of character development; there is a successful and transforming use of the personal experience of religious crisis and conversion; there is a successfully particularized though more personally interested transformation of her sexual crisis; and there is a final unsuccessful resort to solution by fantasy. I want to take these four aspects of the novel in reverse order, beginning at the end.

The case against the concluding Providential fantasy has perhaps been won too easily, whether by Henry James or Joan Bennett or Dr. Leavis, who have all written finely but not lengthily on the subject. I assume that all readers of George Eliot will agree on the importance of a sense of unity and continuity in her life and her novels. The two major crises of her life, the one a crisis of belief and the other a crisis of ethical choice, and many less climactic occasions of depression and anxiety, were all marked by a frightening sense of dislocation and loss of identity. Behind the loving chronicle of childhood and the fantastic problem-solving in *The Mill on the Floss* lies the estrangement from her early past. The breach with her brother Isaac was not mended until 1880, when she married John Cross, and received the famous letter of forgiveness:

> I have much pleasure in availing myself of the present opportunity to break the long silence which has existed between us.

To which she replied:

> It was a great joy to me to have your kind words of sympathy, for our long silence has never broken the affection for you which began when we were little ones.[1]

It is no act of wild speculation which finds personal pressures at work in the childhood scenes of *The Mill on the Floss*, in the nostalgic and analytic treatment of brother and sister, in some aspects of Tom's character, and in the subject of the break and the reconciliation. The emotional centrality of the relationship is significant, and so is the intensity of the final embrace – 'In their death they were not divided'.

The conclusion still needs to be closely evaluated. We can only defend it, I think, on very restricted aesthetic grounds. We may say that the novel's ending is prepared from its beginning, in the doom-laden references to death by drowning, in the river-imagery, and in the threads of pagan and Christian lore that run through the reminiscences of past floods, the legend of St. Ogg and the folk-superstition that 'when the mill changes hands the river's angry'. George Eliot is all too plainly preparing for her denouement. This is what Henry James had to say about that denouement in his essay, 'The Novels of George Eliot', in *The Atlantic Monthly*, October 1866:

> The denouement shocks the reader most painfully. Nothing has prepared him for it; the story does not move towards it; it casts no shadow before it.

James is wrong about nothing preparing us, wrong too about no shadow being cast, but he is quite right to say that 'the story does not move towards it'. Almost everything moves except the story. Even the characters are ingeniously though artificially involved in the pre-echoes as Mrs. Tulliver fretfully worries about her children being brought home drowned, or about Maggie tumbling in some day, and as Philip teases Maggie about selling her soul to the ghostly

boatman on the Floss. The foreshadowings strike us as artificial because they are uninvolved with action. There is the sense of a restless preparation in rhetoric which does not move dynamically with
events and characters. Mrs. Tulliver's nagging worries attach themselves clearly enough to the Maggie who pushes Lucy into the mud,
but scarcely to the flood and the heroic rescue. If Maggie were to fall
in carelessly, or throw herself in recklessly, there would be a relation
between prolepsis and action. Or if those legends about the river
and the great set-piece descriptions of its transiently tamed powers
were part of a presentation of man at work in and against Nature,
there could have been such a relation. But such descriptions remain
figures in the frame, not in the picture. The imagery that Henry
James uses of Isabel Archer not only hints at danger, but is fully
related to the action: Ralph does something very like putting wind
in her sails, and the audacity, responsibility, freedom, and danger
involved in the figure are fully worked out in event and character.
The animation that Thomas Hardy bestows on Nature is revealed
throughout *The Return of the Native* or *Far from the Madding
Crowd*, and Nature and Man are related at every turn of the action.
But the river-imagery and the descriptions of strong Nature in *The
Mill on the Floss* expose instead of disguising those gaps in the
action. Most of the hints and images and descriptions could be cut
without much loss of lucidity; Tulliver is a marvellous study in
reduced pride and love and temper, but not the hero or victim of a
story of economic struggle. The novel has a unity in imagery, and
this has a strong mnemonic force, but it does not prepare us for the
part played by the river in reaching the conclusion and solving the
problem. What we are prepared for is the struggle between the
energetic human spirit and a limited and limiting society: such
struggles are not settled by floods.

The flood is the Providence of the novel. It would not be quite
true to say that religion is rushed in at the end without being earlier
involved with action and character. The community of St. Oggs
is most carefully analysed as a mixed pagan and Christian society,
and a very large number of the characters are placed in religious
tradition, belief, and feeling. Maggie's religious experience is central
to the novel, but I do not think it prepares us for the miraculous
aura, however delicately adjusted, which surrounds her in the last
pages. It is interesting that a scholar who has made a special study of
George Eliot's treatment of religion, Martin J. Svaglic, observes that

'Maggie and Dorothea, in their moments of greatest crisis, do not pray'. Gordon Haight rightly corrects him about Maggie (in a footnote to the reprinted article in *A Century of George Eliot Criticism*). Yet there is a sense, I think, in which we can see why Svaglic can say that Maggie, like Dorothea, does not pray. Her prayer is in no way formal, her God can merge into the God of our anguished cries to no God, her voice is not raised to be heard – only compare her prayer with Jane Eyre's. But he is wrong, for the vague appeal is instantly answered, pat, like the prayers in *Jane Eyre*, with comfort and solution. When she is faced with a crisis of decision (which is what Svaglic may have meant by her moment of greatest crisis), she does not make her decision by referring to any laws or values that are not human. Dorothea's critics knew very well that her decisions and values were revealingly humane, void of supernatural reference, and Maggie feels, thinks, and chooses in the same humanly reliant way. True, there is the conversion by the aid of Thomas à Kempis, but there is absolutely nothing in it that does not pertain to George Eliot's Feuerbachian creed. Here is the third Positive, Duty, which she allowed to Myers in the garden of Trinity, Cambridge, but no trace of the first two, God and Immortality. If we look carefully, we see that George Eliot makes the religious conversion insistently human: the value is that of selflessness; there is a conversion of ethic, not of belief. George Eliot's emphasis is on the human agents, on Thomas himself, but also on the conveying human agent, whose 'hand' made the marginal marks and helped Maggie read and emphasize. There may be some slight trace of her own Evangelicalism in Maggie's adolescent histrionics, and it is, of course, interesting that this is the part of the conversion that is criticized and rejected. But the chief emphasis is human, though by this stage George Eliot could take and indeed represent human duty and fellowship in a solvent of religious symbolism and association. What is emphasized in the conversion is the human element, but what is emphasized at the end in the final chapter, despite the tactful and tactical ambiguities of 'almost miraculous effort divinely-protected', and the dream of the Virgin in the boat, is the super-human:

> Her soul went out to the Unseen Pity that would be with her to the end. Surely there was something being taught her by this experience of great need; and she must be learning a secret of human tenderness and long-suffering, that the less erring could hardly know?

'O God, if my life is to be long, let me live to bless and comfort. . . .'
At that moment Maggie felt a startling sensation of sudden cold
about her knees and feet: it was water flowing under her.

What turns a great psychological novel into a Providence novel
at the end is not simply this magical coincidence of prayer and
answer in the 'water flowing under her': it is the appearance of
exactly the wrong kind of problem-solving. Throughout the novel
there have been two chief implications in the action and relationships – implications which at times rise into explicit formulation:
one, that 'character is destiny – but not entirely so', which emphasizes not only social determinism and large human influence,
but the sheer chanciness of life; the other, that 'the highest election
and calling is to do without opium', a belief central to George Eliot's
rejection of Christianity, which remained with her all her life,
which is fully and strongly borne out in all her novels, and which
seems to be the standard by which maturity is described and mea-
sured in *The Mill on the Floss*. Maggie's 'process' is more complex
than any extracted pattern, but one of the strands in the extracted
pattern must be her rejection of the opiates of daydream, literature,
and religion. When she is able to make no dream-worlds any more,
and when literary dream-worlds fail her, she finds a new and subtly
effective drug in the religion of self-denial. Philip – and the novel's
course – make it plain to her that she is now substituting another
harder fantasy for the older fragile ones. She acts her renunciations,
and Philip prophesies, while the novel's course reveals that she has
fallen into the fantasy of choosing renunciations – little ones that
will not hurt too much. The final experience is the lengthy pain-
fulness of renunciation, and George Eliot takes great pains to show
this, even in the last foreshortened book of the novel, by making
Maggie try to live with the renunciation, and by making her go
through it a second time. She dramatizes most movingly the difference between giving up passion in passion and giving it up in deprivation. Laurence Lerner, in *The Truthtellers*, seems to me to be
right off the track when he says that the second renunciation is
theoretic, because the actual presences of the victims have gone. The
second renunciation is, on the contrary, a proof of the untheoretic
nature of her choice: she has lived with it. Imagination can people
Maggie's world with her victims, just as it makes her 'hear'
Stephen's voice as she reads his letter – a true and acute touch about
the physiological pressures of imagination. George Eliot is showing

implicitly what she made Philip tell Maggie explicitly – that renunciation hurts, that pain is unpleasant, that deprivation is destructive. My reason for making such an elaborate attack on the end of this novel is not a high regard for aesthetic unity and distress over an unprepared ending: it is an objection to the bad faith that contrasts so strongly with the authenticity of everything that comes before. George Eliot insists that renunciation does not make you feel noble and striking and secure, but empties life, depresses the spirit, and destroys a sense of meaning. Little renunciations and sacrifices, such as doing plain sewing and being nice to your mother, are enjoyable because painless, and are no kind of rehearsal for the real thing. George Eliot makes this point as toughly as James was later to do in *The Portrait of a Lady*, but she then goes back on it, softens it, tacks on the least appropriate conclusion. She gives Maggie rewards and triumphs after all, not just by answering the despairing prayer, but by taking her to Tom and allowing her, before they drown together, to see that change of vision in his eyes. The novel has been about living without fantasy and opiate, and ends with a combination of several strong fantasies. There is the fantasy of death, the fantasy of reconciliation, and the fantasy of being finally righted and understood. Henry James's suggestion that Maggie might call back Stephen was nowhere within range of the novel's contingencies: Maggie could either have thrown herself into the river or carried on, and the point which the whole novel had been sharpening would then have been driven against the reader's breast.

I do not see this novel as sharply divided into 'realism' and fantasy. We can see the way the end undermines the strength of the analysis of moral choice, and we can see personal reasons behind the shift into such blatant fantasy. In the rest of the novel there are other visible personal pressures at work, which are far from being destructive and falsifying. If the final fantasy is a response to her personal break with the past and her brother, so the crisis of renunciation seems also to be propelled by a personal need. There is some relation, at each stage in the novel, between a great personal need and the artistic shaping. The renunciation of Stephen seems to me to be a typical and successful instance of personal problem-solving: in it George Eliot transfers the ethical issues involved in her own sexual choice to a different situation which will generalize, justify, and explain. George Eliot violently and predictably rejected the renunciation in *Jane Eyre* – a renunciation made in the interests of 'a

50

diabolical law which chained a man soul and body to a putrefying carcass'. *The Mill on the Floss* reverses the situation in *Jane Eyre* in a way that can be seen as an argument with Charlotte Brontë. But I would scarcely wish to put it so theoretically. George Eliot went to live with Lewes in what was technically an adulterous union; her heroine refuses to marry a man who is unofficially engaged. George Eliot is not affecting moral delicacy (as some hostile readers thought) but inventing a situation which brings out her own defence, which eliminates all the personal particulars and invents new ones which generalize her argument. In her own case there is the breaking of a social, moral, and religious 'law'; in Maggie's case nothing approaching law or contract. In her own case there are no human victims, but George Eliot's own freedom and isolation, and Lewes's already wrecked relationship with his unfaithful wife; in Maggie's case there are two human beings, Lucy and Philip, out of whose painful deprivation would be taken her joy. The novel's apologia says, in effect: had human ties been involved, I would not even have broken the faintest commitment; since there were none, I was prepared to break social laws and commandments. Here is another personal pressure shaping the novel, but it works lucidly, logically, and imaginatively: the argument is sharpened as artistic argument must be, through particulars of feeling and relationship.

George Eliot's presentation of sexual-ethical choice is very far from being disinterested, but it in no way distorts the solidity and effective particularity of the novel. The same may be said for her presentation of religious conversion. Here we have something which seems also to have a source in personal experience, though George Eliot's change of faith is probably further 'behind' Maggie Tulliver's conversion than her sexual choice lies 'behind' Maggie's. At this point in the novel, we are midway between invention and experience, and it is, of course, true that crises of decision and vision which are to be found in most of the other novels can also be so described. Romola's decision to reject Savonarola's rigid doctrine for her human ethic is very close to George Eliot's arguments for Maggie's renunciation, but the situation in which Maggie is placed is plainly closer to personal experience. There is the continuity and stability of the ethic: her moral arguments are not purely pragmatic, and her reasons for living with Lewes are perfectly compatible with her humanist ethic as reasons, not as rationalizations. But just as the inventions are closer to the personal crises elsewhere, so they are, I think, in the religious crisis. Once again there is involvement, but no loss of clarity. The artist seems to be using invention in order to see experience straight, or in order to validate fantasy. Maggie's conversion to an ethic of love and sacrifice draws on George Eliot's own conversion from Christianity. As in *Silas Marner*, the religion to which she gives fullest sympathy is a religion of personal love, so that it is not true to say that experience is reversed. Characteristic of her own experience is the sense of false conversion and the restoration to continuity: George Eliot dramatized her 'conversion' in much the way Maggie does, by refusing to go to church, by taking the risk of a break with her father. Afterwards came not only a loving need to compromise and conform, but a tolerance which refused to draw lines between right and wrong belief. The element of egoism in Maggie's altruism, of new fantasy in her apparent rejection of fantasy, makes the presentation psychologically alive and morally interesting.

But this interestingness depends on much more than the ability to criticize and generalize moral experience. It depends also on the imaginative representation of ethics and psychology, on the ability to make us feel that the artist is enlarging investigation, not restricting it. At the end of the novel we feel this restriction with particular force, not simply because it goes against the grain of the truths the novel is trying to utter, but because the presentation of character has been remarkably open and unformed by the usual *Bildungsroman* conventions. E. S. Dallas, in his review of the novel in *The Times* (19 May 1860), spoke with fine penetration of George Eliot's 'effortlessness', observing that 'even when she has reached her climaxes she is entirely at her ease'. Maggie's character is presented in the medium of pity which has made it possible for Dr. Leavis and other critics to see in it elements of indulgence and self-gratification, but it also comes very close to an Existentialist openness, freedom, and pragmatism. Right up to the bad faith of the conclusion, we are presented with characters who are defined by the process of experiencing. Such closeness to experience is a rich theft from life by art, and all too rare in the great Victorian novelists. There is a tendency in modern criticism to argue or assume that closeness to life has the disadvantage of imperfect externalization, but it may also bring with it the advantage of unformed experience – of intransigence and a denial of form. The characteristic formal movement of novels of education is a progressive and evolutionary one, but even though *The Mill on the Floss* is a very Darwinian novel, its debt to Darwin is to be found in its hard and pessimistic look at struggle and survival, rather than in its optimistic treatment of personal evolutions. If we feel effortlessness in the climaxes, this is to some extent the result of a refusal to let climax determine and change character too markedly. To compare the process of Maggie Tulliver with the process of Janet Dempster or Adam Bede is to see George Eliot presenting character still sunk in the inchoate eddies of living.

Maggie is a character who believes herself to be converted and transformed, but who is incorrigibly herself. I speak relatively: of course, she does learn to live in a reserved and controlled way, but this lesson is scarcely a dramatic change, being a part of social education hard for sane and sensitive creatures to escape. But her change is minimal. George Eliot creates a pattern of apparent *Bildung*, but undermines and flattens its gains and crises. I do not know what Lady Ritchie had in mind when she said in her essay on Mrs. Gaskell (*Blackstick Papers*) that George Eliot seldom becomes subject to her creations, but seems to watch them from afar, except in the case of Maggie, where for once she is apparently 'writing of herself'. Apart from the sources of personal experience I have been speaking of, there is this lack of patterning, which also seems to have come out of the closeness to life. Writing out of personal dreams and urges has many effects, moves art in contrary directions. Here perhaps it moves it in the direction of a static concept of moral character in marked opposition to the models of development and deterioration found in earlier and later novels, where the heroes and heroines seem smoothly and steadily to ascend and descend their moral staircases.

It is possible to describe Maggie's progress in the diagrammatic form of such an ascent: her childhood is marked by the habit of creative and drugging fantasy, by the need to be loved and admired, by recklessness and absentmindedness, by pride and masochism; she moves to more subtly effective fantasies, in art and religion, her need to be loved and admired is controlled and subdued, and modified by her need to argue her values, she softens her pride; but the final stages show the weakness of her masochistic and unreal religiosity, and recklessness and dreaminess are finally triumphed over in the renunciation of Stephen: Maggie emerges from illusion and self-love. My account of her process is the more distorting for being faithfully close to the climaxes of the novel. What happens, however, is that the climaxes are reached and then denied. Maggie ascends and descends. It is a process more like an eddy than a directing current. It is true that Maggie is 'converted' to self-abnegation and the life of duty, and true, too, that Thomas à Kempis brings into her life something which changes it and does not entirely disappear. But it is a much weaker influence than we may remember. Before Philip tells her that fanaticism brings its own perils and that renunciation may have a terrible backlash, she is already moving out of that violent act of histrionic repression. She is very easily persuaded by Philip to move into a world of emotional and intellectual gratification, but a world that is the adult equivalent of her old dream-worlds. George Eliot shows the backward movement very gently and unfussily. The climax of vision and decision is not utterly undone, but its effects are largely erased:

> Could she really do him good? It would be very hard to say 'good-by' this day, and not speak to him again. Here was a new interest to vary the days – it was so much easier to renounce the interest before it came.
>
> (V. 1)

This mild and muted irony does not hold up its hands and exclaim in horror that on the preceding page Maggie had been saying 'it makes the mind very free when we give up wishing, and only think of bearing what is laid upon us, and doing what is given us to do'. George Eliot does not shirk showing the dividedness of Maggie's mind, and the shifting dialogue between the two voices, one sweet, one stern, which comes close on the passage just quoted, is Clough-like in its refusal to set a good angel against a bad. Maggie postpones conflict and drifts with the conversation, until she hits against 'an old impression' revived 'with overmastering force'. Philip offers to lend her *The Pirate*, and she feels the old wind blowing on her from Scott's rough sea, and puts the book aside: 'It would make me in love with this world again . . . it would make me long for a full life.' Philip tempts her then with sacredness and purity of 'poetry and art and knowledge', relying ruefully on the lack of sexual temptation his friendship offers. Maggie replies with fair self-knowledge, and a better instinct about the sacredness and purity of the arts, 'But not for me. . . . Because I should want too much. I must wait – this life will not last long.' The debate is lengthily repeated once more in the third chapter of Book V, and

54

once more there comes an interval in which it is dropped. In the less intense and argumentative talk in the interval there is another aesthetic temptation as Philip sings 'Love in her eyes sits playing'. The argument and the song end very undramatically, with little comment from the author, as Philip offers his sophistry, 'If I meet you by chance, there is no concealment in that?' which Maggie snatches at. The long, reflective passages which follow do not exclaim at the shortlived nature of Maggie's renunciations, but are given up to Philip. And in the following chapter (4), which moves on nearly a year, Maggie is back again reading Scott, identifying with the dark-haired heroines, telling Philip that their renewed friendship has indeed made her restless and occupied with 'the world', and referring to the time when she was 'benumbed' as past time. What happens next is one of those unexpected eddying movements: Philip asks her to love him, she accepts and assents, and what has seemed a source of dream and love and richness for the mind is set out as a new renunciation: 'If there were sacrifice in this love, it was all the richer and more satisfying' and 'The tissue of vague dreams must now get narrower and narrower'.

The web is a complex one: just when Maggie seems to be most enticed by the old voice 'that made sweet music', George Eliot shows that the relation with Philip is made up of renunciation as well as indulgence. At each step of apparent progress, when Maggie says most confidently, 'I have made up my mind,' she is shown, very quietly, as moving back on her word. This eddying process shows itself not only in each detail of apparent change, but throughout the whole broad pattern of growing up. The Maggie who pushed Lucy into the mud, who ran away, who used her doll as a scapegoat, who cut off her hair, who wanted to give Tom the bigger half of the jam-puff and immediately forgot his existence in devouring it, this Maggie is still present in the older Maggie, with adult appetites, adult control over trivial acts, and adult lack of control over grave ones. The strength of personal love which animates her sense of duty as she renounces Stephen owes something to the stern voice she listened to in Thomas à Kempis, and forgot, and heard again, but much to the generous lovingness that was there in the little girl. Her *experience* changes: she finds that renunciation is hard and destructive, but her *character* is not transformed by this discovery. Character is not cut in marble, George Eliot tells us in *Middlemarch*, but although the motion of Maggie's character is dynamic, it is no case of progress, like Silas Marner's. It is not very easy to say what George Eliot is doing in creating this oscillation and eddy. It may be that she saw herself as writing a tidy *Bildungs-roman*, as she was in her other novels, but that the very closeness to life, so falsifying at the end, paradoxically broke the pattern by its fidelity to the stubborn and unchanging nature of human character. It may have been Maggie's refusal to be a tragic and evolutionary heroine (like Morel's refusal to be a villain in *Sons and Lovers*) that brought about the final swing into dreaming and wishing.

One last word. It is not a novel where one character shows this openness and freedom while others remain conventionally grouped around that live centre. The stubborn and unchanging nature of character is shown dynamically, not statically, and the whole psychological notation of the novel keeps us in touch with mobility and complexity. This stubbornness is seen outside Maggie, for instance, in Tom, and perhaps most movingly in Mr. Tulliver. One of the finest examples, to my mind, comes in two adjacent scenes, which show Tulliver's recovery after his stroke. One marks a crisis of change, the other undercuts and makes an almost cancelling movement. 'Almost cancelling' – it is necessary to say 'almost', because although the novel is constantly showing characters apparently changing and thinking themselves changed, it is also showing that what seemed so influential is not utterly to pass without trace. Maggie does hear the stern voice at the end. And though Mr. Tulliver feels the Christian sacramental demands of his family Bible, and is led to an action which he tries to cancel in an act of pagan revenge, set out in that same Bible, the first submissive act does hold good, does affect events. It is rather that George Eliot shows people acting out of character, in obedience to strong external pressures, and then shows the recoil, in the obedience to the principle of self. In Book III, Chapter 8, Mr. Tulliver is apparently transformed, rather like Maggie, on the day when he comes down from his sick-bed to face the daylit emptiness of his house after the bankruptcy and sale. He picks up the family Bible and traces in it the cyclical history and ritual of birth, marriage, and death: his mother's death, his own marriage, his children's births. His wife wails in terms reduced to sacrament and proverb, speaking in the urgent voice of traditions larger than herself:

'We promised one another for better or for worse. . . .'
'But I never thought it 'ud be so for worse as this. . . .'

'If there's anything left as I could do to make you amends, I wouldn't say you nay.'

'Then we might stay here and get a living, and I might keep among my own sisters... and me been such a good wife to you, and never crossed you from week's end to week's end.'

'Give me a kiss, Bessy, and let us bear one another no ill-will: we shall never be young again.... This world's been too many for me.'

There is a strange unreality and foreignness in Tulliver's feelings in these extracts: he speaks in a voice of feeling unnaturally enlarged by awe and suffering and responsibility and illness. What George Eliot knows, and clearly shows that she knows, is that such high tide-marks of feeling, as she calls them elsewhere, when speaking of Maggie's deceptive acquiescence on Philip's love, may take us out of character, but do not transform us. It is the same intuition about moral change which lets her show Rosamond briefly and warmly responding to Dorothea, then living on to be Lydgate's basil plant. In the very next chapter, Tulliver's return to health and routine, his habituation to what shocked him out of character, makes him speak and act from the feelings of an older and for him more native religion of vengeance, curse, and feud:

The first moment of renunciation and submission was followed by days of violent struggle... he had promised her without knowing what she was going to say.

(ch. 9)

Here again it is easy to set out a plain, unblurred antithesis, missing the nuances. George Eliot does not show a straight swing of the pendulum, any more than she does with Maggie's 'submission' to Philip. Tulliver's old vigour returns, not simply to show him the difficulty of that vow made out of character, but also to bring up feelings that argued on the side of that vow, feelings that were not relevant when it was made, but which crop up later to arrest the pendulum, feelings of practical advantage, feelings of love for his past and his home. Here too, George Eliot uses her authorial reserve, saying nothing to interrupt the swing from tugging nostalgia to the violent decision to curse Wakem. There are times when her refusal to comment on the relation between two contrary states of mind points to the subterranean workings of conflict and decision. Tulliver repeats that vow out of character, 'I'll be as good as my word to you,' but makes Tom write — in that same Bible whose

57

ritual influence helped to take him out of character – the words of unforgiveness and hate: 'I wish evil may befall him.'

The novel whose chapters and divisions are so marked by quotations and images from Bunyan is no simple pilgrim's progress, but is indeed the least progressive of all George Eliot's studies in character and morality. This denial of progress in character, this flattening and erasing of the conventional diagram of moral evolution (conventional in moral thinking as well as in art) is a source of the truthfulness of a great but flawed novel, a novel whose merits and flaws show how art can tell difficult truths and consoling lies.

NOTES

1. *Letters*, vii, 280, 287.

IV

'SILAS MARNER'
Lilian Haddakin

'THE FIRST 100 pages are very sad, almost oppressive . . . I wish the picture had been a more cheery one,' John Blackwood regretfully, and rather regrettably, observed after reading – 'with the greatest admiration', nevertheless – the manuscript of the first part of *Silas Marner*.[1] Perhaps he was less ready than he should have been to trust the author's assurance, given as early as the final paragraph of Chapter 2, of a happy ending:

> But about the Christmas of that fifteenth year, a second great change came over Marner's life, and his history became blent in a singular manner with the life of his neighbours.

Blackwood's comment shows the naïvety of one who regards a novel as something like an extension of life. The sentence quoted from *Silas Marner* has naïvety of a different order; it is the note of the legendary tale, in which it is permissible – and, indeed, proper – to indicate in advance the broad pattern that is going to emerge.

Silas Marner perhaps gives more unalloyed pleasure to the modern reader than any of George Eliot's other works. It is both fresh and mellow, and it wins much goodwill. Not that the often-remarked 'fairy-tale' element in the book discourages the exercise of the critical faculty and lulls the reader into over-facile acceptance. *Silas Marner* has also won critical approval and has been acclaimed a 'minor masterpiece'. And the strain of realistic pastoral typified by the scenes at the Rainbow Inn has been remarked no less than the strain of 'fairy-tale'.

Minor it doubtless is in comparison with that major masterpiece, *Middlemarch*. But what I wish to do in this essay is not to ask what makes the later work 'major' and the earlier one 'minor', but to define the peculiar quality of *Silas Marner*. It clearly stands apart from *Romola* and the works that follow. And although, no less clearly, it has a good deal in common with *Adam Bede* and *The Mill on the Floss*, which immediately precede it, the satisfaction it offers is in some important ways different from that which we get from these two works.

Some readers may think that to analyse *Silas Marner* is to break a butterfly upon a wheel. But *Silas Marner* is not a butterfly. It is a big thing, except in the number of pages needed to tell the story. It is strong and profound, and, although evidently very simple in some ways in comparison with nearly all George Eliot's other works, it has its own complexity. As a whole, it is as firm as it is delicate, and the sense it gives of a rounded rendering of simplicities is achieved by a complex literary art that unites several heterogeneous elements. It deals with great and 'difficult' issues under the guise of a legendary tale, realistically treated, so that the outcome is, from one point of view, a tale of old-fashioned village life. The 'great questions' – of the 'primary affections' and their workings, of religion and superstition and class – are embodied in the story of an obscure weaver who, expelled from one community through a false accusation of theft, and finding himself an alien in the community to which he migrates, first becomes a miser, then is robbed of his gold, but 'blessed' with a foundling child in its place, and at length, through her, is emotionally healed and firmly linked with the village community.

We know, because George Eliot has said so, that *Silas Marner* had a different kind of origin from that of her other works. I do not propose to elaborate an argument along the lines of *post hoc, ergo propter hoc*; but it is a significant fact that *Silas Marner* reads as if it had a different origin from, say, *Adam Bede*. While it is partly the result of sustained reflection ('my mind dwelt on the subject', George Eliot characteristically says), and is marked by the deliberate and thorough craftsmanship that, in this author, always accompanies such reflection, it also – and this is obviously what sets it apart from her other fiction – comes from something spontaneous and unreflective, something not only chronologically prior but, I think, logically so as well. This 'something' – the author writes of a 'sudden inspiration' – not only is not lost as a result of later reflection, but apparently guides the reflection and does a great deal to determine the total structure of the book.

Some of the author's comments in her letters and journal may help us to see more clearly, by disengaging them, some of the strands that make up this fiction (which she consistently refers to as a 'story', not a 'novel'). In using these comments I am not concerned with their bearing on the evolution of the work during what she felt to be its slow advance, but with what they can suggest as we scrutinize the finished work with them in mind.

On 28 November 1860 George Eliot records in her journal[2] that she is writing a story, the idea of which has recently come to her and 'thrust itself' between her and the other book that she was meditating. It is already named: *Silas Marner, the Weaver of Raveloe*. She first mentions the work to her publisher in a letter of 12 January 1861:

> I am writing a story which came *across* my other plans by a sudden inspiration ... It is a story of old-fashioned village life, which has un-folded itself from the merest millet-seed of thought.[3]

On 24 February, after learning his reaction to Part I, she tells him more about the 'sudden inspiration'. The idea for the story sprang from a visual recollection:

> It came to me first of all, quite suddenly, as a sort of legendary tale, suggested by my recollection of having once, in early childhood, seen a linen-weaver with a bag on his back.[4]

That she remembered something else besides the bag on his back we learn from Blackwood's account of a conversation with her a few weeks after the publication of the book: ' "Silas Marner" sprang from her childish recollection of a man with a stoop and expression of face that led her to think he was an alien from his fellows.'[5] Part of what she remembered seeing was a facial expression which she had instantaneously 'construed'. The symbolism proper to a legen-dary tale was already potentially there in the burdened man with the alien look. And for the mature George Eliot the condition of being alien from one's fellows (in itself a metaphorical burden) was a rich theme to explore.

As her mind dwelt on the subject, she tells Blackwood in the letter of 24 February 1861, she 'became inclined to a more realistic treatment'. In its immediate context this must mean, primarily, 'more realistic than the treatment of the subject to be expected in a legendary tale', which squares with her earlier description of *Silas Marner* as 'a story of old-fashioned village life'. The linen-weaver gained a local habitation and a name, and also a quite precise historical setting.

But 'a more realistic treatment' has other implications as well, if we take the phrase in conjunction with certain other remarks, which come immediately before it:

> I should not have believed that anyone would have been interested in it but myself (since William Wordsworth is dead) if Mr Lewes had not been strongly arrested by it. But I hope you will not find it at all a sad story as a whole, since it sets – or is intended to set – in a strong light the remedial influences of pure, natural human relations. The Nemesis is a very mild one. I have felt all through as if the story would have lent itself best to metrical rather than prose fiction, especially in all that relates to the psychology of Silas; except that, under that treatment, there could not be an equal play of humour.[6]

I shall not waste time in speculating on what might have happened if George Eliot had tried to write *Silas Marner* in verse, on the model of 'Michael', the poem from which she took her epigraph. The book has strong Wordsworthian affinities, which I shall come to later, though in some important respects it is very far indeed from being a kind of 'Michael' in prose. The author's feeling that 'the story would have lent itself best to metrical rather than prose fiction' seems to me to raise questions quite distinct from Wordsworth.

A desire for the play of humour was evidently an important factor, even if not the sole decisive one. Mrs. Joan Bennett (who puts in a word for Wordsworth's humour) believes that George Eliot 'shared the widespread mid-nineteenth-century view that "metrical composition" implied a peculiar solemnity'.[7] But even if the novelist was blind to Wordsworth's humorous vein it is unlikely that the humour of, say, Chaucer, Crabbe, and Browning could have escaped her. Nor would their realism have been likely to do so, or their ability to render speech in verse with an air of authenticity. I would prefer to connect George Eliot's impulse towards the free play of humour with her inclination to 'a more realistic *treatment*' and to see the humour of *Silas Marner* as part of its realism. And 'realism', for George Eliot, would presumably also involve a much fuller use of homely circumstantial detail than she herself could well have managed in a verse-tale (which is not, of course, to suggest that all the homely details in *Silas Marner* are 'realistically' used – the broken pot that Silas sticks together and keeps as a memorial shows that this is not so). More important still, 'realism', for George Eliot, involves rendering the spoken word with an air of authenticity. Numerous poets – as well as the ones I have named above – have given us successful metrical renderings of speech; but George Eliot's verse never does so.

It is significant that she felt the appropriateness of verse 'especially in all that relates to the psychology of Silas'. ('Psychology', we must remind ourselves by the way, connotes the 'real', but not necessarily the 'realistic'.) On the printed page, after he leaves Lantern Yard at the end of Chapter 1, Silas is given nothing in direct speech until he bursts in upon the company at the Rainbow in Chapter 7 gasping the words 'Robbed! I've been robbed!' (His only previously recorded piece of direct speech during his life at Raveloe is in Chapter 1, when he says 'Good night' to Jem Rodney, the mole-catcher, upon emerging from a cataleptic trance.) Between Chapter 2 and his appearance at the Red House with Eppie in his arms in Chapter 13 he is laconic in the extreme, as his encounters with Mr. Macey and Dolly Winthrop show. It is scarcely an exaggeration to say that in looking after Eppie he is compelled virtually to relearn the use of speech ('the tones that stirred Silas's heart grew articulate, and called for more distinct answers'). Or, rather, he recollects it, for this development illustrates the author's statement that 'As the child's mind was growing into knowledge, his mind was growing into memory' (ch. 14). In the second part of the book he is, necessarily, much more fluent.

The psychology of Silas during almost fifteen mute years is powerfully rendered by other means than dialogue. Other means were needed, for he is alone when he discovers the theft of his gold and when he finds the infant Eppie on his hearth (the two big 'scenes' in the rendering of his psychology). Those developments in him which are gradual – his insect-like obsession with his loom and his habit of sitting counting his loved guineas – are also solitary.

Not all of the means by which we are enabled to see into Silas's nature are 'realistic', though several of the most impressive passages are starkly factual. Some of the material could, no doubt, have been expressed by George Eliot in competent, if rhythmically unexciting, blank verse. The rendering of Silas's psychology, especially in Part I, is 'poetic' partly in that it freely employs devices more usually associated (at least before the age of George Eliot) with metrical composition. When we say this we are not merely repeating the time-worn truth that the use of metre does not of itself produce a poem and, conversely, that 'the poetic' can be articulated without metre. 'Poetry', said Walter Bagehot, 'should be memorable and emphatic, intense, and *soon over*.'[8] We expect to find these qualities in a metrical fiction to a greater degree than we find them in *Silas Marner*. But it does seem that, both because of its near-poetic conception and because of its free employment of devices more usually associated with verse than with prose, *Silas Marner* is *more easily* memorable, *more* emphatic, *more* intense and *sooner over* than it could otherwise have been. One of the notable things about this work is that it expands in your memory, and individual parts of it expand, so that when you turn back to the book itself you are surprised by its brevity. (Yet it gives an impression of leisureliness, too – one can fairly say that no man ever wished it shorter.)

It seems clear that nothing essentially 'poetic' is lost by Silas's being presented in prose. Moreover, the 'poetic' impinges significantly, though unobtrusively, on the texture of those chapters in which the treatment is more realistic.

The presence or absence of authentically rendered direct speech in this or that chapter in Part I seems to me to have an interesting bearing on the form of the work in another way, too. The absence of direct speech from the chapters devoted to Silas provides a verbal analogue of solitude. At the same time, contained in the solitude/society contrast which Part I as a whole expresses, there is a 'class' contrast, rendered in speech, exemplifying the barriers that exist within the tightly-knit community of Raveloe. There is an abundance of dialogue in Part I. The speakers fall into two groups, each with its distinctive mode of speech: the Cass family and their associates, and the villagers. In much of Part I (broadly, up to Chapter 11, which presents the New Year's Eve dance at the Casses' home, where representatives of both groups are assembled by the author in readiness for Silas's entrance with Eppie in Chapter 13), 'upper' and 'lower', though both groups are articulate, are almost wholly insulated from each other on the printed page. The villagers themselves are given nothing in direct speech until the conversation at the Rainbow (ch. 6), though – as if they could be heard talking in the distance – the flavour of their speech has been conveyed in such 'reported' locutions as 'if you could only speak the devil fair enough, he might save you the cost of the doctor' or 'No, no; it was no stroke that would let a man stand on his legs, like a horse between the shafts, and then walk off as soon as you can say "Gee!"' It is in this 'distant' talk that we chiefly see the subdued play of humour in the first two chapters.

On the other hand, some of the methods (notably metaphor) which are used to reveal Silas's psychology are also used, though more sparingly, in the other chapters, the 'social' chapters. They constitute one of the linking devices in a most intricate pattern of interlocking contrasts and parallels – a pattern that requires the reader to grasp the many juxtapositions of literal and metaphorical, and also to make numerous transpositions and transvaluations. There is no hard and fast line between fact and symbol in the work as a whole. Gold is both factual and symbolic. W. J. Harvey has shown[9] that an image may be converted into literal fact later, as is the comparison between weaver and child:

> A weaver who finds hard words in his hymn-book knows nothing of abstractions; as the little child knows nothing of parental love, but only knows one face and one lap towards which it stretches its arms for refuge and nurture.

> (ch. 2)

And Silas's feeling that half-earned guineas are like unborn children foreshadows 'the close symbolic connection between the golden-haired Eppie and the miser's hoard'.[10]

The Wordsworthian affinities of *Silas Marner* seem to me to go far beyond what is conveyed in the epigraph from 'Michael', important as this is:

> A child, more than all other gifts
> That earth can offer to declining man,
> Brings hope with it, and forward-looking thoughts.

Mr. Peter Coveney observes: 'The force of the book lies in the presentation of Silas Marner, the "declining man" in question'; and he adds, more debatably: 'The weight, however, of the moral must fall on the protagonist, on the agency of Marner's redemption, on the child who bestows the "forward-looking thoughts".'[11]

This is a fair enough comment only if one accepts the epigraph as a clue to the whole 'moral' of the book. In fact, however, George Eliot would have needed several epigraphs to epitomize her complex moral. The choice of this particular one seems to owe something at least to Blackwood's finding the earlier chapters of the work 'sombre'. The author reassured him very promptly, and the epigraph, which she sent him a little later, when *Silas Marner* was nearly finished, seems designed, in part, to reassure the public, too, that the picture is not going to be wholly gloomy. She was only anxious lest her epigraph indicated the story too distinctly, and it was now Blackwood's turn to reassure her: 'The motto giving to some extent the keynote to the story does not I think signify in this case, as whenever the child appears her mission is felt.'[12]

Had she decided upon a multiple epigraph (a practice adopted by Crabbe and Clough, for example), she could have chosen several other passages from Wordsworth, all of them equally relevant to *Silas Marner*, though not all relating to the *story*.

To begin with, Silas himself is 'Wordsworthian'. He is the kind of man Wordsworth might have come across on the 'lonely roads', one of those

> Souls that appear to have no depth at all
> To careless eyes.[13]

Hence, no doubt, George Eliot's feeling that no one but herself would be interested in the story, 'since William Wordsworth is dead'. Many touches – especially in Chapter 2 – confirm such a view of Silas.

Moreover, the world of *Silas Marner*, notwithstanding its 'fairy-tale' aspect, is

> the very world, which is the world
> Of all of us, – the place where, in the end,
> We find our happiness, or not at all![14]

And we may add that the world seems to have been so for George Eliot in a more thorough-going sense than it was for Wordsworth. After he leaves Lantern Yard, Silas's treasures, of both kinds, are laid up on earth.

The list of possible Wordsworthian epigraphs could be much extended, but one other quotation will suffice here (it is from 'The Old Cumberland Beggar'):

> We have all of us one human heart.

In *Silas Marner* this statement is qualified, without being eroded. The unity of the human heart in the central Wordsworthian sense is there. The 'essential passions' link man with man; and 'pure, natural human relations' exert 'remedial influences'. But (as well as, most evidently, showing us different individual hearts and different types of heart) George Eliot qualifies the poet's statement by revealing another kind of 'oneness'. She reveals a unity – or better, a whole range of unities – beneath apparent differences. They are not all soothing to contemplate. Godfrey Cass, for instance, though somewhat scornful of the credulity of the villagers, is no less credulous than they in his personal 'religion' of 'Favourable Chance'. He is Everyman, too, in his everyday, unconscious superstition, as we see from his way of dealing with his fears that his brother has stolen his horse:

> Instead of trying to still his fears he encouraged them, with that superstitious impression which clings to us all, that if we expect evil very strongly it is the less likely to come; and when he heard a horse approaching at a trot, and saw a hat rising above a hedge beyond an angle of the lane, he felt as if his conjuration had succeeded.
>
> (ch. 8)

And there are parallels to Silas's narrowing and hardening in his solitude:

> His life had reduced itself to the functions of weaving and hoarding, without any contemplation of an end towards which the functions tended. The same sort of process has perhaps been undergone by wiser men, when they have been cut off from faith and love – only, instead of a loom and a heap of guineas, they have had some erudite research, some ingenious project, or some well-knit theory.
>
> (ch. 2)

The unities may be some way beneath the surface, and they may easily be overlooked or unsuspected, as the Wordsworthian unity seldom can be. Often George Eliot is explicit in pointing her parallels, but she has less direct methods, too, of saying '*De te fabula*'.

She is Wordsworthian also in her insistence on the great power of memory to help the working of the affections and to bind the life of the individual into a unity. Backward-looking thoughts are as important in Silas's development as forward-looking ones, even though it is to the latter kind that the epigraph directs our attention. Indeed, it is, to an important extent, the power of memory that enables the 'forward-looking' situation to develop, for Silas momentarily indentifies the newly-found Eppie with his long-dead little sister — an identification as crucial, in its way, as the more conspicuous gold-and-curls identification.

His remembered knowledge of 'medicinal herbs and their preparation' has its importance, too, on more than one occasion and in very different ways. I choose this example partly because it shows George Eliot telling us that the care of the foundling was not the only means by which Silas could have been reunited with his fellow-men; partly because it involves the relation of man to inanimate nature, which is one of the themes of *Silas Marner*, even if not a major one; and partly because it illustrates how the author can use a motif both as a recurrent element in a formal pattern (this motif links diverse phases in Silas's life) and as the conveyor of a 'moral' (the herbal lore is made to bear a different moral and emotional significance each time it appears).

Silas has gained this knowledge from his mother ('a little store of wisdom which she had imparted to him as a solemn bequest'), but in his Lantern Yard days 'his inherited delight to wander through the fields in search of foxglove and dandelion and coltsfoot, began to wear to him the character of a temptation' (ch. 1). Then, quite early in his life at Raveloe, at about the time that he begins to love guineas, he recognizes in the cobbler's wife 'the terrible symptoms of heart-disease and dropsy, which he had witnessed as the precursors of his mother's death', feels 'a rush of pity at the mingled sight and remembrance', and brings her 'a simple preparation of foxglove' (ch. 2). This 'resurgent memory', which could have led to 'some fellowship with his neighbours', has unfortunate aftereffects, for the villagers (in accordance with the 'old demonworship' which is part of their total religion) flock to him for charms and cures and do not believe him when he says that he knows no charms and can work no cures, so that the 'repulsion' between him and his neighbours is heightened. The herbs are then forgotten until years later, when he is out in the fields with Eppie. She brings him flowers, whereupon

> Silas began to look for the once-familiar herbs again; and as the leaves, with their unchanged outline and markings, lay on his palm, there was a sense of crowding remembrances from which he turned away timidly, taking refuge in Eppie's little world, that lay lightly on his enfeebled spirit.
>
> (ch. 14)

Finally, how far is Eppie herself Wordsworthian, and in what ways? She seems to me to be connected not only with the Wordsworthian Child but also with the Wordsworthian Maid. I should like to consider the implications of a passage in Part II on the education of Eppie before dealing with her as a type of Childhood, for the latter theme will take us a long way from Wordsworth as we relate the Child to the total context in which she appears.

The passage from Part II shows how Eppie, now eighteen, became the 'village maiden' that she is:

> The tender and peculiar love with which Silas had reared her in almost inseparable companionship with himself, aided by the seclusion of their dwelling, had preserved her from the lowering influences of the village talk and habits, and had kept her mind in that freshness which is sometimes falsely supposed to be an invariable attribute of rusticity. Perfect love has a breath of poetry which can exalt the relations of the least-instructed human beings; and this breath of poetry had surrounded Eppie from the time when she had followed the bright gleam that beckoned her to Silas's hearth; so that it is not surprising if, in other things besides her delicate prettiness, she was not quite a common village maiden, but had a touch of refinement and fervour which came from no other teaching than that of tenderly-nurtured unvitiated feeling.
>
> (ch. 16)

Eppie's education (apart from her two hours daily at the dame school, for we are in 'the very world') is the work of Nature. But George Eliot insists firmly that the Nature which chiefly counts here is human nature, not inanimate nature, and that country life is not, *per se*, ennobling. The 'passions' of her rustics in the book as a whole are not conspicuously 'incorporated with the beautiful and permanent forms of nature', and while she would agree with Wordsworth that the manners of rural life 'germinate' from 'elementary feelings', the elementary feelings of *her* rustics appear to come largely from being 'pressed close by primitive wants'. Whatever is idealized in the account of Eppie's education, the manners of rural life are not (though there are no grounds for supposing that the author is taxing Wordsworth, whose poetry she knew well, with the false supposition that freshness of mind is 'an invariable attribute of rusticity').

Silas, like Nature in Wordsworth's poem, 'Three years she grew in sun and shower', has taken the Child to himself; she 'kindles'

69

him more than she is kindled by him, perhaps, and he does not 'restrain' her as Nature restrains Lucy; but the Stone-pits, where they live together, may be seen as a version of Wordsworth's 'happy dell'.

It is with Eppie the representative of Wordsworthian Childhood that Mr. Coveney is concerned in his discussion of *Silas Marner*. Eppie is a 'presence', stirring tenderness and awe in Silas, feeding his sense of a Power presiding over his life, forcing his thoughts onwards and 'warming him into joy'. 'In idea', says Mr. Coveney, 'the meaning of Romantic childhood is well enough conveyed', but he finds the presentation of the child as a character in the novel inadequate: 'But the object called upon to sustain the poetic weight staggers beneath it, totters, in fact "toddles" beneath it. There is a failure in the characterization of the central image.'[15]

I doubt whether, for George Eliot's purposes, artistic and moral, Eppie needs to be very firmly established as a 'character' in Part I. (In Part II she does need to be, and is.) She certainly has to be established as a 'blessing' – welcomed by Silas and rejected by Godfrey – and as a 'blessing' in this sense she is firmly established, for you can present a blessing in terms of the man who is blessed. And this is what George Eliot does. From the beginning of Chapter 12, when the child first appears in the Raveloe lanes in her mother's arms, to the end of Part I is little more than one-seventh of the whole work, and much of this seventh is occupied with other people's attitudes to Eppie (those of her mother, Silas, Godfrey, Dolly Winthrop, the Kimbles and numerous unnamed persons) and also with many people's reactions to Silas after he has adopted her. Admittedly there is some idealization in this at certain points, which, nevertheless, the tone of the legendary tale, never wholly laid aside for very long, does something to render acceptable.

Mr. Coveney's objection to the rendering of the child Eppie, in so far as it is a literary one, seems to be an objection to the author's reliance on a too-easy response from the reader. Baby-talk is used; in effect, when Eppie says 'gug-gug-gug' we are expected to find it 'sweet'. Sometimes this reliance is ill-concealed under the guise of factuality; the word 'little', Mr. Coveney notices, is seldom used solely to convey a fact when George Eliot applies it to children. There is certainly substance in his literary objections, though they do not seem to me to be as weighty as he makes them out, since I think he exaggerates Eppie's prominence in the fiction as a whole.

I doubt, however, whether the matter is purely literary. There clearly is an element of sweetness and softness in *Silas Marner*; and it is vitally necessary both to the moral conveyed and to the picture of life given in the work. Sweetness and softness are not qualities that twentieth-century readers accept very readily in morals or in pictures of life; so that, when we are confronted with a Victorian fiction in which these qualities are conspicuous, it is perhaps difficult for us to exercise that discrimination which constitutes critical justice. But to equate sweetness and softness with sentimentality would be obtuse.

To put it in another way, there is a strain of 'cosiness' in the book. Silas's joys, when he gets them, are small and confined in so far as they come from 'eating o' the same bit, and drinking o' the same cup'; little things are suffused with sentiment. But George Eliot seems to me to have answered the objection to 'cosiness' as connoting triviality:

> Nancy, used all her life to plenteous circumstances and the privileges of 'respectability', could not enter into all the pleasures which early nurture and habit connect with all the little aims and efforts of the poor who are born poor: to her mind, Eppie, in being restored to her birthright, was entering on a too long withheld but unquestionable good.
>
> (ch. 19)

In this chapter, in which Godfrey and Nancy come to claim Eppie, the girl could certainly not be adequately described as 'cosy'.

But the Wordsworthian affinities of *Silas Marner*, important as they are, should not be exaggerated. Ultimately, what a scrutiny of these affinities shows is that the work is something far more original than simply a Wordsworthian tale in prose. And if we give undue prominence to the motif of the Child we distort both the theme and the design of the whole. *Silas Marner* has a broader theme. To state this in the most abstract and general terms, the book is about feelings and the forms in which they incorporate themselves. Silas's quasi-paternal love is one feeling among many; his fostering of the child is one form among the many forms that embody feeling. George Eliot is explicit about religious feelings and religious forms:

To people accustomed to reason about the forms in which their religious feeling has incorporated itself, it is difficult to enter into that simple, untaught state of mind in which the form and the feeling have never been severed by an act of reflection.

(ch. 1)

In *Silas Marner* as a whole, many feelings are shown incorporating themselves in many forms; and few of the characters sever feeling and form by an act of reflection (to some extent, Silas himself and Dolly Winthrop eventually do). The same kind of feeling may be differently incorporated in different communities (the religious forms of Lantern Yard are strikingly different from those of Raveloe); the feelings of the same man may be incorporated in different forms at different times, as those of Silas most notably are. His story is that of feeling ('the sap of affection') all but dried up as his life is nearly reduced to the 'unquestioning activity of a spinning insect' – non-human existence, both animate and inanimate, is a constantly-tapped source of metaphor – yet surviving, nevertheless, and making fresh growth as it partly finds and partly creates forms which can supply it with both framework and nourishment.

His 'strange history' (the narrative form of the book) is that of a double metamorphosis. The first metamorphosis into a miser, following his expulsion from the Lantern Yard community, is essentially, though not solely, a change in his inward life, 'as that of any fervid nature must be when it has fled, or been condemned to solitude'. This is the phase in which natural affection almost withers away, though he still *has* feeling for the earthenware pot in which he fetches water from the well; it has been his 'companion' for twelve years,

> always lending its handle to him in the early morning, so that its form had an expression for him of willing helpfulness, and the impress of its handle on his palm gave a satisfaction mingled with that of having the fresh clear water.

(ch. 2)

So, after accidentally breaking it, 'he stuck the bits together and propped the ruin in its old place for a memorial'. This 'little incident' illuminates the drab phase in which the monotony of daily drudgery at his loom alternates with 'nightly revelry' as he pours out his hoarded guineas, bathes his hands in them and rejoices in them as in a 'golden wine'. The loom works on his outer form, which is all his neighbours know: his 'face and figure shrank and bent themselves into a constant mechanical relation to the objects of his life, so that he produced the same sort of impression as a handle or a crooked tube, which has no meaning standing apart' (ch. 2). The guineas on which his nightly ritual centres provide a repository – an unnatural one, and therefore bad – for his feelings: 'His gold, as he hung over it and saw it grow, gathered his power of loving together into a hard isolation like its own' (ch. 5).

His second metamorphosis, into a loving foster-father, with all that this implies in the way of reciprocal 'blessings' and 'gifts', is swifter than the first, but by no means instantaneous. It depends initially on the agonizing loss of his gold, and then on 'pure, natural human relations', the growth of which is necessarily gradual and involves a multitude of interconnecting forms, domestic, social, and religious; and being, in the broadest sense, 'social', it also involves verbal forms, as the first metamorphosis did not.

The image of the alien-looking man with the burden, which provides the 'millet-seed of thought', thus grows into a legendary tale which is also a picture of 'real life'. It does so by answering the questions that the appearance of the man suggests: How did he become alien, and hence solitary? How can he cease to be solitary? What does the burden mean, and how can he get rid of it?

Among other things, the burden symbolizes the unjust accusation of having stolen 'treasure'. Silas later amasses treasure, which is stolen from him. The child comes in place of the treasure, and he ceases to be solitary. Later still, the treasure he hoarded is recovered, but it now has a different value because it is associated with other feelings and can be used on behalf of the child.

One of the chief links between the legendary sphere and that of real life is Godfrey Cass. As a character he is 'realistic' (though some of the local means by which he is presented are not). So far as the design of the work goes, he is the figure who forms the principal contrast with Silas: Godfrey rejects the child; Silas accepts her. Other contrasts follow from this. The plot becomes twofold – Silas's story and Godfrey's story being linked by the child – and it has a very marked pattern. This markedness of pattern might not be wholly acceptable in a work of single-minded realism. True, double stories are common enough in novels of the nineteenth century; but as the brevity of *Silas Marner* (largely a consequence of its 'legendary' element) throws more emphasis on the plot, the pattern appears with unaccustomed clarity. The obviousness of the pattern, with all its coincidences and other improbabilities, is acceptable only partly as 'the narrative means to a moral end';[16] it is acceptable also as belonging to a non-realistic literary mode – a neat and strongly marked pattern is something we associate with a legendary tale; and a legendary tale, though it can contain plenty of 'moral', or poetic justice, does not exist for the sake of its moral.

The legendary conception thus plays an important part in determining the narrative organization of some of the 'real-life' material, though clearly not all of it. It does little towards organizing the Nancy Lammeter element. But Nancy, a sensitive and firm character sensitively and firmly presented, is vitally important in the rendering of 'feeling and form' on the realistic level. Her feeling is incorporated in various traditional forms, some of them important in their implications (she would have accepted Godfrey's child at any time if she had known it was his), and some trivial (sisters should dress alike). Her forms, even the trivial ones, are living forms because they are suffused with feeling. They are generally adequate for Nancy in all that relates to her own social sphere, but they are inadequate for dealing with the actuality, social and emotional, that she confronts in the persons of Silas and Eppie in Chapter 19, when the forms to which she is accustomed prevent her from entering into the feelings of 'the poor who are born poor'.

If Godfrey is one of the chief links between the legendary and the realistic, Dolly Winthrop is a 'realistic' character charged with the important function of helping Silas to evolve and to articulate a view of life that will 'explain' his own history. She and Silas are the two characters in the work who most desire an adequate 'view of life', and who *do* speculate, however 'untaught' and 'simple' they may be. Mr. John Holloway has an interesting discussion of this aspect of *Silas Marner* in *The Victorian Sage*. He remarks that, in Dolly's 'speculative pronouncement' to Silas in Chapter 16, arising from her feeling that 'Them above has got a deal tenderer heart nor what I've got', 'we have in all essentials a version of the author's own world view', and he adds: 'To be expressible in a simple or in a subtle form, so as to suit the needs and capacities of the most sophisticated people and the least, is perhaps essential to any significant view of life.'[17] But it is not quite true to say that 'We see ... how things move according to a hidden plan'.[18] We see how Silas and Dolly come to feel that things move according to a hidden plan. George Eliot always 'places' the views of her characters (as Mr. Holloway, indeed, observes). An 'adequate' view is adequate for particular characters in particular circumstances; and the circumstances in which they formulate the view, as well as the terms they use, are part of the author's method of conveying *her* view. To say this is not to quibble. Silas's and Dolly's formulations are made in broadly religious terms. George Eliot's formulation, in *Silas Marner*, is made by means of a legendary tale (roughly, a literary analogue of religious myth) combined with a picture of the actualities of religious life and religious forms.

Dolly is notably free from the 'demon-worship' in which George Eliot shows most of the villagers participating whenever their words and actions are concerned with charms, cures, a fear of the 'evil eye', and so forth. Characteristically, she includes other forms of demon-worship, too – metaphorical forms – and this is wholly consonant with both the message and the method of the work. Godfrey's first wife is 'enslaved' to the 'demon Opium'; and Godfrey's heart (in a sentence of biblical reminiscence) is 'visited by cruel wishes, that seemed to enter, and depart, and enter again, like demons who had found in him a ready-garnished home' (ch. 3).

In one of its aspects *Silas Marner* is a web in which religion (including superstition), viewed as part of 'real life', crosses the threads of fairy tale. The opening paragraphs, for instance, contain all the elements of the author's initial 'childish recollection' (the linen-weaver bent under the burden of his bag, the alien look), and they have a certain tone of 'once upon a time'. But we soon learn that the action is to take place, not just in a 'far-off time', but 'in the early years of this century'; and Silas is 'such a linen-weaver' as the whole race of weavers of his day. It is made clear, too, that the mystery attaching to the race of weavers is put there by the superstitious fears of rustics who are actually living a life that, psychologically, contains some of the grimmer elements of a fairy tale. And, in the local phrasing throughout the work, religion, superstition, fairy tale, and hard fact are all combined.

Silas's cataleptic trances epitomize the method. George Eliot could have devised some other means of bringing about the unjust accusation and the entrance of Eppie into the cottage, so we are justified in asking why she has chosen this one. The trances are variously explained by different people at different points in the story. In Lantern Yard they are generally believed to show that Silas is 'a brother selected for a peculiar discipline', though William Dane disingenuously says that 'to him, this trance looked more like a visitation of Satan than a proof of divine favour'. The Raveloe villagers are unsure whether to call them 'fits' or to suppose that 'there might be such a thing as a man's soul being loose from his body . . . and that was how folks got over-wise, for they went to school in this shell-less state to those who could teach them more than their neighbours could learn with their five senses and the parson' (ch. 1). Silas himself does not understand them, and apparently gives up trying to do so. Eppie does not try to explain them, but accepts them as something that has to be dealt with; when she and Silas go to look for Lantern Yard and find it has vanished, she is 'on the watch lest one of her father's strange attacks should come on'. In the 'legendary tale', catalepsy is a curse or spell, something corresponding – at first – to the gift of the wicked fairy in the story of the Sleeping Beauty. Shortly before Eppie enters his cottage, Silas is standing by the open door, and he puts his hand on the latch to close it,

> but he did not close it: he was arrested . . . by the invisible wand of catalepsy, and stood like a graven image, with wide but sightless eyes, holding open his door, powerless to resist either the good or evil that might enter there.
>
> (ch. 12)

But in the long run it does not matter whether good or evil fairies, whether Chance or Fate or Providence or 'Them above' are the mental 'forms' favoured by the interpreters. The solution for human problems, George Eliot is saying, must be looked for in human nature itself. To apply the notion of feeling and form to the literary work as a whole, *Silas Marner* is the imaginative form in which the author has incorporated her feeling about human nature and the human condition.

Silas Marner is a very tightly integrated work of art. One finds this experimentally in trying to convey one's sense of what it is and of the author's mode of proceeding. I fix my attention on what seems to be a significant piece of the whole. But this piece is like the centre of a spider's web. It has not one significance, but many, radiating in all directions. And I am left with an awareness that, for many of the pieces I have chosen for comment, there are others that would have served equally well, and, further, that in the course of exploring these others I might have come upon facets of the work, or manifestations of George Eliot's literary power, which the selection that I have in fact made has left unexplored.

NOTES

1. 19 February 1861, *Letters*, iii. 379.
2. *ibid.*, iii. 360.
3. *ibid.*, iii. 371.
4. *ibid.*, iii. 382.
5. [15] June 1861, *ibid.*, iii. 427.
6. *ibid.*, iii. 382.
7. Joan Bennett, *George Eliot: Her Mind and Her Art* (Cambridge U.P., 1948), p. 132.
8. Walter Bagehot, 'Wordsworth, Tennyson, and Browning; or, Pure Ornate and Grotesque Art in English Poetry', *Literary Studies*, first published 1864 (Everyman's Library Edition, 1944), ii. 317.
9. W. J. Harvey, *The Art of George Eliot* (Chatto & Windus, 1961), p. 139.
10. *ibid.*
11. *The Image of Childhood*, p. 172.
12. 5 March 1861, *Letters*, iii. 386.
13. *The Prelude* (version of 1850), xiii. 167–8.
14. *ibid.*, xi. 142–4.
15. *The Image of Childhood*, pp. 173–4.
16. 'Even where [George Eliot] uses coincidence in the ordinary narrative conventions of discovery and accident, it is hardly ever interpreted as a version of Fate, . . . but merely as a narrative means to a moral end.' *The Novels of George Eliot*, p. 116.
17. John Holloway, *The Victorian Sage* (The Norton Library Edition, 1965), pp. 133–4.
18. *ibid.*, p. 134.

V

'ROMOLA' AS FABLE
George Levine

THE INITIAL and inescapable fact about *Romola* is that of its
failure. There is no quarrelling with Henry James's argument that
the novel 'does not seem positively to live'. And yet *Romola* is a
far better – at least far more interesting – book than the conventional
and ultimately correct placing of it would suggest. Clearly, as Joan
Bennett has said, it 'could only be the work of a gifted writer'.[1]
But how is the 'gift' manifested in the novel? Many bad novelists
have been, like George Eliot, deeply serious and highly intelligent,
but they remained utterly incapable of investing their art – as art –
with interest. Certainly, when *Romola* is viewed as a novel of the
kind generally taken as characteristic of George Eliot – that is, on
the terms its own circumstantial density and analytic elaboration
seem to propose – there is little that can be done to save it. James,
seeking the life and verisimilitude which George Eliot apparently
attempted to achieve in it, saw the novel's defects as ultimately the
defects of novelistic imagination: 'A twentieth part of the erudition
would have sufficed,' he said, 'would have given us the feeling and
colour of the time, if there had been more of the breath of the
Florentine streets, more of the faculty of optical evocation, a greater
saturation of the senses with the elements of the adorable little
city.'[2]

The implications of the judgment are apparent in the key phrases
– 'feeling and colour', 'saturation of the senses'. What James sought
is the essence of the traditional novel: more genuine showing; less
scholarly and intellectual scrupulosity and more imaginative selec-
tivity; details functioning to evoke the feeling of place and the

quality of life. The implicit ideal is that of a quite traditional realism of the kind one might find in Jane Austen, or, for that matter, in *The Mill on the Floss*: realism which depends very much on the sensitive recording of the apparently trivial details of ordinary life and manners. It is notorious that George Eliot laboured over the details of the novel, so scrupulously researched and recorded in her 'Quarry for *Romola*', precisely in order to achieve this kind of realism. Her commitment was always to avoid lapsing from the 'picture' to the 'diagram'. But in *Romola*, somehow, the picture is always strained, always gives the impression of being artificially contrived, and the result is that the 'diagram' shows through with unwanted clarity.

The failure fully to 'realize' the action and characters of *Romola* in novelistic terms is, however, only partly the result of a failure on George Eliot's part to do what she set out to do. *Romola* is the book which most clearly marks the transition from the 'early' to the 'late' George Eliot. In it she was dealing with new materials (not merely the historical setting) of greater complexity and entailing a development both in style and form. In *Silas Marner*, which interrupted her work on *Romola*, she used much of her characteristic English setting; but she wrote what has, essentially, been accepted as a fable. *Silas Marner* is governed by two patterned stories that might be diagrammed – stories given substance, to be sure, by the vividness of the carefully selected details. But the actions and the narrative are unabashedly symbolic, and the degree to which the events of the novel are happily coincidental causes no difficulty. The difficulty with *Romola* is not so much that it is as strictly controlled by fabulous and symbolic events as *Silas Marner*, but that it seems to be struggling to be a different kind of work – to be, that is, a traditional novel. The different modes do not mesh. Being asked to take Romola and Baldassarre as real characters in a real world, the reader balks at Romola's idealization and Baldassarre's melo-dramatic function as Tito's Nemesis.

The nature of the criticisms of *Romola* through the years tend to confirm this judgment. Barbara Hardy has demonstrated that analysis preponderates over demonstration in ways thoroughly un-characteristic of George Eliot.[3] Joan Bennett, among others, has complained that the Florentines speak a language never heard in Italy or England. George Lewes, on the other hand, having per-suaded George Eliot of the value of the subject, tried to convince her that her relation to fifteenth-century Florence was not, in fact, much different from her relation to the English life of her early novels. She knew, he wrote, 'more about Savonarola than she knew of Silas'.[4] But what she knew and what she felt and could dramatize were different things. And as early as R. H. Hutton's brilliant review in the *Spectator*, it was clear that George Eliot could not engage her readers with 'the light Florentine buzz with which so great a part of the first volume is filled. Its allusions are half-riddles, and its liveliness a blank. . . .'[5]

George Eliot's justification of this 'buzz' in her famous letter to Hutton suggests how very much within the tradition of the realistic novel she was attempting to work in *Romola*:

> It is the habit of my imagination to strive after as full a vision of the medium in which a character moves as of the character itself. The psychological causes which prompted me to give such details of Florentine life and history as I have given, are precisely the same as those which determined me in giving the details of English village life in *Silas Marner*, or the 'Dodson' life, out of which were developed the destinies of poor Tom and Maggie.[6]

Within the tradition of the novel that this view implies there is an interaction between character and background which makes the two essentially inseparable. The supreme example of this tradition in George Eliot's novels is Lydgate's history – the history of his gradual entrapment by his surroundings. And this entrapment is a function of his own character – which is itself partly a product of his *milieu* – as well as of the society in which he moves. Indeed, it was George Eliot herself who developed most carefully and scrupulously the tradition in the novel which makes 'plot' (the external narrative action of the novel) a function of 'character': 'Our deeds determine us as much as we determine our deeds.' The belief that it is possible somehow to escape the consequences of one's actions and act without reference to one's relations to the larger community becomes, within the realistic framework of George Eliot's novels, a crucial kind of moral blindness and, therefore, a central thematic preoccupation.[7] On the other hand, her mention of *Silas Marner* as one of the books in which this conception works suggests that she accepted the possibility of creating the theme in fable as well as novel. But it should be noted that, within the tradition of the novel, character and narrative tend to coalesce, and perhaps the typical novelistic plot is one which shows a character forced to accept the limitations imposed upon him by a densely realized society. In the tradition of romance, on the other hand, the central preoccupation tends to be narrative rather than character, and character tends to operate without relevance to the constricting pressures of an outside world.

At any rate, in *Romola* the theme of the need to submit to the larger community is embodied in a novelistic way (to which I shall refer again later) in the character of Tito Melema. Yet it is even more complexly – if less satisfactorily as experience – treated in the character of Romola herself. The novel, in fact, tends to build up a tension between the stories of the two characters, the one out of a tradition of realism, the other out of romance. Observing this tension, and, in particular, the peculiarly abstract but occasionally powerful history of Romola, forces us to call into question the strictly Jamesian grounds of our disapproval. *Romola* needs to be seen as a genuinely experimental work, closer in mode to *Silas Marner* than to *Middlemarch*, and more closely anticipating *Daniel Deronda* than any other of the prose works.[8] It is a fable, if a fable only half-embodied, and it moves in the direction of a vision far more complicated than any she had worked with hitherto. *The Mill on the Floss* had taken her beyond the simple village life she had treated in *Adam Bede* and posed correspondingly more complex moral questions: the conclusion of the novel could not handle those questions in George Eliot's characteristic mode, and the realistic *Bildungsroman* needed to end with a symbolic action. The retreat to village life in *Silas Marner* was a retreat with a difference. Everything was simplified, and yet the simplification entailed a frank exploration of the fabular symbolic mode to which *The Mill on the Floss* seems to have taken her. 'The habit of her imagination' was, to be sure, manifest there. But the connection between character and action which emerges is as much symbolic as naturalistic and has a kind of diagrammatic quality rather than a circumstantial inevitability. Within the moral schema all the particular events are explicable and effective, but they are not inevitable reflexes of character. In this respect, *Silas Marner* is but a short step to *Romola*, and from *Romola* it is not a long way to *Daniel Deronda*, which works out another moral fable (in juxtaposition, also, it should be noted, with a 'realistic' one), more complexly and self-consciously, but with equal reliance on action external to character, yet somehow profoundly related to it.

The disparity between character and action in *Romola* is partly a result of its being an historical novel. Such a novel entails treating many events that occur quite apart from any 'deeds' of the major characters. Lorenzo would have died whether or not Tito had come to Florence, and the French would have invaded had Romola – had even Savonarola – been a different kind of person. Unity and coherence within such a novel (unless the historical events are not really relevant to the characters) must depend considerably on non-naturalistic modes of connecting character and event. Tito may become part of the plot to destroy Savonarola, but his crucial relation to the history is metaphoric or symbolic: his particular kind of corruption is a reflection of a general Florentine corruption.[9] And, moving down to the narrative, which is less concerned with history than with the private destinies of fictional characters, we find that relations and events are frequently equally as metaphorical. Coincidences are central in *Romola* as they are in *Silas Marner*,[10] and they work out the underlying moral schema in symbolic ways.

Barbara Hardy has suggested that part of *Romola*'s failure is to be accounted for by the absence of what she calls 'free scenes' – scenes which function 'to give the central illusion that the action is rooted in normal space and time'.[11] And this, put another way, means that the diagram of the action, which is the embodiment of the meaning, is dominant: the mode is fable, not realistic novel. When the book achieves its power, it does so poetically: that is, for example, when Romola and Savonarola meet for the third crucial time, repeating the earlier problem of flight, the power resides more in the imagined moment than in the larger psychological context out of which the moment is supposed to grow. Two forces, largely impersonal, confront each other, and the working out of the possibilities of that confrontation, regardless of context, carries the imaginative weight. Romola, we know, was consciously idealized (and therefore impersonalized). And such idealization is incompatible with a realistic novel, where everything must be conditional, contingent, enmeshed.

The curious uncertainty of *Romola*, hovering between novel and fable, is suggested by a letter George Eliot wrote to Sara Hennell, replying to the idea that Romola, the character, is 'pure idealism':

> You are right [George Eliot agreed], in saying that Romola is ideal.... The various strands of thought I had to work out forced me into a more ideal treatment of Romola than I had foreseen at the outset

– though the 'Drifting Away' and the village with the plague belonged to my earliest vision of the story and were by deliberate forecast adopted as romantic and symbolical elements.[12]

Even the earliest conception of the novel, then, must have entailed fabular elements, actions which function symbolically rather than naturalistically, and which grow rather out of '*strands* of thought' than out of the inevitabilities of fully-realized characters.

At the same time, we can see in the details of the novel that the original conception of Romola is of a novelistic character. It is the technique rather than the conception that makes Romola so thoroughly and painfully ideal. Her history is an education. She begins, like Adam Bede, a clearly noble figure whose defects of knowledge about the possibilities of human experience are meant to be reflected in certain kinds of intolerance and incapacities to respond to weakness and failure. At the outset,

> It was evident that the deepest fount of feeling within her had not yet wrought its way to the less changeful features, and only found its outlet through her eyes.
>
> (ch. 5)

We are prepared, by the likeness between Bardo and Romola – which suggests that she too is implicated in his blindness and his aloofness from life – to follow through the novel the gradual moral education which moves her beyond her father and, indeed, beyond the Florence which is a condition of his existence. The anticipated pattern is characteristic of George Eliot: we find it in Adam Bede before Romola and in Dorothea Brooke afterwards. Moreover, the nature of her particular moral adventures *are* anticipated by that early description: 'There was', in father and daughter 'the same refinement of brow and nostril . . . counterbalanced by a full though firm mouth and powerful chin, which gave an expression of proud tenacity and latent impetuousness' (ch. 5).

But working out the strands of her thought, George Eliot was apparently obliged to state rather than create these qualities in Romola. Almost every character who views Romola sees in her something more than human. To the citizens of Florence and the plague-ridden village, she is 'Madonna'. But even Tito, at the start, sees her as a goddess:

> he felt for the first time, without defining it to himself, that loving awe in the presence of noble womanhood, which is perhaps something like

the worship paid of old to a great nature-goddess, who was not all-knowing, but whose life and power were something deeper and more primordial than knowledge.

(ch. 9)

The actual events in which Romula partakes demonstrate not only that she has a desperate need for love and a consequent softness which distinguish her from Bardo, but that she has little of the firmness, pride, and latent rebelliousness she is asserted to have. Because she is *the* moral sensibility in the book, she fails utterly on almost every occasion to live up to the supposed Bardo-like pride. Every attempt at rebellion is abortive. The pride and rebelliousness are asserted far more than they are created. Until the last encounter with Savonarola, they tend rather to be ideas than qualities of character. In each conflict with Tito she succumbs very quickly; in the crucial meeting with Savonarola after she first decides to leave Tito her rebelliousness survives no more than an instant. In fact, Romola has from the start a highly complex moral sensibility, and the education she undergoes is only growth in knowledge, which makes the sensibility richer, a working out of that sensibility's implications and possibilities. Her moral nature is, indeed, so refined and complex that it cannot be embodied dramatically within the limits of the naturalistic method towards which George Eliot leaned. Adam Bede's morality, on the contrary, even after his education, is fundamentally simple and straightforward. But Romola's moral perplexities bear an enormous weight in a highly sophisticated and insidiously corrupt society.

Even before she meets Savonarola, who will persuade her to accept the marriage tie as sacred, we are given this characteristically impressive passage, which reveals that Romola, in the very moment of rebellion, has a sensibility prepared for submission:

There was still something else to be stript away from her belonging to that past on which she was going to turn her back for ever. She put her thumb and forefinger to her betrothal ring; but they rested there, without drawing it off. Romola's mind had been rushing with an impetuous current towards this act, for which she was preparing: the act of quitting a husband who had disappointed all her trust, the act of breaking an outward tie that no longer represented the inward bond of love. But that force of outward symbols by which our active life is knit together so as to make an inexorable external identity for us, not to be shaken by our wavering consciousness, gave a strange effect to this

simple movement towards taking off her ring – a movement which was
but a small sequence of her energetic resolution. It brought a vague but
arresting sense that she was somehow violently rending her life in two:
a presentiment that the strong impulse which has seemed to exclude
doubt and make her path clear might after all be blindness, and that
there was something in human bonds which must prevent them from
being broken with the breaking of illusions.

(ch. 36)

An instant later, to be sure, Romola does feel that 'It cannot be!
I cannot be subject to him. He is false. I shrink from him. I despise
him!' And she snatches the ring from her finger. But the whole
powerful sequence is conducted in such a way that we are engaged
utterly on Romola's side. When Romola behaves in ways counter to
her own best lights she is never treated with the ironic detachment
which at once humanizes Dorothea Brooke and engages our sympathy for her on a higher level than such directly engaged language
can do. There is in this scene, as in almost every scene in which
Romola figures, so high an intensity of crisis and unrelievedness of
thematic relevance that she emerges not so much a complicated
human being as a romantic heroine. And the consequent failure to
create the experience (as the 'experience' of Dorothea Brooke's
choice of Casaubon is created) moves the moral issue – which is the
central issue of Romola's history – sharply into focus. The absence
of 'free scenes'[13] tells strongly here in transforming the experience
from novelistic to fabular. One understands what Sara Hennell,
meant when she wrote to George Eliot that 'in Romola you have
created a goddess and not a woman'.[14]

The point is not that the passage is ineffective: like many others
in *Romola*, it has in itself considerable power and carries conviction.
Rather, we should see that it operates in a different kind of work
from that which James was seeking. Psychologically and realistically, it loses power as it is seen in the context of Romola's un-
deviatingly idealized behaviour. But when seen in the context of a
whole sequence of analogies and equally symbolic moments which
give the fable its shape and meaning, it is considerably enriched.
These analogies emphasize the highly patterned nature of the narrative, and force upon our attention the fact that the novel is controlled more by moral and intellectual preoccupations than by
George Eliot's submission to the possibilities of her created world.

The full moral complexity of the passage can only be understood in the context of other similar situations in the novel. The first, most obvious, and most important is Tito's relation to Baldassarre, symbolized also by a ring. Here is the parallel passage in which Tito readies himself to sell Baldassarre's ring:

> Why should he keep the ring? It had been a mere sentiment, a mere fancy, that had prevented him from selling it with the other gems; if he had been wiser and had sold it, he might perhaps have escaped that identification by Fra Luca. It was true that it had been taken from Baldassarre's finger and put on his own as soon as his young hand had grown to the needful size; but there was really no valid good to anybody in those superstitious scruples about inanimate objects. The ring had helped towards the recognition of him. Tito had begun to dislike recognition, which was a claim from the past. This foreigner's offer, if he would really give a good price, was an opportunity for getting rid of the ring without the trouble of seeking a purchaser.
>
> (ch. 14)

Here too an external symbol knits together an active life and makes an 'inexorable external identity'. And we recognize, when Romola snatches the ring from her own finger, that she is implicated in Tito's guilt, although the language does not judge Romola as it does Tito. Like Tito, she is about to rend her life in two. Later on we will see Romola preserving for Tessa – significantly, from Savonarola's *piagnoni* – the necklace and clasp which are for her, in however inarticulate a way, the symbols of her marriage to Tito. (Much later, Romola's discovery of these in the possession of Bratti allows her to find Tessa and her family and bring them under her protection – to knit past and present together for both of them.) And we will see Baldassarre tearing off the locket that links him with his mother and using the amulet within it to buy the knife with which he wants to kill Tito. By this time the pattern is far more important than the dramatically realized action: Baldassarre's relation to his mother has no other presence in the novel. She is invoked for the sake of the moral direction of the action. Savonarola will ultimately defy his Church, but this parallel is too complicated to be useful at this point, and will be returned to later. All the parallels, however, not only amplify the moral resonances of Romola's reflections about the ring and complicate the moral significance of the action; they establish a characteristic pattern within the book – a set of relationships in character and action which is dependent not simply (sometimes not at all) on natural relations within a real world, but upon symbolic and thematic correspondences. The intricacy and yet clarity of the design of Romola tends to set it off from the tradition of realism; it also is one of its great virtues.

But the extraordinary richness of its moral implications is even more important than its patterned intricacies for the value of Romola as art. Traditionally, we think of fable and romance as being so schematic that their meanings are immediately reducible to simple formulae: fables are, in a way, embodied ideas whose peculiar strength lies in the radical emotional intensity with which heroes and heroines are seen as typical aspects of the human psyche.[15] In Romola, the 'grave moralizing strain' of the romance, as Northrop Frye calls it, does not, however, issue in any simple moral reflections. To be sure, Romola gives the appearance of resolving the difficult moral problems it poses; but, in fact, the whole work is imagined as art, not discursively, and the particular actions of its heroine do not resolve themselves into moral aphorisms. It may be easy enough to settle for vaguely general assertions, such as that George Eliot is arguing that egoism is evil, that love, loyalty to family and community, self-sacrifice, duty are the supreme values. But none of these vague catch-phrases approaches the complexity of the explanation of the problems in the book.

It is useful to return here to the ramifications of Romola's initial decision to leave Tito. These will demonstrate both the intricacy and brilliance of the patterning of the novel and the fact that this skill does not operate in the service of an ultimately simple and schematically clear set of moral assertions. Each crucial relation in the novel is symbolized by one or more 'outward symbols'. Rings symbolize the relations between Tito and Romola and Tito and Baldassarre. The money Tito earns from the sale of Baldassarre's ring he proposes to invest in a miniature painting by Piero de Cosimo to be made on a wooden case, the painting to depict him as Bacchus and Romola as Ariadne. This device, of course, symbolizes for Tito his relation with Romola, a relation he believes possible only because he has destroyed his relations with Baldassarre. Into this box Tito gets Romola to place the cross she took from the hands of her dying brother, Dino (whose relation to his father needs to be examined in this connection). And this cross has come to symbolize for Romola another kind of life, one which, at the start of the book, she is incapable of understanding because she

knows nothing of it from the inside. The cross is her connection
with Savonarola, 'whose very voice', she tells Tito, 'seems to have
penetrated me with a sense that there is some truth in what moves
[men possessed with fervid belief that seem like madness to their
fellow-beings]: some truth of which I know nothing' (ch. 18).
When Tito cuts himself off from Baldassarre, he builds a new life
with Romola. When Romola cuts herself off from Tito, she unlocks
the 'tabernacle' and appropriately reflects on the foolishness of the
picture Tito had Piero paint. '"Ariadne is wonderfully transformed",
thought Romola. "She would look strange among the vines and
roses now"' (ch. 3). But, having taken off the ring, she puts on the
crucifix, although without fully understanding its symbolic significance. It is important, however, that she sees it as a connection
with her past: '"For Dino's sake", she said to herself.' Shortly
thereafter, however, Savonarola will make it clear to Romola what
the cross really signifies:

> 'Conform your life to that image, my daughter; make your sorrow an
> offering: and when the fire of Divine charity burns within you, and
> you behold the need of your fellow-men by the light of that flame, you
> will not call your offering great.'
>
> (ch. 40)

The symbol that Romola chooses after rejecting the ring is thus not
directed towards a rejection of her past, but towards a fuller absorp-
tion into it. Taking up the cross leads her once again to take up the
ring, to return to Tito and Florence. It entails not only the rejection
of the pursuit of joy, of Bacchus and Ariadne – Romola had already
seen the need for this. It entails the active sacrifice of self in the
interest of others.

It brings Romola, moreover, to the discovery of a new father, a
spiritual father. Following Savonarola's last appeal for Romola to
return to her place, she answers, 'Father, I will be guided' (ch. 40).
It should be noted, moreover, that the whole sequence of Romola's
rejection of the ring and ultimate acceptance of Savonarola's appeal
is constructed around the scene in the Rucellai Gardens in which
Tito finally and brutally rejects his father. And, with another twist
of irony in the pattern of the narrative, Tito departs immediately
thereafter to Rome, where he will begin to hatch the plot of his
betrayal of Savonarola. The sequence marks the hopeless divergence
of Tito and Romola, although, in the sequence, the two never
confront each other.

To this point, the intricacy of the patterning may seem to be operating very largely in the tradition of the fable: the moral lessons seem clear, if more profound in their details than is customary. But in fact, the pattern is more intricate and the moral problems more complex. The parallel (and then the contrast) by which we see Tito and Romola juxtaposed in relation to family loyalties carries beyond them to the very source of the 'outward symbol' of the cross, Dino. The book persistently enforces the parallel between Tito and Dino. When we first meet Bardo, we learn quickly of his bitterness at what he takes to be his son's desertion to mysticism and fanaticism. This bitterness is barely different in intensity from that of Baldassarre at his discovery of Tito's desertion. Both figures are juxtaposed against Romola, who has sacrificed her life to the arid and – the images in the library confirm – fragmented scholarly pursuits of Bardo. (The similarity between Romola's relation to Bardo and Dorothea Brooke's to Casaubon has frequently been noted.) The ultimate parallel is worked out when Tito sells the library (the final outward symbol of his and Romola's relation to Bardo). Dino, who characteristically for this book figures in it less as a character than as a symbol somewhat akin to the death's head that frightens Gwendolen in *Daniel Deronda*, introduces the earliest blurring of the moral scheme. If Dino is the source of the cross and the provider of the vision of Romola's marriage which ultimately comes true, he is also a betrayer of his father, as inadequate to the full demands of human relations as Tito himself. His total refusal on his deathbed to speak about his relation to Bardo or even to treat his sister as a sister rather than as the subject of a vision cannot be taken as Savonarola takes it. When Savonarola's arresting voice insists that 'every bond of your life is a debt', Romola asks, 'How, then, could Dino be right? He broke ties. He forsook his place.' His answer, especially when seen in the heavily humanist terms of the whole book and in the light of his later career, is altogether inadequate: 'That was a special vocation. He was constrained to depart, else he could not have attained the higher life. It would have been stifled within him' (ch. 40). One of Dino's functions is to suggest that the tension between duty and rebellion, which we have seen is the central concern of Romola's career, is a real tension, not to be resolved in any schematic way.

Dino's fanaticism and narrowness are in part a symbolic manifestation of Savonarola's own failings, his narrowness. Romola's almost visceral revulsion from the other fanatic *piagnoni* and her dissatisfaction with Fra Silvestro imply early that Savonarola is not a totally adequate guide and that ultimately there will be 'a moment for her when', as Savonarola says and she reiterates, 'the soul must have no guide but the voice within' (ch. 59). And it is crucial to one's understanding of the novel that the scene in which Romola accepts Savonarola's appeal that she return to Tito is not to be taken as a conclusive moral statement. The moment recurs in which Romola feels she must leave Tito and Florence, and, after the full experience of Savonarola's teaching, Romola finds herself in a precisely similar moral situation. This time, however, Savonarola himself is implicated in the corruption of Florence. Stronger and wiser, while Savonarola's spots of commonness have shown through, she can and does reject him and her life in Florence. She finds that the rejection of Tito, which had once, in the terms of the book, made her morally analogous to Tito and Dino, is now possible and distinctly different from their kind of betrayal. It is at this point that the inescapably symbolic sequence begins. When Romola drifts away, the book can no longer be regarded as a novel in the traditional sense. It is as though the moral education of Romola must begin again, as though the whole circumstantial world of Florence and the history of her life have not existed. Romola must be born again, and she can be reborn only by moving through a ritual repetition of her first departure from Florence, and by entering a setting which is frankly unrealistic. She becomes clearly what she has always implicitly been: the romantic heroine whose problems are universal and ultimately not dependent on the contingent and the conditional. The novel's 'Proem' had insisted on the continuity of human life regardless of its local conditions. Romola enacts a fate which is neither Renaissance nor Victorian, but human.

Inevitably, then, the dramatization of this culmination of Romola's career comes in scenes quite self-consciously 'romantic and symbolical'. Without excusing the rather arbitrary way in which George Eliot seems at this point to construct her symbols – having Romola drift conveniently, not out to sea and death, but to the plague-ridden city which will once again engage her in life – it is crucial to recognize that the 'romantic and symbolic' qualities are built inextricably into the whole conception of the novel. Romola's full moral experience depends on her liberation from external guidance and on absolute confrontation with self, regardless of the pressures of the external world. This liberation grows from the tension between Romola's story and Tito's. Tito's story, as we have noted, is very much a novelistic one: it dramatizes with heavy irony the futility of the attempt to achieve a 'romantic' condition, free from entangling relationships and obligations, and it reveals how clearly one's actions are dependent on one's own past. In other words, Tito's movement in the novel is heavily determined. Hard as he struggles to free himself, he is increasingly enmeshed in the local and the contingent; Romola, on the other hand, struggling hard to accept her obligations, finds that her past is withdrawn from her, and that she is liberated from the pressures of her community and of her past to decide her own fate. The irony of the narrative pattern of the novel is that Tito's actions, attempting to disentangle him, in fact operate to disentangle Romola.

If any aspect of *Romola* is exempted from the general critical condemnation, it is usually the story of Tito's progressive fall into evil. This has been, until recently, the most commonly discussed part of the novel, and little needs to be said here about its psychological fidelity and the appearance of inevitability Tito's progress gives. Determinism plays its rôle most fully in Tito's story:

> But our deeds [George Eliot says] are like children that are born to us; they live and act apart from our own will. Nay, children may be strangled, but deeds never: they have an indestructible life both in and out of our consciousness; and that dreadful vitality of deeds was pressing hard on Tito for the first time.
>
> (ch. 16)

Tito's story is that of Arthur Donnithorne, worked out in more detail and carried to a higher extreme of evil.

In fact, however, though it has a measure of artistic success — especially as George Eliot begins to develop those tools of psychological analysis that will be indispensable to *Middlemarch* and *Daniel Deronda* — Tito's story is considerably less interesting than the story of Romola, at least from the point of view of the fable of *Romola*. Tito was a kind of character George Eliot found it relatively easy to do, and she managed throughout her career to work elaborate refinements on the study of the kind of egoism he represents. What she always found difficult to create is the character whose egoism is an aspect of his capacity for goodness. Romola is a not quite successful study for Dorothea Brooke, who is eventually etherealized and idealized back into Daniel Deronda himself.

But before returning in more detail to Romola's progress, it is worth noting briefly how Tito operates to intensify her freedom. Tito sells Bardo's library, and cuts her last link with her father; he is involved in the plots which ultimately cause the death of Bernardo by compromising Savonarola, who is thus also lost to her as a guide. Tito's life, after the marriage, is deeply interwoven with the plots and counterplots of Florentine politics, while Romola, utterly passive in regard to these plots (although she manages to thwart Tito's first attempt on Savonarola's life), finds that the conditions of a corrupt Florence entail deep personal sorrow and move her towards estrangement. In Romola's story, the details of Florentine life are largely irrelevant. It is through Tito's life that most of George Eliot's knowledge of Florence and its history finds expression: the discussions in the barber's shop, the descriptions of pageants, the analysis of the political structures and parties within the community. Even Savonarola's story, which seems so closely integrated with Romola's, actually moves in the novel as a reflex of Tito's world. The deepest analysis of Savonarola comes in the third book as a result of two of Tito's tricks, the one leading to the death of Bernardo, the other to Savonarola's trial by fire. For Romola, Savonarola is a personal guide; for Tito he is an historical figure. And Romola's rejection of Savonarola is a function of the fact that he is a public figure.

While Tito progressively entangles himself in public life, hoping all the time to get free to leave Florence, each step in Romola's progress back to Florence makes her relation to the 'real' – that is, novelistic – world more tenuous. Savonarola had, to be sure, persuaded her of the value of the ordinary man who is a believer, who 'feels the glow of a common life with the lost multitude for whom that offering was made, and beholds the history of the world as the history of a great redemption in which he is himself a fellow-worker, in his own place and among his own people' (ch. 40). But, in fact, Romola's relation to Florence upon her return is almost entirely a willed relation, growing out of no natural ties, but her faith in Savonarola himself: 'She had no innate taste for tending the sick and clothing the ragged, like some women to whom the details of such work are welcome in themselves, simply as an occupation.' Her relation to Tito, moreover, 'brought a doubt whether, after all, the bond to which she had laboured to be true might not itself be false' (ch. 44). She sees the 'miserable narrowness' of Savonarola's followers. And she stays this side of lawlessness and despair, we are told, because 'No soul is desolate as long as there is a human being for whom it can feel trust and reverence' (ch. 44).

But only when, as I have suggested, Romola comes to have 'no guide but the soul within', when her choice, that is, becomes absolutely free and spontaneous, can the genuine relations between her and her world be discovered. Thus, when she loses her faith in Savonarola, the inevitable crisis of the fable is achieved. She is free to choose. The contrast with George Eliot's usual novelistic treatment of choice is sharp. Gwendolen Harleth makes her decision to marry Grandcourt under severe pressures which grow out of the various entanglements of her life – her love of her mother, her need to become a governess if she does *not* marry, the easy acquiescence of the society in Grandcourt's eligibility, her belief that she can dominate, and so on. The tradition of romance provides an alternative treatment of choice – James's Isabel Archer consciously rejecting all advice, undirected by material need, choosing Osmond out of her ignorance. Romola is one of the few characters in George Eliot's novels (Dorothea is an interesting though qualified exception) who reaches a stage where she is utterly on her own to choose which way to go. She has nothing to decide with but her own nature, her own sense of life.

Romola's progress to this point of crisis has, moreover, been curiously uninvolved in the wider life of the novel. In relation to the political activities in Florence, she is an utterly passive figure, although she is active in helping the poor and suffering. Her story is very much a personal one, and it moves not with the inevitability of a determined world, but with the inevitability of symbolic fable, controlled by a vision of moral value, by a sense of what lies behind nature, not on the surface of it. Romola sustains her purity by remaining in the world of romance; but in both the subject and technique of the novel romance is forced to confront the 'real' world. It may be one way to account for the unsatisfactory quality of the novel that the romance is never reconciled to the real, and that this is a result of the fact that the moral positions established by the two different worlds are not reconciled in the novel itself.

The intrusion of the dense world of Florentine public life on Savonarola causes his particular tragedy, and further demonstrates

93

the way the book is split between the realistic and the romance. Savonarola's ethic, although it has a public and visionary guise, is a personal one. At least it operates on Romola in that way. Although, as we discover, Savonarola's preaching can feed the visionary fanaticism of some of his followers and the passionate lust for vengeance of Baldassarre, Romola listens only to the direct voice of human feeling which makes her aware that Savonarola is greater than she and can, therefore, be taken as a guide. But when one of the fanatic *piagnoni* accuses her of knowing secrets about her uncle which might, if revealed, save the state, Romola is forced to reconsider her relation to Savonarola.

> Why, with his readiness to denounce wrong from the pulpit, did he not publicly denounce these pretended revelations which brought new darkness instead of light across the conception of a Supreme Will? The answer came with painful clearness: he was fettered inwardly by the consciousness that such revelations were not, in their basis, distinctly separable from his own visions; he was fettered outwardly by the foreseen consequences of raising a cry against himself even among members of his own party, as one who would suppress all Divine Inspiration of which he himself was not the vehicle. . . .
>
> (ch. 52)

In Savonarola's story we have the beginning of George Eliot's explicity dramatized distrust of politics, hinted at in *Janet's Repentance* and fully explored in *Felix Holt*. The public life is inevitably corrupting. It brings out, in *Romola*, Savonarola's spots of commonness.

The power of the final confrontation between Savonarola and Romola lies precisely in the unresolved tension between novel and romance, between public and personal ethics, between the social, conditional, enmeshed life of the ordinary man and the personal, free, uncontingent life of the romantic heroine. And by the time the novel arrives at that confrontation, Savonarola and Romola have moved through a set of experiences which make their symbolic force extraordinarily rich and complex. The fable, by means of an elaborate pattern of contrasts and juxtapositions, repetitions and variations (only a small part of which has it been possible to discuss here), moves to its inevitable symbolic climax in such a way that the moral problems with which it is engaged cannot be resolved discursively or in terms other than those of art. The last part of that pattern that needs to be discussed is the parallel, already suggested, between the moral dilemmas of Savonarola and Romola. In her famous letter to R. H. Hutton, George Eliot pointed out that Savonarola and Romola were faced with the same problem: 'The question where the duty of obedience ends, and the duty of resistance begins, could in no case be an easy one' (ch. 55). In the context of the novel, this refers directly to Savonarola, who refuses to accept his excommunication. But it obviously applies also to Romola in her relation to Savonarola.

In the chapter 'Pleading', we are given the closest direct look at the mind of Savonarola. Hitherto, the view has been largely from the outside; now we discover how thoroughly enmeshed in the dense and tangled affairs of man he is. Savonarola's resentment towards opposition is thwarted for a moment, as Romola argues with him, 'by that hard struggle which made half the tragedy of his life – the struggle of a mind possessed by a never-silent hunger after purity and simplicity, yet caught in a tangle of egoistic demands, false ideas, and difficult outward conditions, that made simplicity impossible' (ch. 59). Although it is difficult, with Romola, not to be angered by Savonarola, George Eliot's handling of the scene attempts to sustain impartiality, to feel the difficulty of the confrontation between two forces, both admirable. Savonarola's crucial remark can serve in part as a judgment of the entire book: ' "Be thankful, my daughter, if your own soul has been spared perplexity; and judge not those to whom a harder lot has been given. *You* see one ground of action in this matter. I see many" ' (ch. 59). This is a powerful voice, but it is the voice of compromise, emerging from a real world in which human relations are so complex that no moral questions are easily soluble and in which any answer will have some morally repugnant effects. The novel, through Savonarola, is speaking against the purity of romance and pleading for tolerance.

Romola herself learns tolerance of Savonarola after his death, but the failure of her book resides centrally in George Eliot's impatience with the world of compromise, of which, in *Middlemarch*, she became the great master. *Romola* expresses a great yearning for justice: in its very technique it is a manifestation of the validity of one of George Eliot's most moving aphorisms: 'Justice is like the kingdom of God – it is not without us as a fact, it is within us as a great yearning' (ch. 67). But within *Romola* justice finally emerges as 'a fact': Tito meets his Nemesis and is destroyed in a way that looks sharply forward to the kind of externalizing of visions we get in *Daniel Deronda*. Mordecai waits on Blackfriars Bridge and out of the water comes the man – Daniel – whose existence he has almost willed; Baldassarre wills Tito into being:

> Baldassarre, looking up blankly from the search in the runlet that brought him nothing, had seen a white object coming along the broader stream. Could that be any fortunate chance for *him?* He looked and looked till the object gathered form: then he leaned forward with a start as he sat among the rank green stems, and his eyes seemed to be filled with a new light. Yet he only watched – motionless. Something was being brought to him.
>
> (ch. 67)

And Romola, like Daniel gliding on the river and discovering Mirah, glides to a new engagement in life – an engagement which gives her life meaning and direction. She rescues the plague-ridden village as Daniel rescues Mirah:

> She had felt herself without bonds, without motive; sinking in mere egoistic complaining that life could bring her no content; feeling a right to say, 'I am tired of life, I want to die.' That thought had sobbed within her as she fell asleep, but from the moment after her waking when the cry had drawn her, she had not even reflected, as she used to do in Florence, that she was glad to live because she could lighten sorrow – she had simply lived, with so energetic an impulse to share the life around her, to answer the call of need and do the work which cried aloud to be done, that the reasons for living, enduring, labouring, never took the form of argument.
>
> The experience was like a new baptism to Romola.
>
> (ch. 69)

The completion of the symbolic pattern is clear enough. But even more clear is the fact that George Eliot herself has put justice in the world. Her own great yearning for it sought a method by which to embody it: the method was romance.

But the romance, while appearing to resolve the problems which the book raised, resolved, in fact, nothing. The need and the will clearly triumphed over the possibilities which, even within the terms of the kind of romance *Romola* might have been without its ending, the book allowed. The sporadically brilliant, architecturally stunning exploration of large moral issues which *Romola* provides is its great virtue: the book's power and its capacity still to interest lie in its refusal to simplify the question, though its conclusion seems to falsify an answer. The question, indeed, could in no case be an easy one. And the book ends as divided as Romola and Savonarola were at the conclusion of their last interview – unassimilated novel and romance – 'the two faces were lit up, each with an opposite emotion, each with an opposite certitude' (ch. 59).

NOTES

1. *George Eliot: Her Mind and Her Art*, p. 140.
2. Henry James, 'George Eliot's Life', *Atlantic Monthly*, LV (May 1885), pp. 668–78.
3. *The Novels of George Eliot*, p. 59.
4. *Letters*, iii. 420.
5. R. H. Hutton, 'Romola', *Spectator* (18 July 1863), pp. 2265–7; reprinted in *George Eliot and Her Readers*, ed. John Holmstrom and Laurence Lerner (Bodley Head, 1966), pp. 56–64. See pp. 56–7.
6. *Letters*, iv. 97.
7. In a letter to Mrs. Bodichon, George Eliot comments on the general moral problem of freedom from pressures of external relations: 'It seems to those who are differently placed that the time of freedom from strong ties and urgent claims must be very precious for the ends of self-culture, and good, helpful work toward the world at large. But it hardly ever is so' (*Letters*, iii. 365–6). In a way, this is what Romola discovers. But the condition of such freedom is a condition of romance; and Romola's story must be worked out in terms of romance in order for her fully to comprehend the inadequacy of 'freedom'.
8. Barbara Hardy has noted how the emphasis on the visionary in *Romola* anticipates *Daniel Deronda* (*The Novels of George Eliot*), p. 176. This is a crucial point that merits further exploration. Given the limits of the argument of this paper, I cannot adequately discuss the visionary elements here, but that they do anticipate *Daniel Deronda* is one of my working assumptions.
9. See, on this point, Lawrence Poston, 'Setting and Theme in *Romola*', *Nineteenth Century Fiction*, XXI (March 1966), pp. 225–33.
10. Silas's catepleptic fits, which leave him vulnerable to betrayal and theft, have their parallel in Baldassarre's loss of memory. Manipulation of these lapses need not rely at all on the qualities of character (although George Eliot tries to explain them in terms of the action). Both kinds of lapses are essentially symbolic, and function also to assist the narrative's movement through mysterious injustice to ultimate poetic justice. Eppie's fortuitous (and happily symbolic) entrance through Silas's door has a kind of parallel in Romola's drifting to the plague-ridden village. Both events re-engage the characters in their communities.
11. *The Novels of George Eliot*, p. 185.
12. *Letters*, iv. 103–4.

13. Jerome Thale puts this criticism, essentially Barbara Hardy's, in a different, equally useful way: 'The trouble with the character of Romola ... is not that she is too good – though she is. The trouble is that everything about her – pride, noble sentiments, humility, self-will – is seen only from a lofty moral plane. She is judged only by the highest moral standards. . . . She is too epical – and the epical simply will not do in a realistic novel' (*The Novels of George Eliot* (Columbia, U.P., 1959)), pp. 81–2.

14. *Letters*, iv. 104.

15. See Northrop Frye, *Anatomy of Criticism* (Princeton U.P., 1957), pp. 304–5: 'The romancer does not attempt to create "real people" so much as stylized figures which expand into psychological archetypes. It is in the romance that we find Jung's libido, anima, and shadow reflected in the hero, heroine, and villain respectively. That is why the romance so often radiates a glow of subjective intensity that the novel lacks, and why a suggestion of allegory is constantly creeping in around its fringes. . . . If Scott has any claims to be a romancer, it is not good criticism to deal only with his defects as a novelist.'

VI

'FELIX HOLT THE RADICAL'
Arnold Kettle

Felix Holt the Radical begins magnificently. We are taken right
into history, into the England of 1832, after the passing of the Reform Bill. But there is nothing musty about the history, no sense of
a retreat into the past. On the contrary, by choosing as her subject an
England thirty-five years gone, George Eliot's instinct, as in *Middlemarch*, may well have been wise. It is not easy for a highly self-
conscious and responsible novelist to absorb quite contemporary
experience with the kind of assurance which ultimately creates good
art. Such a writer often does best with the material he has stored
from his youth; then recollection in tranquillity brings forth a freshness of emotion which has yet passed, unselfconsciously, through the
toughening of experience. That George Eliot was able to draw on
the memories of her Midland childhood and youth no doubt helped
avoid a repetition of the conscientious but rather arid sort of history
behind *Romola*: that she should have chosen a period and a subject
so closely interwoven with the England of 1866 prevents – at the
outset at least – any loss of urgency, for to understand 1832 was,
after all, an essential part of understanding 1866.

For the England in which George Eliot was writing was itself on
the brink of a new Parliamentary reform, and one which raised far
more immediately than the Bill of 1832 the question of working-class
suffrage, one of the preoccupations of *Felix Holt*. To appreciate how
contemporary a book this was one has only to see George Eliot's
novel in association with non-fictional works like Bagehot's *English
Constitution* (1867), Matthew Arnold's *Culture and Anarchy* (1869),
and the *Studies in Parliament* (1866) of R. S. Hutton, who himself

reviewed several of her novels for *The Spectator*. *Felix Holt* was published in the year that Robert Lowe – himself the author of the 'revised code' for the administration of education under which Matthew Arnold operated as a school inspector – warned the House of Commons: 'Once give working men the votes, and the machinery is ready to launch those votes in one compact mass upon the institutions and property of this country.' Arnold's fear of the cultural attitudes of the populace, symbolized for him by the tearing down of the Hyde Park railings in 1866, is closely connected with Lowe's famous remark, after the passing of the 1867 Reform Bill, that it was essential 'to compel our future masters to learn their letters', and it was in this context that George Eliot brought Felix Holt out of fiction into actual public life by publishing the 'Address to Working Men by Felix Holt' in *Blackwood's* in January 1868.

The triumph of the opening chapters of *Felix Holt* is threefold: the general evocation of post-Reform Bill Britain (especially in the Introduction and Chapter 3, but permeating the whole enterprise); the vivid and remarkably intense and finely dramatized presentation of a number of personal relationships and tensions; and the linking of the two – the general and the particular – by the revelation of certain patterns which are at once private and public, personal and typical. In a sentence that has become well known, George Eliot showed her consciousness of what she was doing:

> These social changes in Treby parish are comparatively public matters, and this history is chiefly concerned with the private lot of a few men and women; but there is no private life which has not been determined by a wider public life, from the time when the primeval milkmaid had to wander with the wanderings of her clan, because the cow she milked was one of a herd which had made the pastures bare.
>
> (ch. 3)

It is a sentence we shall return to.

The sketching-in of the general social situation is extremely well done. George Eliot, like Hardy, looks at a landscape historically and sees the social forces behind the visual changes, and this, as in a Breughel picture, is what gives the visual effect its point and significance. The changes brought about by the Industrial Revolution – the coalmines, the canals and their consequences – are most effectively suggested. (It is interesting to compare the use of similar material by another Midlands novelist, Lawrence, in *The Rainbow*.) Before these changes the social separation in Treby between the County aristocracy and the well-to-do traders and richer farmers had been complete. The Debarry and Transome families owned the estates and supplied the rectors, while the prosperous middle class 'played at whist, ate and drank generously, praised Mr. Pitt and the war as keeping up prices and religion, and were very humorous about each other's property' (ch. 3). Now, as Treby Magna

> gradually passed from being simply a respectable market-town – the heart of a great rural district, where the trade was only such as had close relations with the local landed interest – and took on the more complex life brought by mines and manufactures, which belong more directly to the great circulating system of the nation.
>
> (ibid.)

the old divisions alter. On the one hand landed and industrial interests begin to come into open conflict; on the other the nature of the working people changes. Trebian Dissent alters its character. Political Radicalism becomes an urgent issue. 'There were Dissenters in Treby now who could not be regarded by the Church people in the light of old neighbours to whom the habit of going to chapel was an innocent, unenviable inheritance' (*ibid.*). Radicalism is seen here by George Eliot not simply as a set of opinions: it is a social force arising out of basic economic changes.

The return to Treby of Harold Transome after fifteen years of successful money-making in the Middle East and of Felix Holt after a period of study in Glasgow opens up the personal interest of the novel. Harold Transome is heir to the estate of Little Treby. His return home is a superb scene. His mother, weighed down by the burdens of an incapable husband, a dissolute elder son, and a series of ruinous law-suits, has kept the estate going. She is proud, energetic, intensely Tory, intensely bitter – and the bitterness is gradually revealed to be bound up with her secret: that her son Harold was fathered, not by her feeble husband, but by a bold and able young lawyer named Matthew Jermyn. Now, the hated elder son dead, Harold comes home, rich, to take over the estate. Mrs. Transome, uncompromising in so much, has built up over the hard and lonely years a powerful compensatory illusion: when Harold comes back everything will be well. Not only fortune will come back to Transome Court, but honour and joy. And then Harold comes and he is his father's son, an energetic, insensitive second-rater. He brings with him foreign habits, a little son of dubious parentage, plenty of ambition but no sense of the past, in which his mother lives. He is not consciously unkind nor especially un-scrupulous, but he has no understanding whatever of the kind of person Mrs. Transome is. And to cap her humiliation he announces that he intends to stand in the forthcoming election as a Radical.

Felix Holt is also a Radical, but of a quite different kind. His father has been a relatively successful quack doctor, so that he could afford to study, but his whole *milieu* is in entire contrast to Transome Court – plebeian, Dissenting, respectable. He too dis-appoints his mother: for he insists, on getting back to Treby, that they will not live on the proceeds of quack medicine, which he believes to be fraudulent, but on the money gained by honest work as a watch-maker. Felix, indeed, takes his Radical stand on the fundamental question of class allegiance: he is a worker and will remain one. 'Why should I want to get into the middle class be-cause I have some learning?'[1] he asks. Advance must come through the raising of the working class as a class, and for that he feels an intense responsibility, and he will not compromise, either in his personal life or in his principles, with the rich. 'I want the working men to have power' he is to tell the Nomination-Day crowd (ch. 30).

Harold Transome's Radicalism is, of course, something quite different from this. He is a Radical because the future looks that way, because

> nothing was left to men of sense and good family but to retard the national ruin by declaring themselves Radicals, and take the inevitable process of changing everything out of the hands of beggarly dema-gogues and purse-proud tradesmen.
>
> (ch. 2)

And he wins an important round by gaining the support of his old Tory clergyman uncle with the assurance, 'I am a Radical only in rooting out abuses':

> 'That's the word I wanted, my lad!' said the Vicar, slapping Harold's knee. 'That's a spool to wind a speech on. Abuses is the very word.'
>
> (ch. 2)

It is this contradiction between two kinds of Radical, the ruling-class kind, who is in fact just about as revolutionary as Disraeli's Tory Democrats, and the working-class sort, who is wanting a fundamental change in social organization, that is the real core of George Eliot's novel. And it is a marvellously promising subject,

for not only is the contradiction at the heart of it a real one historically, bearing the closest and most searching general consideration,
but it also opens up in its personal aspects an enormously rich and
fruitful field of human observation, dramatically and psychologically, as the early sections of *Felix Holt the Radical* indicate.

I have said that the triumph of the opening chapters of the novel
is threefold. The general evocation of England in 1832, which it is
inadequate to describe as 'background' (personal lives are not
acted out against a backcloth of social life; the interdependence is
closer and subtler than that), has been touched on. So has the
magnificent presentation of a personal situation, that of Mrs.
Transome, her son, and the lawyer Jermyn. What is rather more
difficult to establish – chiefly, I think, because our tools and vocabulary of analysis are either too 'literary' or not literary enough – is
the nature of the artistic pattern of the book at this stage.

I have said that the core of George Eliot's novel is the contradiction between two kinds of Radical, that this is indeed a novel
about Radicalism. I think this is shown by (*a*) the title of the novel,
with its gratuitous emphasis on Felix's politics, (*b*) the direction of
emphasis in the general historical passages, (*c*) the way, at the end
of Chapter 3, Felix Holt is introduced as a contrast-cum-parallel to
Harold Transome, with their relationship to their respective
mothers as well as their Radicalism stressed, and (*d*) the development in the early structure of the book, of two main contrasting
areas of interest – the Transome-Jermyn area and the Holt-Lyon
area – with other episodes and characters subsidiary to these two.
This general view of the pattern of *Felix Holt* is, it seems to me,
borne out by the passages of detailed analysis of the formal organization of the novel by Barbara Hardy in her interesting book, *The
Novels of George Eliot.*[2]

Harold Transome's Radicalism is not presented simply as a
personal opinion: the operation of it involves a whole area of social
life – the support of the clerical uncle, the bringing into play of a
'machine' run, though scarcely controlled, by Jermyn and his
satellites. Similarly, Felix Holt, though a strongly individualistic
and non-conforming character, is presented as a part of the whole
Dissenting community: his relationship with the Lyons, the Dissenting minister and his daughter, is as socially inevitable and firmly
grounded as Transome's relations with Matthew Jermyn. All this produces, in the first hundred or so pages of *Felix Holt*, a deepening

sense that the personal stories within the novel are not subsidiary to (that would give a false impression), but, to use George
Eliot's own word, essentially determined by the wider public life
of Treby. She makes the point explicitly in the sentence:

> There could hardly have been a lot less like Harold Transome's than
> this of the quack doctor's son, except in the superficial facts that he
> called himself a Radical, that he was the only son of his mother, and
> that he had lately returned to his home with ideas and resolves not a
> little disturbing to that mother's mind.

(ch. 3)

The problem about this sentence is whether the word 'superficial'
is used ironically. As W. J. Harvey has remarked, 'These facts, of
course, turn out to be anything but superficial',[3] and there would
not, one might assume, be any point in stressing the parallels which
give the book its peculiar structure unless they were in fact significant. But I think there is an ambiguity here, and am not sure that
George Eliot's use of the word is really ironical.

It is necessary to stress this point because it is my argument that
George Eliot fails to develop or fully realize the pattern which is
the core of her book. The obvious retort, of course, is that it
evidently isn't really the core of the book, that George Eliot's intention and preoccupation is somewhat other than I have suggested,
and that I am not only foisting my own pattern on the novel, but
unreasonably blaming the author for not sticking to it. I agree
that this would be a silly thing to do. The point at issue is not, it
should be added, precisely what George Eliot consciously intended
to do or not to do. One can scarcely ever measure the exact degree
of self-consciousness of an artist, or anyone else. The important
thing about a work of art is not what its author may at some point
or other have intended, but what is there.

What happens in *Felix Holt* is that George Eliot, having made
clear what her novel is about, having revealed its incipient pattern,
then fails to fulfil the promise she has hinted at.

I have already suggested that the developing pattern of the book,
even in its early stages, is not without its ambiguities. Though the
central theme is expressed primarily in the historical terms already
discussed, there are, right from the start, indications that within
George Eliot's mind other and perhaps contradictory forces are at
work.

An example of what I have in mind comes at the end of the

Introduction. The general line and tone of the writing has, in the first pages, been historical. The use of the coachman as a kind of choric figure, at once character and *compère*, permits George Eliot a degree of irony which is immediately 'placed' by the reader within an objective context. The processes of social change are thus rendered and commented on in a way which is at the same time personal and impersonal: the historical forces evoked are envisaged in terms of actual living people and their individual destinies. Abstraction is thus avoided and an objectivity at once concrete and intimate achieved. Then, in the last two paragraphs of the chapter, we notice a change of method, accompanied by a significant change in tone, a certain hushed intensity which tells us that the author's feelings are in some way peculiarly engaged.

Sampson the coachman has been hinting that

some 'fine stories' lie behind the public fortunes of the Transome family. And such fine stories often come to be fine in a sense that is not ironical. For there is seldom any wrong-doing which does not carry along with it some downfall of blindly-climbing hopes, some hard entail of suffering, some quickly-satiated desire that survives, with the life in death of old paralytic vice, to see itself cursed by its woeful progeny – some tragic mark of kinship in the one brief life to the far-stretching life that went before, and to the life that is to come after, such as has raised the pity and terror of men ever since they began to discern between will and destiny. But these things are often unknown to the world; for there is much pain that is quite noiseless; and vibrations that make human agonies are often a mere whisper in the roar of hurrying existence. There are glances of hatred that stab and raise no cry of murder; robberies that leave man or woman for ever beggared of peace and joy, yet kept secret by the sufferer – committed to no sound except that of low moans in the night, seen in no writing except that made on the face by the slow months of suppressed anguish and early morning tears. Many an inherited sorrow that has marred a life has been breathed into no human ear.

Readers will, I think, be divided in their reactions to such a passage. To some the shift into an emotionally-charged tone raptly generalizing upon the secret sufferings of humankind will bring a sympathetic sense that here at last the true depths are being sounded. George Eliot has moved, such readers will feel, from the relative superficies of material development to the deeper mysteries of the human heart and its sorrows. This, they will feel, is the real thing.

Other readers will note the change with a certain suspicion as a move from a controlled objectivity to a vaguer and perhaps self-indulgent expression of an attitude of mind not altogether free of abstract generalization and the preacher's tone of voice. I do not want to attempt to adjudicate between two hypothetical reactions; but I think the texture of the writing here is worth examining. What gives the prose its curious density is not simply the piling up of a multiplicity of issues and images, many of which are somewhat mystifying to anyone reading the book for the first time; there is also a slipping into a characteristic rhythm based on deeply-held convictions about the unchanging sadness of the human lot. George Eliot's artistic intentions in *Felix Holt* seem to me rather basically unresolved. Is this to be a novel about Radicalism or a novel about Mrs. Transome? The logic and structure of the book point in one direction, the emotional engagement of the author in the other.

This is why, despite some excellent things in the later part of the novel, the promise of *Felix Holt* is not really fulfilled. The area in which Mrs. Transome appears is never less than distinguished;[4] and Mrs. Transome extends to the other characters closest to her personal tragedy – Harold, Matthew Jermyn, even her poor husband – a dimension of artistic vitality they do not always have in other parts of the book. But it has to be said that this considera-tion of the Transome situation – fine and moving as it is – is not linked organically with the rest of the novel. Even the Transomes' relations with Esther in the part of the book in which she is living at Transome Court have little of the conviction one associates with most of the scenes in that house and the increasing tendency of the author to fall back into a 'sweet Esther Lyon' rhapsody tells its own tale. The political part of the book too is almost incidental to the Transome drama, the essence of which could have been achieved without the introduction of the theme of Radicalism as anything but a relatively trivial matter. The development of Harold's re-lations with Jermyn and the whole bitter humiliation of Mrs. Transome need not have been significantly different if Harold Transome had stood as a Tory candidate.

Clearly, with Mrs. Transome George Eliot had got hold of a situation which engaged her deeply. Put in general terms, this has something to do with the position of woman *vis-à-vis* men; but chiefly it involves the question of moral responsibility and the sense – so deep in George Eliot – that we get nothing on the cheap in this severe world and no past action can be obliterated. Mrs. Transome, like Mrs. Alving, is trapped by ghosts. The revelation of her situation is done with fine artistry, great psychological insight and dramatic power; but it remains peripheral. As Leslie Stephen remarked years ago, one would really need to know a little more about that early love-affair to have the sense of even Mrs. Transome's story being fully explored. As it is, even the presentation of this, the finest, area of the latter part of the novel suffers from the nature of the plot.

Felix Holt the Radical begins clearly to deteriorate from the time (about the twelfth chapter) when the complexities of the plot start to take over control and to undermine the development of the wide and significant conflicts which George Eliot has earlier established. This plot is excessively tortuous and involves not only two mysteries of parentage, but a most formidable paraphernalia of legal detail over which the author (assisted by the eminent Positivist lawyer, Frederic Harrison) was excessively conscientious. Its most obvious disadvantage is that it is almost impossible on a first reading to be quite clear as to who knows what about whom. But this would not really matter very much if the plot were doing its job in reinforcing the main image or pattern of the novel. The plot of *Bleak House* is, we recall, enormously complex and dependent on a number of chances – to say nothing of legal complications – which no one demanding naturalistic probability could be likely to accept. Yet the plot of *Bleak House* triumphantly serves the total design and meaning of Dickens's novel, while that of *Felix Holt* continuously detracts from the seriousness of George Eliot's.

Why is this? In literary terms, because the forces brought into play in the unravelling of the plot do not correspond with those which have been set in motion by the statement, in the opening chapters, of what the novel is about. This is to be a novel about the personal fortunes of people whose lot is organically bound up with the condition of England, with class-conflicts and the moral problems involved in social advance, with the two faces of Radicalism and what political responsibility implies. Yet it is all worked out in terms of legal niceties, unexpected inheritances and complex intrigues in which little or no conflict of principle arises. The law, which dominated the plot, is never itself given any serious moral or historical consideration. It is simply there. Compared with the consideration of the law in *Bleak House*, that in *Felix*

Holt is superficial and inadequate. Jermyn, as a 'convincing character' abstracted from his place in the novel, may be superior to Tulkinghorn, who exists primarily as a visual image reinforced by an idiosyncratic rhetoric; as a significant figure in an achieved work of art he is greatly inferior.

That Felix should be imprisoned for his part in a riot he has tried to quell is a fact conveyed by George Eliot without a breath of irony;[5] the whole episode is treated entirely in terms of individual characters' motives and consciences. The trial scene has no more moral profundity and almost as much conventional melodrama as the one in *Mary Barton*. A certain irony is directed upon the stupid Mrs. Holt, who is convinced that the gentry can get her son off if they feel so inclined. Yet when this in fact happens the episode is treated entirely unironically and its moral and social implications ignored, not only by the morally uncompromising Felix, but by the omniscient author, who is not averse to moral reflection at other moments of the book.

There is, indeed, almost no resolution to this novel at all – and such as there is comes near to seeming a mockery in the light of the issues that have been raised, the depths sounded. Esther, it is true, marries Felix, putting behind her the vanities on which she has fed herself; but her moral choice, as has been truly said, does not carry the conviction of a tragic ordeal.[6] This is not only because too much self-interest is involved, but because at the trial, as throughout almost all the latter part of the novel, the actual implications of Felix's Radicalism are lost sight of. It is to his 'nobility' that Esther testifies at his trial, not his principles: what she gives him is a high-grade character-reference. And her ability at the end to provide 'a little income for your mother, enough for her to live as she has been used to living; and a little income for my father, to save him from being dependent when he is no longer able to preach' (ch. 51), this not merely softens the end of the book, leaving it in a comfortable glow of cosy compromise, but undermines the whole moral position on which Felix has originally taken his stand. Why it should be better to accept Esther's money than his father's is not revealed.

What would seem to be involved in all this is a failure on George Eliot's part to face, morally or artistically, the problems she has set in motion in undertaking this particular novel. W. J. Harvey has drawn attention[7] to the rather odd abandonment, in the course of the book, of the projected debate between Mr. Lyon and the curate, Mr. Sherlock. The episode as it stands is so disproportionate to any furthering of the plot achieved by it that it is hard to believe that George Eliot had not originally intended an actual confrontation. Why did she draw back? Our suspicions of something incompletely realized have, of course, been aroused even in the excellent early reaches of the book by the presentation of Felix himself and the lack of 'bite' in the Holt-Lyon sections as compared with the Transome-Jermyn ones. There is something dangerously near a musical-comedy, *Quaker Girl* atmosphere about the whole conception of Esther. Yet there is also in the early chapters that involve Felix and Esther a good deal of strength. The tendency to idealize is counteracted by much that is shrewd and true. The presentation of Felix at this stage seems to me, despite the warning lights, successful, the rather absurd and even repulsive aspects of him – the priggishness and pedantry – are, by and large, 'placed', and a genuine strength and simplicity emerges. And the tendency to idealization does not matter much in this context where the pattern of the book is firmly established. The most important thing about Felix and Esther at this stage is that they should be there at all, embodying a way of life firmly contrasted with the Transomes'. And though the realization of Mr. Lyon is weak compared with that of, say, Mark Rutherford's Dissenting ministers, I cannot feel that Dr. Leavis's dismissal of him as a bore is the last word.[8]

I am arguing, it will have become apparent, that the basis of George Eliot's failure in this novel is a drawing back from certain of the realities of the social situation which the book is about. Of these the most important is the nature of the common people and their problems, particularly in the light of the new possibilities of democratic advance. She is sympathetic. She sees clearly enough the limitations of Transomian Radicalism and she feels deeply the necessity for something different. She recognizes indeed that a more genuine Radicalism must be based, not on the fears of the ruling class, but on the aspirations of the working people; and this recognition gives what strength it has to her presentation of Felix. But the weakness of the recognition is that it is so theoretical and idealistic. And this is why the idealization of Felix becomes *in the end* a serious artistic flaw.

Felix cannot, of course, be, for George Eliot's purposes, a typical working man. The typical working men in *Felix Holt* are crude, brutal, and stupid. They are incapable of any real foresight, let alone idealism. It would be a mistake to write off George Eliot's picture as simple middle-class prejudice, though one might well accuse her of not seeing the trees for the wood. But the brutalization of whole sections of the working class is not just the invention of a too-refined imagination; it is a fact of the times and had to be reckoned with. George Eliot, however, does not reckon with it: she accepts it as a fact and turns away. Again, this would not matter (for the novel is not *about* working-class life in the way that *Mary Barton* or *Alton Locke* is) if Felix himself were conceived differently. His weakness as a hero is not that he is not just like the miners he meets at the 'Sugar Loaf' at Sproxton. A working-class leader is never a typical worker in the sense of being an average one. Felix's necessary part in the book is not to be an average representative of the working people: his part is to be a Radical, a leader. And it is here that the element of idealism in George Eliot's conception of her hero is fatal. For Felix is not allowed to be a leader; he is not allowed to grapple in a serious way with the actual problems of popular leadership, and his very inadequacies in this respect are paraded as virtues. It is *because* he is an ineffectual idealist that Esther respects him. George Eliot did not in the final analysis want a hero that could be a hero.

Experience of misunderstanding leads me to wish to emphasize that my criticism of the presentation of Felix is not based on some kind of irrelevant personal disagreement with the principles with which his author endows him. I am not trying to rewrite George Eliot's novel for her. Felix is an inadequate hero simply because he does not in fact play a hero's part in the novel, though it is essential to the structure and conception of the book that he should do so. Unless what Felix stands for as a Radical emerges as more convincing than what Harold Transome stands for, the conflict between them becomes, artistically, an unfruitful conflict and Esther's choice a mere matter of personal preference. By disarming Felix as an effective moral agent, George Eliot commits the blunder of disarming him as an effective force in the book.

George Eliot cannot really plead ignorance or historical limitation for her failure here. It is true, of course, that it was more difficult to be an effective Radical in 1832 than a few years later, when the Chartist Movement was in full swing. But Chartism did not arise overnight, and it is worth noticing that in Chapter 30 of

Felix Holt, the Nomination Day scene, a Radical speaker is allowed to put forward, eloquently enough, the Chartist demands for universal suffrage, annual Parliaments, secret ballot and equal electoral districts, and advises the workers to use their influence on behalf of Transome, even though he doesn't have much faith in liberal artistocrats. It is at this point that Felix gets up and makes a critical speech denouncing the demand for the franchise.

His arguments are not silly, and it is not the mere mouthing of them that disqualifies Felix from carrying forward effectively the pattern of George Eliot's book:

'I should like to convince you [he says] that votes would never give you political power worth having while things are as they are now. . . .'
(ch. 30)

As late as 1871 George Eliot's Radical friend, Frederic Harrison, was arguing against universal suffrage on the grounds that in a class-divided society the ruling class can bribe, confuse, and nullify the voting power of the masses. And this is indeed a real problem and one which, especially in the early days of democratic aspiration, was bound to give the strategists of social change serious pause. Felix is obsessed by the thought that the people have been so deeply corrupted that any change that is less than fundamental – a change of heart – merely perpetuates in differing forms existing corruptions. But such thinking can, of course, have more than one implication. Frederic Harrison in 1871 was arguing in the context of the defeat of the Paris Commune, with which he felt a deep sympathy: what he was feeling towards is a more thorough-going revolutionary analysis of the nature of the State than Radicalism could provide. Whereas what Felix Holt offers as an alternative to the vote is defined only in the vaguest and least practical terms. His chief concern is lest the drunken and stupid 70 per cent. should be in a position perpetually to outvote the sober and thoughtful 30 – an argument which reflects a rather fundamental lack of confidence, not simply in the franchise, but in any possibility of social change at all, especially when the alternative to the Chartist programme is seen, not as some sort of non-Parliamentary revolutionary action, but simply as the changing of 'public opinion'. Felix is a 'moral force' man: but here again George Eliot gives him less than a fair chance. For the actual division in the 1830s and 1840s between those Radicals who put their faith in 'moral force' and the 'physical force' men was *within* the Chartist Movement, and the 'moral force' advocates were those who had most, not least, faith in Parliamentary action.

By depriving him of faith in both Parliamentary action and the creation of a popular, revolutionary 'mass movement', George Eliot ensures that Felix by the end of the book is not only an ineffectual Radical, but a deficient hero.

What Felix is in fact left with is not much more than a vague hope in the powers of good books and personal example – and his own clear conscience. All that has happened in the course of the novel is that Harold Transome has failed to win a seat in Parliament; Mrs. Transome's secret has been revealed; Jermyn has been ruined; and Felix and Esther have settled down to a life of modest good works and high moral principles, a culmination which George Eliot invests, not only with approval, but with a novelettish kind of coy cosiness.

And lest there should be any doubt as to what has happened to the great human issues raised so impressively in the early pages of the book there is included in the Epilogue, for those who like their tale to have a moral, the following paragraph:

> As to all that wide parish of Treby Magna, it has since prospered as the rest of England has prospered. Doubtless there is more enlightenment now. Whether the farmers are all public-spirited, the shopkeepers nobly independent, the Sproxton men entirely sober and judicious, the Dissenters quite without narrowness or asperity in religion and politics, and the publicans all fit, like Gaius, to be the friends of an apostle – these things I have not heard, not having correspondence in those parts. Whether any presumption may be drawn from the fact that North Loamshire does not yet return a Radical candidate, I leave to the all-wise – I mean the newspapers.

Perhaps one should not pause too long on such a passage, remembering that, in rounding off her novel, George Eliot felt herself trapped in a convention she did not relish. Yet I think it is quite a significant paragraph. The first sentence, in its unembellished irony, its rather grim simplicity, goes to the heart of George Eliot's dilemma. England has prospered: the successful 1850s and 1860s have succeeded the unstable 1830s and 1840s; but nothing has been solved. She can neither accept nor reject the word 'prosper' and her ambiguous attitude invests the word with interest. But neither can she close with this bare, rich statement.

The sentences that follow have a different tone, apparently more explicitly ironical, actually nearer in flavour to cynicism than to a fruitful irony. The paragraph as a whole is tired writing, weary and dispirited, without the vitality of a controlled despair.

I do not want to labour or belabour the weaknesses of *Felix Holt*, but I think the sort of failure indicated here, and the artistic failure to create a figure commensurate with the needs of her central theme, is bound up with George Eliot's whole position in relation to the England of the 1860s and the future of democracy. Felix is conceived not historically as a figure of the 1830s expressing the tensions and dilemmas of a Radical at that stage of English history, but rather as the author of the 'Address to Working Men' which George Eliot was to publish in 1868.

One of the striking features of that 'Address' is how very unhistorical it is in its approach. The argument is conducted almost entirely in terms of general principles and attitudes and an emotional conviction of 'the supreme unalterable nature of things'.[9] The principles invoked are very much the same as those which Matthew Arnold was at the same time formulating in *Culture and Anarchy*, and the two works make an illuminating example of the strengths and weaknesses of the high-minded mid-Victorian intellectual. In certain respects they represent a genuine liberation of the sensibility – especially in their critique of the characteristic attitudes and opinions of the aristocracy and middle class. But when it comes to the question of change, of tackling the real problems implicit and explicit in the democratization of British society, what stands out is a fear of the 'mob' – the sinister people who tore down those Hyde Park railings – which incapacitates both writers from facing creatively the very issues which on one level of consciousness they recognize to be the essential ones. Raymond Williams puts the point well when he notes that when George Eliot 'touches, as she chooses to touch, the lives and the problems of working people, her personal observation and conclusion surrender, virtually without a fight, to the general structure of feeling about these matters which was the common property of her generation, and which she was at once too hesitant to transcend, and too intelligent to raise into any lively embodiment. She fails in the extension which she knows to be necessary, because indeed there seems 'no right thread to pull'.[10] And I feel sure that Mr. Williams is right in associating this inadequacy particularly with 'the fear of a sympathetic, reformist-minded member of the middle classes at being drawn into any kind of mob-violence'.[11]

I am not, of course, primarily concerned with George Eliot's social and political attitudes as such. Nor would I wish to dismiss her fear of violence as an incomprehensible lapse without any objective basis, though I think it has to be said that she finds it easier to excuse or ignore the use of violence if it is associated with the defence of an established order. What concerns me, in discussing *Felix Holt*, is to try to isolate the quality of sensibility which seems to lie behind the successes and weaknesses of this particular book; to try, in other words, to answer the question: Why does this novel, which begins so well, peter out into so weak an ending? I do not think we can answer this question, which is an aesthetic one, without exploring issues which may seem at first to have little to do with aesthetic values. And central to the whole question, I believe, is the tendency of the writers of the 1860s – including George Eliot and Matthew Arnold, but not, significantly, Dickens – to look at life more and more from the point of view of the modern middle-class intellectual with his own peculiar mixture of high-mindedness and blindness, social conscience and irresponsibility, realism and idealism, his contradictory support and fear of democracy, his contempt for privilege and wish for privilege.

If *Felix Holt the Radical* did not give evidence, in its early reaches, of so rich an apprehension of central nineteenth-century dilemmas, an attempt to analyse the causes of its collapse would be merely tiresome. As it is, this flawed but often impressive book does indeed tell us a good deal about the nature of Victorian Radicalism, its very failure as an historical novel reflecting a deeper and perhaps more interesting failure, the inability of George Eliot to see herself as a character in history.

NOTES

1. (Ch. 5.) Bernard J. Paris, in his *Experiments in Life, George Eliot's Quest for Values* (Detroit, 1965), p. 199, says that Felix Holt 'feels bound by heredity to the working class'. But though George Eliot, like most Victorian novelists, is in general very conscious of heredity, this is scarcely the issue here. Felix's allegiance is based on *values*, not heredity.

2. Two passages (pp. 89–93, 137–9, 1959 ed.) are particularly relevant.

3. *The Art of George Eliot*, p. 174.

4. The best appreciation of this part of the book is in F. R. Leavis, *The Great Tradition* (Chatto & Windus, 1948), pp. 52 foll.

5. What Barbara Hardy refers to as 'narrative irony' (*Novels of George Eliot*, p. 93) operates only by implication. *We* may see the irony in the plot, but George Eliot makes little or nothing of these possibilities. It is interesting that in her chapter on 'The Ironical Image', in which Mrs. Hardy examines the deeper and more telling irony of George Eliot, *Felix Holt* is not mentioned.

6. *ibid.*, p. 62.

7. *op. cit.*, p. 134.

8. *op. cit.*, p. 52

9. From 'An Address to Working Men, by Felix Holt' in *Essays of George Eliot*, p. 429.

10. Raymond Williams, *Culture and Society 1780–1950* (Chatto & Windus, 1958), p. 109.

11. *ibid.*, p. 104.

VII

'MIDDLEMARCH': A NOTE ON
GEORGE ELIOT'S 'WISDOM'

Isobel Armstrong

By 'WISDOM' I do not mean a set of philosophical or intellectual beliefs – George Eliot's peculiar version of Determinism, for instance, or her 'conviction as to the relative goodness and nobleness of human dispositions and motives'.[1] I mean by it what Alexander Main intended when he collected George Eliot's *Wise, Witty and Tender Sayings* in 1873. Main's book belongs to that group of writings which Robert Preyer called, in his article on 'Victorian Wisdom Literature', the prudential wisdom of the maxim and the proverb, writings which attempt to say something, consolingly and didactically, about the human condition.[2] Preyer treated these writings as a sub-literature to be distinguished from the High Wisdom of the fragmentary insight. I feel that George Eliot's wisdom partakes of both categories and perhaps I place a higher value on prudential wisdom than Preyer does: certainly whether they are to called aphorisms or the fragmentary insights of High Wisdom, it is true that the sayings *are* detachable. Her 'sayings', sage-like, discursive generalizations about the nature of human relationships, about what it is like simply to be alive, emerge from the narrative with a delicate, oracular dogmatism. They have a curious equanimity; they often assume a majestic eloquence and slow down the novel in an almost processional way. In a parenthetical discussion in *Middlemarch* George Eliot regrets the passing of Fielding's easy, discursive conversations with the reader as a means of narrative technique. The pace of a modern novel has to go more quickly, she says. Nevertheless, by the standards of present-day criticism her sayings do create pauses, punctuating the novel with gravely reflective meditation:

> For the egoism which enters into our theories does not affect their sincerity; rather, the more our egoism is satisfied, the more robust is our belief.
>
> (ch. 53)

> Life would be no better than candlelight tinsel and daylight rubbish if our spirits were not touched by what has been, to issues of longing and constancy.
>
> (ch. 54)

This way of becoming chorus to her own novel and using choric comment to provide a moral gloss on the action has, of course, never been very popular with twentieth-century critics. George Steiner thinks of it as an inept 'personal interference' in the action: even W. J. Harvey, in his perceptive discussion of this technique, looks at George Eliot's skill in handling it rather than at its possibilities; but I do not think there is any need to consign these sayings altogether to the dim sub-regions of Victorian wisdom literature. They are a necessary constituent of George Eliot's art. In this essay I shall discuss how they are presented in such a way as to gain the reader's assent. I believe, indeed, that far from being dispensable, far from retarding the narrative, they are the growing-point of the novel. It is through them that George Eliot commands the reader's most intense imaginative involvement with the world of the novel. She was herself very much aware that art must create pictures, not diagrams, to be successful. But discursive comment and dramatic representation are intricately linked in her novels. Diagram is almost continuously superimposed on picture or picture is superimposed on diagram in her work with a subtle interaction. By the time she wrote *Middlemarch*, George Eliot could exploit this interaction with mature assurance and it is instructive to look at the possibilities of this manner of proceeding, not the least because it raises the question how we talk about didactic art – in this case highly successful didactic art.

I have talked of George Eliot's 'sayings' or 'wisdom' in preference to the more usual description of it as 'authorial comment' or 'the convention of the omniscient author' because I would like to retain some of the claims implied by this terminology. It suggests that these sayings have the status of truth, or, as Keats would have said, a truth, an insight. Most critics would prefer to see authorial comment as validated by the novel, by the aesthetically meaningful structure of the work as a whole and by the interrelationships of particular events evolving as the novel proceeds. The implication is that this truth need be true only for the life of the novel and may last only so long as the novel lasts. I have already said that the sayings can be detached from the novel and I believe that they can sustain themselves on their own, as truths. W. J. Harvey has called them moral commonplaces, generally acceptable comments about which we do not need to reflect: to reflect about them, indeed, would be fatal to George Eliot's artistic purpose. They are 'bridges between our world and the world of the novel. They are not ends in themselves, not the proper objects of contemplation. And we are meant to pass easily and quickly over these comments, these bridges.'³ Some insights are insights simply *because* of their truistic nature, and to say that they are truistic is not to condemn them. Many of George Eliot's sayings are of this kind, but by no means all. It is not possible, for instance, to pass quickly over her comment on the virtual death of Lydgate's marriage to Rosamond, that 'fracture in delicate crystal' – 'In marriage, the certainty, "She will never love me much", is easier to bear than the fear, "I shall love her no more" ' (ch. 64). Indeed, the comment generally slows the novel down in such a way that it is not possible to pass over any of it 'easily and quickly'. I should like to reverse W. J. Harvey's description and say that the authorial comment creates bridges, not between our world and the world of the novel, but between the world of the novel and *our world*, for, as I shall suggest, George Eliot's procedure depends upon the constant corroboration and assent of the reader to her sayings. In other words, the status of moral comment inside her novels is the same as any moral comment outside any novel. It demands inspection. The pressure on the reader to agree can best be shown by a negative example at present. After Sir James Chettam's disappointment over Dorothea, George Eliot generalizes his patient fortitude in this way, explicitly including us all in her comment:

We mortals, men and women, devour many a disappointment between breakfast and dinner-time; keep back the tears and look a little pale about the lips, and in answer to inquiries say, 'Oh, nothing!' Pride helps us; and pride is not a bad thing when it only urges us to hide our own hurts – not to hurt others.

(ch. 6)

But one's reaction to this is not corroboration, but sharp dissent. We may well endure disappointments, but some of us want to complain, and we may even complain a good deal. There are often occasions when nothing helps us and the question of hurting others is irrelevant. This is one of the occasions when one is in sympathy with those critics who wish George Eliot had managed the James-ian conjuring trick of the disappearing author. The source of the irritation, I think, is that this statement is simply not wise. It is not sufficiently inclusive – it is not, indeed, truistic, and that is partly what is wrong with it. It is moralizing and preachy instead, sug-gesting that we *should* swallow disappointment, not that we *do*. It looks too much as if it is drawn from George Eliot's personal experience and that she is showing the reader how to be wise.

On the whole, though, these comments, jutting as they do out of the novel, are peculiarly satisfying. How does George Eliot achieve this? It is partly a matter of tone. There are many kinds of didacti-cism in *Middlemarch*, apart from her own. There is Dorothea's dogmatism, Caleb Garth's honest, simple morality, Farebrother's sophisticated judgments, and Bulstrode's pontifications – 'Those who are not of this world can do little else to arrest the errors of the obstinately worldly' (ch. 36). George Eliot reserves for herself a tone of generous compassionateness, considered and fairminded. When there is anything harsh to be said, somebody else in the novel says it. It is Mrs. Cadwallader, Chettam, and Celia who say the harshest things about Casaubon; it is Celia who says the harshest things about Dorothea.

> 'I suppose it is being engaged to be married that has made you think patience good,' said Celia, as soon as she and Dorothea were alone together, taking off their wrappings.
> 'You mean that I am very impatient, Celia.'
> 'Yes; when people don't do and say just what you like.'
>
> (ch. 9)

Mrs. Cadwallader is also very useful for voicing the sharpest views of Dorothea and Casaubon:

> 'Really, by the side of Sir James, he looks like a death's head skinned over for the occasion. Mark my words: in a year from this time that girl

will hate him. She looks up to him as an oracle now, and by-and-by
she will be at the other extreme. All flightiness!'

(ch. 10)

George Eliot's sayings very rarely take the form of judgments;
they are offerings, observations made, sometimes with a hint of
tentativeness, towards assessing a predicament.

Early in the morning – about six – Mr. Bulstrode rose and spent some
time in prayer. Does anyone suppose that private prayer is necessarily
candid – necessarily goes to the roots of action? Private prayer is in-
audible speech, and speech is representative: who can represent himself
just as he is, even in his own reflections?

(ch. 70)

The beautifully poised persuasiveness of this comment is achieved
by the movement from question to statement to question. About
the nature of prayer itself, George Eliot can afford to make a categorical statement, and this is made in the strongest possible way –
the present tense and the double use of 'is' (the verb 'to be' is the
most categorical of all verbs) reinforce the absoluteness of her sentence. But this is framed by questions – questions which are a
direct appeal to the reader's honesty and psychological experience.
Where his honesty is invoked, the question is doubled and doubly
qualified – 'necessarily . . . necessarily . . .?' The saying is at once
categorical and tentative. One has only to think of the extremes to
which authorial comment can go – Charlotte Brontë's embarrassing
confidentialness or her aggressive apostrophes to the reader to confirm an angry judgment, for instance, or Jane Austen's confident
assumption that the reader will and can only share her norms
(the more confident a writer is the more epigrammatic he can be) –
to see how subtly George Eliot's sayings work upon the moral
consciousness of the reader.

Yet the success of George Eliot's sayings is more than a matter of
tone, more than a matter of giving the impression of having pondered and of being able to manipulate the reader. Her success
depends, I think, upon her capacity to move beyond the moral
universe of the novel, turn outwards towards the reader and to
invoke a general body of moral and psychological knowledge or,
rather, *experience,* which can be the corporate possession of both
writer and reader; this shared experience is continually being
brought to bear on the novel. She constantly asks for an assent, a

corroboration from the reader, before she proceeds. Her way of extending and enlarging the imagination or the 'sympathies' of her readers through her art is to move between the known, the common experience, and the unknown, the unique and particular predicaments of the novel: she moves, in effect, between diagram and picture. I can begin to describe this procedure best by comparing George Eliot's authorial comment first with that of Thackeray. Geoffrey Tillotson says, surprising though it may seem, that she learned a good deal from Thackeray in the way of authorial comment, but in fact Thackeray's commentary works in the opposite way.[4] It rarely moves beyond the universe of the novel (though it makes a feint at doing so), but asks for an exactingly rigorous examination of the truth of the comment in the light of what has gone on in the action. Thackeray's summing-up (in fact, a refusal to sum up) of Pen's affair with Fanny is a good example:

> What respectable person in the world will not say he was quite right to avoid marriage with an ill-educated person of low degree, whose relations a gentleman could not well acknowledge, and whose manners would not become her new station? – and what philosopher would not tell him that the best thing to do with these little passions if they spring up, is to get rid of them, and let them pass over and cure themselves: that no man dies about a woman, or vice versa: and that one or the other having found the impossibility of gratifying his or her desire in the particular instance, must make the best of matters, forget each other, look out elsewhere, and choose again? And yet perhaps, there may be something said on the other side. Perhaps Bows was right in admiring that passion of Pen's, blind and unreasoning as it was, that made him ready to stake his all for his love; perhaps, if self-sacrifice is a laudable virtue, mere worldly self-sacrifice is not very much to be praised; – in fine, let this be a reserved point, to be settled by the individual moralist who chooses to debate it.
>
> (*Pendennis*, ch. 51)

An ironical play with the reader's responses, a deliberate attempt to disarm and disorientate him, is going on here. Pen's conduct is held up for judgment and two extremes of judgment are offered – a worldly and a romantic – without any attempt to predispose the reader to one or the other. The appearance is of an excessive detachment, of a judgment qualified away. No wonder Roscoe was confused enough to say that Thackeray see-sawed between cynicism and sentimentality. The see-saw of this comment begins with the specious reasonableness of 'And yet' following the sweeping assumptions generated by what one might call the negated negative – 'what person will *Not* say?' Thackeray is presenting stereotyped extremes here, and the questions he asks are false questions, questions which are irrelevant to Pen's actual position. They may be the conventional kinds of assessment, but they are not the correct ones. They are there to forestall a facile conclusion: Pen's conduct was not as entirely cynical as the first judgment suggests – he stayed away from Fanny for her own good. His considerations were not social, but sexual – he was fond enough of her not to want to make her into a fallen woman, but not fond enough of her to marry her, and by this stage in his career he was realistic enough to recognize this. On the other hand, his feeling for her was not the blind, romantic passion posited as the other extreme. One should be alerted by the ironical use of perhaps: Pen enjoyed being flattered and he enjoyed being patronizing, and he was master of himself enough to be only too conscious of the embarrassment of being caught up in a vulgar fight in Vauxhall Gardens with a porter's daughter on his arm. These ironically self-cancelling, conventional judgments have a hollow ring. They contradict the action of the novel, and the reader, if he is not to be duped into a lazy and inaccurate judgment, has to go back and revalue the events which have been described as scrupulously as possible. The clarification of his confusion is within the novel itself, and these comments force a retrospective re-examination of the narrative. The reader is not being asked to assent to a statement about life; he is being asked to discover what is in the novel.

Thackeray's sport with truisms makes the reading of his novels an edgy process: I think this is what Bagehot meant when he remarked that Thackeray had been called an 'uncomfortable' novelist. By the same token, George Eliot could be called a comfortable – or at least a comforting – novelist. Her sayings do not play ambiguously with our responses; when she asks a question – as she frequently does — it usually demands the answer 'Yes':

> Poor Mr. Casaubon felt (and must not we, being impartial, feel with him a little?) that no man had juster cause for disgust and suspicion than he.

(ch. 37)

Do we not shun the street version of a fine melody? – or shrink from the news that the rarity . . . is really not an uncommon thing, and may be obtained as an everyday possession?

(ch. 47)

On the other hand, Thackeray's questions provoke, along with disagreement, an uneasy feeling that the wrong question is being asked.

Thackeray's non-participation in his evaluation ought to be clear from his use of hypothetical people and the attribution of views to other people: 'What respectable person . . . what philosopher . . . Perhaps Bows was right . . .'. George Eliot, on the contrary, commits herself to her sayings by frequently allowing them to take a proverbial form, thus making them sound entirely conclusive:

And when gratitude has become a matter of reasoning there are many ways of escaping from its bonds.

(ch. 37)

One must be poor to know the luxury of giving!

(ch. 17)

. . . but our tongues are little triggers which have usually been pulled before general intentions can be brought to bear.

(ch. 37)

Unwanted circumstances may make us all rather unlike ourselves: there are conditions under which the most majestic person is obliged to sneeze, and our emotions are liable to be acted on in the same incongruous manner.

(ch. 32)

There is no general doctrine which is not capable of eating out our morality if unchecked by the deep-seated habit of direct fellow-feeling with individual fellow-men.

(ch. 51)

In Chapter 31 she makes a lightly self-conscious reference to Solomon's proverbs as if she were aware of the deliberation of her procedure: 'Solomon's Proverbs, I think, have omitted to say, that as the sore palate findeth grit, so an uneasy consciousness heareth innuendoes.' This mock proverb comes at the point when Lydgate has just been forced to understand Mrs. Bulstrode's broad hints about Rosamund, and after it the narrative goes on to describe how he responds with hypersensitive irritation to Farebrother's good-humoured jokes. This comment serves many purposes. It is a very

economical way of conveying a particular stage in the evolution
of his feeling, of showing how Lydgate has already changed by the
time he meets Farebrother. It expresses at the same time both the
comedy and the awkwardness of Lydgate's situation. It is also a
very fine way of generalizing his feeling so that his predicament is
enlarged; it comes to indicate not only Lydgate, but a common
human situation – it might include us all. George Eliot has indirectly appealed to the reader's experience here. Once one has
assented to this proverbial saying one cannot but go on to recognize the uneasiness of Lydgate's position. By moving out of the
world of the novel, this saying actually consolidates an imaginative
involvement with the characters.

Even more common than the indirect appeal of proverbial statement is the direct implication of the reader by the simple use of
personal pronouns – 'we', 'our' – a straightforward invoking of
the reader to participate in the choric comment:

> The Vicar's talk was not always inspiriting: he had escaped being a
> Pharisee, but he had not escaped that low estimate of possibilities which
> we rather hastily arrive at as an inference from our own failure.
>
> (ch. 18)

> As he threw down his book, stretched his legs towards the embers in
> the grate, and clasped his hands at the back of his head, in that agree-
> able after-glow of excitement when thought lapses from examination of
> a specific object into a suffusive sense of its connections with all the rest
> of our existence – seems, as it were, to throw itself on its back after
> vigorous swimming and float with the repose of unexhausted strength
> – Lydgate felt a triumphant delight in his studies. . . .
>
> (ch. 16)

> The spiritual kind of rescue was a genuine need with him. There may
> be coarse hypocrites, who consciously affect beliefs and emotions for the
> sake of gulling the world, but Bulstrode was not one of them. He was
> simply a man whose desires had been stronger than his theoretic beliefs,
> and who had gradually explained the gratification of his desires into
> satisfactory agreement with those beliefs. If this be hypocrisy, it is a
> process which shows itself occasionally in us all, to whatever confession
> we belong, and whether we believe in the future perfection of our race
> or in the nearest date fixed for the end of the world; whether we regard
> the earth as a putrefying nidus for a saved remnant, including our-
> selves, or have a passionate belief in the solidarity of mankind.
>
> (ch. 61)

And, of course, there is the famous 'We are all born in moral stupidity . . .'. What gives the weight and solidity to these sayings is their assumption that they speak for more than the experience of the author, that they are inclusive statements. In Chapter 29 George Eliot moves from analysing Dorothea's situation to a consideration of Casaubon and marks the change of direction by asking 'But why always Dorothea?' Her method is to move progressively nearer to the reader as the chapter proceeds. The first indication of this outward movement is the generalizing pronoun 'one'! 'To know intense joy without a strong bodily frame, *one* must have an enthusiastic soul.' A few lines later comes a demonstrative 'that', again with a generalizing force, for 'that thing' implies the thing we all know about, what is familiar, the thing we understand. Hence 'His experience was of *that* pitiable kind which shrinks from pity, and fears most of all that it should be known: it was *that* proud narrow sensitiveness which has not mass enough to spare for transformation into sympathy. . . .' The repetition of 'that . . . which . . .' asks for pity by assuming an intimate familiarity with the state which evokes it. Finally, at the end of the paragraph, George Eliot leans her full weight on the reader, as it were, and appeals directly to a mutually known experience:

> For my part I am very sorry for him. It is an uneasy lot at best, to be what we call highly taught and yet not to enjoy: to be present at this great spectacle of life and never to be liberated from a small hungry shivering self – never to be fully possessed by the glory we behold, never to have our consciousness raptuously transformed by the vividness of a thought, the ardour of a passion, the energy of an action, but always to be scholarly and uninspired, ambitious and timid, scrupulous and dim-sighted.

The movement from 'I' to 'we' is made first of all with a formal gesture of inclusion – 'what we call' – and then 'we' is used in a really positive way, gathered up into the reiterated rhythms of never to be . . .' and followed immediately by the reinforcing 'never to have *our* consciousness'. Again, the insistent definite article assumes a prior knowledge of all that Mr. Casaubon cannot experience – glory, the vividness, the ardour, the energy. The reader is carefully dissociated, carefully uninvolved, from what Mr. Casaubon actually is. The nouns change to a string of anti-climactic adjectives which only apply to Mr. Casaubon – scholarly, uninspired, ambitious, timid, scrupulous, dim-sighted. George Eliot is

invoking understanding and pity by assuming a privileged experience on the part of the reader which enables him to grasp a
negative and impoverished state of mind. What one may not know
– or may not feel sympathy with – is approached through what one
knows. This kind of comment is particularly frequent, as I shall
show, whenever there might be possible failure of empathy on the
part of the reader. In much the same way, a generalizing image is
used to intensify involvement. Lydgate's accommodation to the
limitations of his marriage, his recognition that he must make
fewer and fewer demands on it, and the consequent constriction of
his emotional life is expressed through an appropriately surgical
simile – 'the ideal wife must be renounced, and life must be taken
up on a lower stage of expectation, as it is by men who have lost
their limbs' (ch. 64).

It is this deliberate attempt to reach agreement between author
and reader which enables George Eliot to make emphatic judgments which will carry a reader's assent. Her remark, for instance,
that Lydgate is 'morally lovable' is acceptably emphatic because
it is made in the context of this relationship of confidence. Henry
James, I think, is far less successful when he attempts to do something like this for Isabel Archer in *Portrait of a Lady*. There is a
certain archness about the way James apologizes for her here – suddenly emerging from behind the corner where he has been waiting
unseen. Because no continuous authorial relationship has been
established, such comments are bound to seem anomalous:

> Altogether with her meagre knowledge, her inflated ideals, her con-
> fidence at once innocent and dogmatic, her temper at once exacting
> and indulgent, her mixture of curiosity and fastidiousness, of vivacity
> and indifference, her desire to look very well and to be if possible even
> better.... She would be an easy victim of scientific criticism, if she
> were not intended to awake on the reader's part an impulse more tender
> and more purely expectant.
>
> (ch. 6)

But, of course, everything depends on the *placing* of these comments, and their relationship to the narrative. It is by skilfully
juxtaposing her 'sayings' with other elements of her story that
George Eliot makes them such an important part of her art – makes
them, as I have said, the growing-point of imaginative involvement
in the novel. She will move from the particular facts of the story
into an enlarging generalization. Or she will begin with a general-

ization from common experience and carefully modify it until it is precisely applicable to the world of the novel. The movement outwards and back often happens so unobtrusively that it is hardly noticed, as in this account of Will's feelings, where the generalization moves into *oratio obliqua* almost imperceptibly. It is separated from the particular description of Will's state only by a semicolon. The reader's world and the world of the novel are bound together syntactically and by the overriding continuity of 'and':

> Our good depends on the quality and breadth of our emotion; and to Will, a creature who cared little for what are called the solid things of life and greatly for its subtler influences, to have within him such a feeling as he had towards Dorothea, was like the inheritance of a fortune.

(ch. 47)

In general, however, the extension outward slows down the novel, as I have said, and I would like to examine one or two examples of George Eliot's skill in placing these comments before passing on to look in detail at Chapter 42, where Casaubon's tragedy is described with a marvellous blending of discursive, generalizing sayings and particular detail, where diagram and the picture of 'felt life' interpenetrate.

In Chapter 20 George Eliot first begins to describe Dorothea's doubt and revulsion about her marriage. She begins with the strange fact of Dorothea weeping so early in her married life, and in order to make this *not* strange and to convince the reader that it is appropriate she moves tentatively into explanation by appealing to common generalizations about marriage – difficulties of adjustment are to be expected, people are always different when you live with them:

> Nor can I suppose that when Mrs. Casaubon is discovered in a fit of weeping six weeks after her wedding, the situation will be regarded as tragic. Some discouragement, some faintness of heart at the new real future which replaces the imaginary, is not unusual, and we do not expect people to be deeply moved by what is not unusual. That element of tragedy which lies in the very fact of frequency, has not yet wrought itself into the coarse emotion of mankind. . . .

She holds such generalizations, such norms, steadily before the reader, but at the same time continuously modifies them by showing that they apply only to a limited extent to the case of Dorothea.

She subtracts from Dorothea's situation what is common, what can be recognized, and then goes on to describe what is not, the things which make her situation unique and pitiable. Dorothea was indeed suffering the bewilderment of change, but her 'stifling depression' was not the result of the conditions of marriage, but the narrow, emotional world Casaubon imposed on her. True enough, 'in court-ship everything is regarded as provisional and preliminary', and Dorothea has taken too much on trust, like most of us, but her disillusion is uniquely painful – 'she had been becoming more and more aware, with a certain terror, that her mind was continually sliding into inward fits of anger and repulsion, or else into forlorn weariness'. Here George Eliot uses generalization, uses platitude if you like, to prize open Dorothea's situation. She sets about particularizing the commonplace as soon as it has been asserted, making careful distinctions of degree and quality. The same thing goes on when she talks of Lydgate's pride in Chapter 15. She moves from asking the reader to recognize and acknowledge Lydgate's vanity – 'Among our valued friends is there not some one or other who is a little too self-confident and disdainful; whose distinguished mind is a little spotted with commonness . . .?' – to warning that it is possible neither to fully understand it nor excuse it at this stage:

> The particular faults from which these delicate generalities are distilled have distinguishable physiognomies, diction, accent and grimaces; filling up parts in various dramas. Our vanities differ as our noses do: all conceit is not the same conceit, but varies in correspondence with the minutiae of mental make in which one of us differs from another. Lydgate's conceit was of the arrogant sort, never simpering, never impertinent, but massive in its claims and benevolently contemptuous.

On other occasions the procedure is the reverse of this careful filling out of the commonplace with the minutiae of particular detail. George Eliot will move from minutiae to a generalized statement which incorporates the reader and which therefore associates him with a strange or alien experience. The movement is from the unknown to the known, reversing the process of moving from the known to the unknown. This is particularly striking when Lyd-gate's frenzied behaviour over Laure is being described (ch. 15). The pain of the situation is that Lydgate, for all his frenzy, knows what he is doing, and it is this double-minded experience – insight without the will to act upon what your insight tells you – that

George Eliot wants to make as a common bond between Lydgate and the reader. Lydgate's psychological state is given in minute detail and then comes the generalizing, extending saying:

> He knew that this was like the sudden impulse of a madman – incongruous even with his habitual foibles. No matter! It was the one thing which he was resolved to do. He had two selves within him apparently, and they must learn to accommodate each other and bear reciprocal impediments. Strange, that some of us, with quick alternate vision, see beyond our infatuations, and even while we rave on the heights, behold the wide plain where our persistent self pauses and awaits us.

These generalizations exert an extraordinary pressure on the particular facts of the narrative. They place them, with a sort of mild and tactful deliberation, *sub specie aeternitatis*. This is particularly the case with the comments which I have already mentioned on Lydgate's disappointment in his marriage. The unique pain of his emotional situation is intensified because it is subtly universalized.

Chapter 42 contains the meeting between Lydgate and Casaubon in which Casaubon learns that he is to die:

> Here was a man who now for the first time found himself looking into the eyes of death – who was passing through one of those rare moments when we feel the truth of a commonplace, which is as different from what we call knowing it, as the vision of waters upon the earth is different from the delirious vision of the water which cannot be had to cool the burning tongue. When the commonplace 'We must all die' transforms itself suddenly into the acute consciousness 'I must die – and soon', then death grapples us, and his fingers are cruel. . . .

This statement is the climax of the chapter and it is not strange that the climax should take the form of a saying, a discursive statement. It is at exactly those points in her narrative where George Eliot needs the maximum emotional involvement from her reader that these sayings increase not only in quantity, but in the pressure they exert on the reader. The force of this saying comes about partly because of the way it has been prepared for in the early part of the chapter, but mainly because of the simple truth of what it says. Its high seriousness is arresting, not because it is a statement about death, but because it contains an insight about a psychological process, about the difference between knowing in an abstract way and feeling imaginatively the truth of a commonplace. In fact, George Eliot commands imaginative understanding here by describing what this really means. We are not here asked to pity a man, a man who is emotionally and morally small, because he is at the point of death; we are asked to understand, to feel what it is like when a stock phrase – 'We must all die' – a part of our habitual knowledge, becomes charged with immediacy and terror. Compassion follows upon this understanding. George Eliot is indirectly describing here what happens when her oracular manner is at its best; a commonplace renews its meaning, truisms become true. Johnson is the only other English writer who can put such intense life into a discursive statement. Thought, for both of them, truly becomes an experience.

This climax is prepared for with tact and delicacy. The chapter begins with Casaubon's proud fear of compassion – the one emotion George Eliot wants from the reader – and attempts to generalize it as far as possible:

> Every proud mind knows something of this experience, and perhaps it is only to be overcome by a sense of fellowship deep enough to make all efforts at isolation seem mean and petty instead of exalting.

'But', the next paragraph begins, and it is clear that Casaubon's feelings have no element of generosity in them. His suspicions, irritations, and fears are then enumerated in some detail, particularly his mean-minded and guilty suspicions of Dorothea. The commentary generalizes with an image his vain attempts to ignore his insistent suspicions. There is at this point something pitiable in his almost well-meant self-deception – deception which is nevertheless dishonesty: 'The tenacity with which he strove to hide this inward drama made it the more vivid for him; as we hear with the more keenness what we wish others not to hear.' But pity at this stage would be too easily won and this comment is followed by a paragraph of rather heavy-handed irony at Casaubon's expense. Even his egotism does not blind him to the suspicion that he was 'not any longer adored without criticism' and even he had suspicions 'that he was not unmixedly adorable'. Then follows a close and extensive analysis of Mr. Casaubon's jealousies and his way of making his feelings and decisions respectable to himself. There is no invitation to the reader to participate in this experience in any way. It is only when Casaubon and Lydgate talk in the Yew Walk that the pressure of the authorial comment mounts. George Eliot is careful not to ask for too much involvement too soon.

The scene in the Yew Walk is beautifully managed in its welding of description, dialogue, and commentary. Mr. Casaubon's pinched figure moves down the Yew Walk, while the sun shines and the limes blow leaves in a way which is at once elegaic and ironic. Then comes Lydgate's pity, the rough pity of the man in animal health combined with the doctor's vision of Casaubon as a physical specimen. This is the first time in the chapter that Casaubon's physical emaciation is given any emphasis. The dialogue between doctor and patient is conducted with delicacy on one side and elaborate reserve on the other as Casaubon asks how long he has to complete his work, and the importance of this work is his sole reason, so he tells Lydgate, for asking for an opinion. The next paragraph moves from Mr. Casaubon's dry, precise movement – he takes one hand from behind his back as if to punctuate his speech – to a reflection, in a rather inflated style, on his situation:

> Nay, are there many situations more sublimely tragic than the struggle of the soul with the demand to renounce a work which has been all the significance of its life – a significance which is to vanish as the waters which come and go where no man has need of them?

But George Eliot deflates her own rhetoric:

> But there was nothing to strike others as sublime about Mr. Casaubon....

Lydgate is both amused and pitying at Casaubon's self-importance. Lydgate, who is also to fail physically and to die around Casaubon's age, who is also to experience the failure of his work and the pain of wasted effort, takes an obstinately (and possibly sanely) unheroic, untragic view of Casaubon, the very reverse of the view George Eliot's rhetoric begins to persuade us to take. Like Thackeray, she presents two possible responses, two possible extremes. But, unlike him, she offers a final judgment explicitly and does not leave the reader, with a moral shrug, to slither backwards and forwards between two extremes. The last sentence describes Lydgate's failure of perception and appeals directly to the reader for more experience than Lydgate can have. 'He was at present too ill acquainted with disaster . . .' – the proviso, 'at present' is ominous – 'to enter into the pathos of a lot where everything is below the level of tragedy except the passionate egoism of the sufferer.' Once again one of the most important and moving moments of the novel is created through a discursive utterance, through the expression of and through an appeal to 'wisdom'. From seeming to be an account solely of Lydgate, the sentence moves into a statement about a larger predicament by way of the generalizing articles – '*the pathos* of *a* lot . . .' – and ends with a precise, paradoxical epigram – '. . . everything is below the level of tragedy . . .' Everything in this case is too trivial to be matter for tragedy, and the only element of large stature is the sufferer's disproportionate response to his fate. Casaubon's tragedy (and this, of course, is to be Lydgate's fate) is that he is not a tragedy, and it is with this subtly paradoxical insight that pity is granted where it was withheld before, and the reader, unlike Lydgate, is given a way to 'enter into' an imaginative understanding of Casaubon's predicament. The smallness and denial of Casaubon's spirit *is* a matter for irony, but it is also tragic. From this it is a short step to the total involvement claimed in the climax of the chapter.

I believe that George Eliot's reflective sayings, her 'wisdom', accord more than is usually acknowledged with the stated aims of her art. She believed that art is a way of 'amplifying experience and extending our contact with our fellow-men beyond the bounds of our personal lot'.[5] She also believed that the aesthetic teaching of the novel is important because it 'deals with life in its highest complexity'. By generalizing the unique experiences portrayed in her fictional world she enables the reader to enter into those experiences. Her utterances, even when they are commonplaces or perhaps most when they are commonplaces, rarely simplify the complexity of experience. In her hands discursive writing is neither thin nor barren.

NOTES

1. *Letters*, iv. 472.
2. *Victorian Studies*, VI (1963), pp. 245–62.
3. *The Art of George Eliot*, p. 81.
4. G. Tillotson, *Thackeray the Novelist* (Methuen, 1963), p. 192.
5. 'The Natural History of German Life', *Essays of George Eliot*, p. 270.

VIII

'DANIEL DERONDA': GEORGE ELIOT AND POLITICAL CHANGE

Graham Martin

I

FEUERBACH STARTS out from the fact of religious self-alienation, the duplication of the world into a religious, imaginary world and a real one. His work consists in the dissolution of the religious world into its secular basis. He overlooks the fact that after completing this work, the chief thing still remains to be done. For the fact that the secular foundation detaches itself from itself and establishes itself in the clouds as an independent realm is really only to be explained by the self-cleavage and self-contradictoriness of this secular basis. The latter must itself, therefore, first be understood in its contradiction and then, by removal of the contradiction, revolutionized in practice. Thus, for instance, once the earthly family is discovered to be the secret of the holy family, the former must itself be criticized in theory and revolutionized in practice.[1]

Marx's *Theses on Feuerbach* maintain that Feuerbach achieves a merely intellectual secularization of religious ideas because he fails to recognize the social pressures which lead to 'religious self-alienation', making it a necessary mystification of social violence and injustice, and at the same time an existential consolation for those who have to endure them. The human condition into which Feuerbach converts religious symbology and categories of thought remains abstract because he fails to grasp it as a complex of 'social relations'. These are the true source of 'religious self-alienation', and until they have been defined, the main task of criticizing them cannot be begun. But since Feuerbach regards 'the *theoretical* attitude as the only genuinely human attitude, while practice is conceived ... in its dirty-judaical form of appearance ... he does not grasp the significance of "revolutionary", of "practical-critical" activity'.[2] For him it is enough to *state* that 'in place of the illusory, fantastic, heavenly position of man which in actual life leads to the degradation of man, I substitute the tangible, actual, and consequently also the political and social position of mankind'.[3] But actually to bring this substitution about means adopting a 'practical-critical' attitude towards political and social reality, by naming specific deformations and working to change them. As the famous concluding thesis puts it, 'The philosophers have only *interpreted* the world, in various ways; the point, however, is to *change* it.'[4]

George Eliot's translation of the *Essence of Christianity* appeared in 1854, and had been written during the period when she was deeply involved in her work for the *Westminster Review*, so that it would be no simple matter to assess exactly what Feuerbach's direct influence amounted to. But, as Basil Willey points out, it is not difficult to recognize the community of attitudes which led her to translate him. 'The supersession of God by Humanity, of Faith by Love and Sympathy, the elimination of the supernatural, the elevation of the natural, the subordination of intellect to heart, thought to feeling ...'[5] — any chapter, and almost any page of her novels would provide some illustration of these aims: her treatment of the clergy, of doctrinal disputes, of characters with 'spiritual' potentiality; her rejection of the conventionally heroic for the hidden poetry 'lying in the experience of a human soul that looks out through dull grey eyes, and that speaks in a voice of quite ordinary tones';[6] the kind of insight contained in the beautiful concluding cadences of *Middlemarch*:

> [Dorothea's] full nature, like that river of which Cyrus broke the strength, spent itself in channels which had no great name on the earth. But the effect of her being on those around her was incalculably diffusive: for the growing good of the world is partly dependent on unhistoric acts; and that things are not so ill with you and me as they might have been, is half owing to the number who lived faithfully a hidden life, and rest in unvisited tombs.

Or — the most general example possible — the fact that the structure of the novels was shaped by her wish to extend the reader's understanding of the common experiences of human life.[7] The issue I want to raise here, then, is not whether or how Feuerbach influenced George Eliot, but whether Marx's criticism of Feuerbach has any application to her novels. How far can it be said of her lifelong project of secularization that it was too theoretically conceived? or that her grasp of human situations was insufficiently alert to their being 'complexes of social relations'? And if these points can be made, how useful would it be to make them? George Eliot was not a Hegelian philosopher, but an English novelist, so that criticism simply of the ideas which affected her work might very well be irrelevant. To put it in Marx's way, it would be difficult for any successful novelist to remain with Feuerbach at 'the highest point attained by contemplative materialism, that is, materialism which does not understand sensuousness as practical activity'.[8] Fictional embodiment of the 'supersession of God by Humanity' necessarily involves the most sympathetic rendering of the 'practical activity' in particular human lives. Even the simplest of George Eliot's stories shows this. The Sad Fortunes of the Rev. Amos Barton turns on the contrast between the doctrinal enthusiasms of its 'hero' and the uncomplicated pathos of the wife's death in childbirth, and, even more explicitly than that, the contrast between other-worldly preaching and this-worldly need in the scene where, on a sleety February morning, Amos practises the cure of souls amongst the workhouse paupers. There is no lack here of a 'practical-critical' attitude, and in this respect at least, one which is entailed by any discussion of her *successful* characterizations, there seems little immediate point in referring to the *Theses on Feuerbach*.

Moreover, far from being a mere interpreter of the world, George Eliot not only believed that it was changing, but hoped that her novels would assist in the process. Recent criticism has emphasized the extent to which her novels are works of art. But it is also useful to remember that, though not in the way her contemporaries understood them, her novels were also social acts, imaginatively reconstructing her own society in a preferred pattern:

The day will come when there will be a temple of white marble where sweet incense and anthems shall rise to the memory of every man and every woman who has had a deep *ahnung*, a presentiment, a yearning, or a clear vision of the time when this miserable reign of Mammon shall end – when men shall be no longer 'like the fishes of the sea', society no more like a face one half of which – the side of profession, of lip-faith – is fair and godlike, the other half – the side of deeds and institutions – with a hard old wrinkled skin puckered into the sneer of a Mephistopheles. . . . You will wonder what has wrought me up into this fury – it is the loathsome fawning, the transparent hypocrisy, the systematic giving as little as possible for as much as possible, that one meets with here at every turn. I feel that society is training men and women for hell.[9]

The novels never strike this unambiguously angry note, but they certainly take sides between the claims of Mammon, 'the systematic giving as little as possible for as much as possible', and those of 'presentiments, yearnings, or clear visions' of a more generous time and condition to come. The significant structure of *Felix Holt*, *Middlemarch*, and *Daniel Deronda* turns exactly upon the contrast between men and women determined to contribute to the 'growing good of the world', and forms of society which, if they do not train 'men and women for hell', put small value upon visions of the ideal, and display the profoundest incongruity between word and deed, professed ethic and real performance.

It is only when we ask how George Eliot conceived the connection between large, ameliorative, historical processes and the moral energies of her characters, working within the deeply flawed conditions of their actual world, that Marx's strictures on Feuerbach can be seen to have application. For example, there is a general contrast between the richly imagined character of what can be called her 'conservative' sympathies in the rendering of society as it is, or was, and the relative vagueness, or thinness, of the symbols of her reforming vision, her idealists. Felix and Daniel offer little real challenge to the energy and power of the worlds they bring into question; and if it is too much to say that they stand merely for the *unsuccessfully* realized Idea of Humanity, products in fact of a merely 'contemplative materialism', they certainly lack the complex depth of realization of their opposite numbers, Harold Transome and Mallinger Grandcourt. Dorothea Brooke and Ladislaw are certainly more successfully conceived, but their actual contribution to the ameliorative process is rather cloudy, and Dorothea's is specifically called 'unhistoric'. In all three novels, in fact, the public realm is only loosely connected with the detailed life of the characters, and it seems fair to ask how and where its progressive momentum is generated, and whether George Eliot's reliance on this is anything more than the gesture of a Victorian optimist. If, in Feuerbachian terms, we think of it as a secularization of the divine will, does this amount to more than a change of names? Again, is not the relative vacuity of her reforming idealists to be connected with Marx's point about human lives existing as complexes of 'social relations'? How far in such characterization has George Eliot been deflected from her habitually penetrating observation by the sort of abstract moralism which she herself has analysed so well? Raymond Williams is, I believe, the first critic to have noticed that George Eliot's favourite metaphor for the pressure of social reality on individual lives – the mesh or web – has an oddly predatory implication.[10] And even though this social pressure destroys or baffles unattractive varieties of aggressive self-absorption, the image itself is a poor vehicle for George Eliot's Burkean faith: that society is a positive informing presence which, far from obstructing individual fulfilment, is the one condition which makes it possible. Do we conclude that the metaphor sometimes works as a substitute for analysis, and reveals an unarticulated feeling that the *actual* 'social relations' are not altogether fertile? We may put this another way by asking what real social content can be discerned within the moral Nemesis which pursues individuals who have sinned against their fellows? This major structural device of the novels ought to represent George Eliot's secularization of the idea of other-worldly judgment, yet in practice does it amount to more than the formal manipulation of the story in the valid but lesser interests of narrative excitement and suspense? Thus, in *Felix Holt*, the train of events which finally brings Esther Lyon to Transome Hall depends on legal circumstances so exceptional as to have no bearing on the real issues of the novel, so that the famous research into the law of entail appears less a matter of effective realism than a thoroughgoing deflection of creative energy from its proper object. There are, in sum, a number of points to take up, and in what follows I want to pursue some of them, first by briefly outlining George Eliot's attitude towards political change, and then by discussing *Daniel Deronda* as her final exploration of that theme.

II

Writing to John Sibree about the first stage of the 1848 French Revolution, George Eliot commented:

> I thought we had fallen on such evil days that we were to see no really great movement – that ours was what St. Simon calls a purely *critical*

epoch, not at all an organic one – but I begin to be glad of my date. I would consent, however, to have a year clipt off my life for the sake of witnessing such a scene as that of the men of the barricade bowing to the image of Christ 'who first taught fraternity to men'. One trembles to look into every fresh newspaper lest there should be something to mar the picture; but hitherto even the scoffing newspaper critics have been compelled into a tone of genuine respect for the French people and the Provisional Government. Lamartine can act a poem if he cannot write one of the very first order. I hope that beautiful face given to him in the pictorial newspaper is really his, it is worthy of an aureole. . . . I should have no hope of good from any imitative movement at home. Our working classes are eminently inferior to the mass of the French people. In France, the *mind* of the people is highly electrified – they are full of ideas on social subjects – they really desire social *reform* – not merely an acting out of Sancho Panza's favourite proverb 'Yesterday for you, today for me'. The revolutionary animus extended over the whole nation, and embraced the rural population – not merely as with us, the artisans of the towns. Here there is so much larger a proportion of selfish radicalism and unsatisfied, brute sensuality (in the agricultural and mining districts especially) than of perception or desire of justice, that a revolutionary movement would be simply destructive – not constructive. . . . Our little humbug of a queen is more endurable than the rest of her race because she calls forth a chivalrous feeling, and there is nothing in our constitution to obstruct the slow progress of *political* reform. This is all we are fit for at present. The social reform which may prepare us for great changes is more and more the object of effort both in Parliament and out of it. But we English are slow crawlers. . . .[11]

The second half of this extract makes a distinction between social and political reform which provides the key to the handling of the political theme in later novels. Social reform, as desired with 'revolutionary animus' by the French, means a thoroughgoing reconstruction of society according to another principle than that of self-interest; while political reform, which is all the English are fit for, *may* contribute to social reform, but is otherwise insignificant. Exactly how far this distinction can be taken is illustrated in the opening comments. What George Eliot finds impressive about the events of February 1848 is not the political achievement so much as the nobly-disinterested moral style with which it has been accomplished, illustrated in the Christian symbolism at the barricade, and the view of Lamartine as a secular saint. Her response is steeped in the abstracting idealism which Marx diagnosed in Feurbach.

Its disengagement from the real history (i.e. the June barricades where 'the fanaticism of the interested counterbalanced the exaltation of the needy' (Flaubert); the exiling of the working-class socialists by the republicans; the subsequent defeat of the republicans by the army; and the Second Empire – though it is fair to add that Louis Blanc's impeachment in 1849 distressed George Eliot, and was the occasion for her outburst in the letter cited on pp. 135–6) is as evident as its intimate connection with the lofty idealism of the heroes and heroines of the novels. Though there are no revolutionary situations, of course, there is a very similar contrast between a disinterested commitment to social reform and the 'selfish radicalism' which is voiced through conscious political activity. Just as the moral-aesthetic response to the French Revolution draws away from the events themselves, so in the novels, idealistic energies find their expression, not in political terms, but in another, morally superior, realm of activity.

III

In *Felix Holt*, political reform is represented by Harold Transome's opportunistic Radicalism, in alliance with the 'brute sensuality' of the election mob bribed by his political agent. In the camp of social reform we find the earliest of George Eliot's reforming idealists, Felix Holt, who attacks the entire political system as working to seduce the working people from their own true good, i.e., the education which would enlarge their moral vision beyond narrow self-interest and low materialism. The contrast between the two men is dramatized in their relationship with Esther Lyon, and her choice of Felix is the culminating event. But the energy of Felix's arguments, and the didactic momentum of the story, are sadly weakened by the vagueness of the future projected for him. We know that this will be devoted to social reform, but in what form, and by what means? The irrelevant legal 'realism' which brings Esther to Transome Hall and her crucial choice is complemented by the implausibility of Felix's connections with the times he lives in, The future of a real Felix Holt could hardly have avoided contact with Chartism,[12] but if George Eliot ever considered this history, which seems improbable, she would have had to forgo it. To the Chartists, education was not an alternative to political suffrage, but part of a programme which made political reform the chief goal.

(The group who initiated the Charter called themselves 'The London Working Men's Association for Benefiting *Politically, Socially* and *Morally* the Useful Classes'. [My italics.]) We have, in fact, to find the explanation for Felix's attitude to politics in George Eliot's view of the events leading up to the 1867 Reform Bill. *Felix Holt* is partly a tract for the times, and in the subsequent pamphlet which George Eliot published under Felix's name, 'Address to Working Men', she reveals a further argument against extending the suffrage: it might give power to semi-criminal working-class elements, destructive of all true culture, the source from which social reform drew much of its inspiration. Felix, in other words, represents an application of George Eliot's idealism to the reform politics of her own time.

Middlemarch evidently reflects the recognition that actual events had contradicted her worst fears. The anxiety at work in *Felix Holt* has been replaced by a distancing irony, a firm confidence that politics has little to do with historical progress. The events of 1829–31 create in Middlemarch only small ripples of disturbance – Mr. Brooke's quarrel with his tenant, his comic attempt at political candidature, Ladislaw's reform journalism on his behalf. Displacing the public history to the margins of the story, we find the personal histories of Dorothea, Lydgate, and Bulstrode, all of whom are closely associated with disinterested efforts for the common good. In other words, social reformers dominate the novel, while political reform is in the hands of the dilettantes, Mr. Brooke and Ladislaw. *Middlemarch* has nothing of *Felix Holt's* political tendentiousness, but it does nevertheless amount to a reinterpretation of Whig history. The 'growing good' of the Victorian future stems not from the 1832 Reform agitation, but from the variously effective altruism of people like Dorothea, Lydgate, Bulstrode, and Ladislaw. But there is one ironic undercurrent. Lydgate's intellectual ambition is defeated, and Dorothea's moral zeal drastically confined, by the tough conservatism of Middlemarch and the narrow life of the gentry. The only heroism which George Eliot allows either of these characters is private – Dorothea's victory over her meaner passions and Lydgate's stooping to the burden of his marriage. In the end, the public world has no place for these valuable adherents to the cause of historical amelioration. The only idealism which survives is Will Ladislaw's, and, set beside the struggles of Dorothea and Lydgate, it is not his future that one remembers.

Both novels, then, adopt the distinction between social and political reform; both relegate political reform to an inferior category; and both identify the cause of social reform with the lives of ardently disinterested characters. But the change of attitude between them is worth noticing. Where *Felix Holt* argues, *Middlemarch* assumes. In contrast with Felix's anger, partly the product of obstructed hope, the confident irony of *Middlemarch* is thoroughly dismissive. Not only does the English political scene offer no scope for 'presentiments, yearnings, clear visions' of a different future, even social reformers find their efforts minutely circumscribed by the habitual self-interest embedded in their own present society.

IV

Daniel Deronda uses a contemporary setting in which formal politics plays no part, but its main structure develops the critical analysis of Victorian society begun in *Felix Holt* and continued in *Middlemarch*. The contrast between its two main characters provides the key to the novel, and through their relationship George Eliot juxtaposes two social images, one actual in the life we see Gwendolen Harleth living, the other potential in the aspirations which Daniel Deronda tries to fulfil. These images are mutually exclusive. Gwendolen's world offers no scope for the achievement of Deronda's purposes, and what these might be she only begins to understand when her own social triumphs have led on to personal disaster. The fact of this contrast is, of course, clear enough from Gwendolen's reaction to Deronda in the opening scene at Leubronn, and his critical rôle there is soon clarified in the account of his early life provided in Chapter 16. We begin, that is, with a moral polarity very familiar to any reader of George Eliot, between Gwendolen's self-absorption and uneasy histrionism, and Deronda's 'subdued fervour of sympathy, [and] activity of imagination on behalf of others'. But the terms of the contrast are not only moral. Consider this account of Gwendolen's awakening to the truth about Deronda's future:

> The world seemed getting larger round poor Gwendolen, and she more solitary and helpless in the midst. The thought that he might come back after going to the East, sank before the bewildering vision of these wide-stretching purposes in which she felt herself reduced to a mere speck. There comes a terrible moment to many souls when the

141

great movements of the world, the larger destinies of mankind, which have lain aloof in newspapers and other neglected reading, enter like an earthquake into their own lives – when the slow urgency of grow-ing generations turns into the tread of an invading army or the dire clash of civil war, and grey fathers know nothing to seek for but the corpses of their blooming sons, and girls forget all vanity to make lint and bandages which may serve for the shattered limbs of their be-trothed husbands. . . . That was the sort of crisis which was at this moment beginning in Gwendolen's small life: she was for the first time feeling the pressure of a vast mysterious movement, for the first time being dislodged from her supremacy in her own world, and getting a sense that her horizon was but a dipping onward of an existence with which her own was revolving . . . she could not spontaneously think of [Deronda] as rightfully belonging to others more than to her. But here had come a shock which went deeper than personal jealousy – some-thing spiritual and vaguely tremendous that thrust her away, and yet quelled all anger into self-humiliation.

(ch. 69)

The geographical imagery has the effect of summarizing the dif-ference between Gwendolen, to whom the world has been a stage, and its people an attentive, partial audience, and Deronda, who has made it the scene of his restless explorations in London and Europe. Gwendolen seeks fuller scope for her self-engrossment than her family can offer, and finds only English county society, and a fashionable marriage on conditions which isolate her from every-body but Deronda. Deronda, on the other hand, searching for his true identity, moves outwards from the Mallingers, to the Mey-ricks, the Cohens, Mirah and Mordecai, and finally the unknown millions of the Diaspora. Thus, in discovering himself, Deronda also discovers history, and if, as an instance, the future of Zionism seems unduly hypothetical, the reference to the American Civil War in the above quotation reminds us that the final perspec-tive which the novel brings to bear on Gwendolen's 'small life' is the world of *real* historical events. Moreover, Gwendolen does genuinely awake to the existence of this world, so that the contrast between her and Deronda also involves its contrary. Without a dim susceptibility to values other than those she usually lives by, there could be no relation between her and Deronda; and it is this relation which activates her painful struggle towards a less self-centred existence. Gwendolen's experience imitates, as well as con-trasts, with Deronda's, so that in their different ways each levels the same kind of judgment against their times. While Gwendolen certainly remains responsible for her choices, it is Victorian England that nourishes in her the expectations which only a Grandcourt can fulfil, and creates the situation in which her refusal of him is almost impossible. And from the worst consequences of that choice, only Deronda appears able to save her.

Deronda's public destiny comes as a shock to Gwendolen, but she had already applied a public criterion to her own life, embodied in the world of cultural achievement, more strictly in the artistic authority of Herr Klesmer, and, as befits its importance, the interview between them (in Ch. 23) is carefully prepared for. Just as Gwendolen stands between the opposite attractions of Deronda and Grandcourt, so in comic contrast, Catherine Arrowsmith, whom Gwendolen sees simply as her rival for local superiority, is wooed by Herr Klesmer, a musician of European reputation, and Mr. Bult, a rising Liberal Party politician. Defying her parents' argument that her fortune ought to be placed in proper hands (i.e. those of a Mr. Bult), Catherine chooses the social outsider, Klesmer, and the significance of this choice is indicated in the exchanges between her two suitors:

> Meanwhile enters the expectant peer, Mr. Bult, an esteemed party man who, rather neutral in private life, had strong opinions concerning the districts of the Niger, was much at home also in the Brazils, spoke with decision of affairs in the South Seas, was studious of his Parliamentary and itinerant speeches, and had the general solidity and suffusive pinkness of a healthy Briton on the central tableland of life. . . . Klesmer he hardly regarded in the light of a serious human being who ought to have a vote; and he did not mind Miss Arrowsmith's addiction to music any more than her probable expenses in antique lace. He was consequently a little amazed at an after-dinner outburst of Klesmer's on the lack of idealism in English politics, which left all mutuality between distant races to be determined simply by the need of a market: the crusades, to his mind, had at least this excuse, that they had a banner of sentiment round which generous feelings could rally: of course, the scoundrels rallied too, but what then? they rally in equal force round your advertisement van of 'Buy cheap, sell dear'.

> 'Herr Klesmer has cosmopolitan ideas,' said Miss Arrowsmith, trying to make the best of the situation. 'He looks forward to a fusion of races.'

> 'With all my heart,' said Mr. Bult, willing to be gracious. 'I was sure he had too much talent to be a mere musician.'

'Ah, sir, you are under some mistake there,' said Klesmer, firing up. 'No man has too much talent to be a musician. Most men have too little. A creative artist is no more a mere musician than a great statesman is a mere politician. We are not ingenious puppets, sir, who live in a box and look out on the world only when it is gaping for amusement. We help to rule the nations and make the age as much as any other public men. We count ourselves on level benches with legislators. And a man who speaks effectively through music is compelled to something more difficult than Parliamentary eloquence.'

(ch. 22)

There is a comic aspect to the whole scene that has to be remembered, but the ideas reverberate nevertheless. Klesmer's Shelleyan vaunt on behalf of creative artists, his view of the Crusades, of the lack of idealism in contemporary English politics, and the contrast between the 'mutuality of races' and the operations of market imperialism (contrast also the quality of Mr. Bult's interest in foreign parts) – all these sufficiently indicate the tradition George Eliot here invokes. And her purpose in so doing is to place, not simply Mr. Bult's political world, but also its social counterpart, the world of Gwendolen's ambition, Mrs. Arrowsmith's salon, where, for all his genius, Klesmer remains a talent to be hired. It follows that it is within this context that we must place Gwendolen's pretension to an artistic career, and when, in the next chapter, she asks for his advice, it is no surprise to hear Klesmer making a particular application of the general case announced to Mr. Bult. His essential point is that, whatever Gwendolen's talent, without the overriding seriousness of the real artist, she can never expect to rise above the level of elegant or, worse, of vulgar 'amusement'; and the reader needs no reminding by this time that devotion to impersonal values is precisely the thing that Gwendolen is incapable of undertaking. This interview belongs, at the personal level, with those other crises in Gwendolen's life where her self-esteem collides with an external judgment that she can neither submit to nor forget. But the context of this collision is more than personal. Moving within but not belonging to Gwendolen's world, Klesmer expresses part of the reason why Deronda must seek his fulfilment out of England, why English politics itself could provide him with no adequate scope. Klesmer's description of himself to Mr. Bult as 'the Wandering Jew' is therefore more than a joke.

Klesmer puts a general case about Victorian England with a clear application for Deronda, but the latter is also the vehicle of a more specific critique of the people amongst whom he lives. (It is in this way that the commentarial perspectives on Gwendolen supplied directly by the author, or indirectly through Klesmer, are given novelistic substance, because the people with whom Deronda is contrasted amount, by and large, to the world of Gwendolen's aspiration.) The novel's social range is, in itself, well worth remarking. The Mallingers and Grandcourt represent the landowning aristocracy. The Arrowsmiths (significant name) are pursuing the familiar English journey from commercial success to a landed estate with some genteel culture, concluding in an alliance in the next generation with the aristocracy, or at least a Mr. Bult. The Rector and Mrs. Harleth present the *rentier* class with fortunes in banking and colonial trade, and the typical *rentier* catastrophe of loss of fortune discriminates Mrs. Harleth from the Rector, who, as incumbent of his parish, belongs also within the class of landowners. The Rector's son Rex illustrates the educated middle class of genteel origin, but without fortune, who turn to the professions for support, and in the family of his Cambridge friend Meyrick we meet another middle-class group, the widow and children of an artist, whose talents and industry save them from the fate that threatens Gwendolen – of being a governess. The introduction of the Meyricks, of course, announces a move away from Gwendolen's world, both physically to London (the description suggests that they are near-neighbours to Thomas Carlyle); and morally, in their connection with Mirah, with Deronda's discovery of the Cohens, Mordecai, and the respectable working men with whom Mordecai discusses intellectual matters.

Deronda's position in this English society is not unlike that of the 'superfluous gentleman' of Russian fiction. In nurture and fortune, he belongs with the Mallingers, but birth and personal endowment set him apart, negatively in the sharpness of his rejection of fashionable society at Leubronn, positively in his search for a significant meaning for his own life, and it is this search which underlies his friendship with the Meyricks, with Mirah, and with Mordecai. But it is his contrasting relationships with Sir Hugo and Grandcourt that best illustrate the kind of criterion George Eliot is bringing to bear upon his *milieu*. Sir Hugo, though a conventional man, without special abilities, conceives his life as a pattern of obligations – to Daniel, and to Daniel's mother, to his wife and heirs, to the tradition of his kind in public life. Grandcourt, on the other hand,

embodies the principle of purely exploitative living. He is an aristo-
crat who has become wholly parasitical in relation to society. Other
people exist only as a means for gratifying his self-conceit at the
social level and, at a deeper, his sadism, with its astonishing mixture
of languor and intensity. His relationship with Lush and Gwendolen show this very fully, but even with Sir Hugo his main,
hardly conscious impulse is to find out what he wants, and deny
him. Deronda's reserved dislike, of course, he can only understand
as envy for his position and fortune, and in so far as these two are
opposite, then clearly Sir Hugo belongs with Deronda. But there
is also the more fundamental contrast between Deronda and his
foster-father. For all his amiability, and for all that he represents
the best of his kind, where Grandcourt represents the worst, Sir
Hugo wholly lacks Deronda's outgoing fervour of sympathy for the
real existence of his fellow-humans. It is this that lies behind Sir
Hugo's significant insensitivity in his dealing with Deronda (the
remark about becoming a singer which crystallizes the young
Daniel's suspicions about his birth, the teasing about his relation
with Gwendolen). And the same lack bears upon Sir Hugo's
politics, and Deronda's loss of belief in 'Sir Hugo's writings
as a standard, and in the Whigs as the chosen race among poli-
ticians'. To take the point of this, we only need contrast the demands Mordecai makes on Deronda with Sir Hugo's suggestions
that he might become a Don:

> 'But talking of Dons, I have seen Dons make a capital figure in
> society; and occasionally he can shoot you down a cartload of learning
> in the right place, which will tell in politics. Such men are wanted. . . .'

Or even go into Parliament:

> ' . . . we want a little disinterested culture to make head against cotton
> and capital, especially in the House. My Greek has all evaporated: if I
> had to construe a verse on a sudden, I should get an apoplectic fit. But
> it formed my taste. . . .'

The connection between this (Sir Hugo is a more serious Mr.
Brooke, in fact) and the genteel culture of the author of *Tasso* need
not be laboured. Sir Hugo's traditions constitute no kind of answer
to Herr Klesmer's speech to Mr. Bult, and Deronda's inability to
find a career stems directly from their limitations. In sum, English
society is so constituted that Deronda has to leave it, not because it

rejects him, but because, threatening to condemn him to a meaningless life, he rejects it. What he finds in its place is certainly more of a promise than a consolidated alternative, but there can be no doubt about George Eliot's wish to draw in as much detail as possible, a supporting contrast between the world he leaves and the world he goes to discover. Klesmer's visit to Gwendolen has already been mentioned: its counterpart is his visit to the Meyricks to pass favourable judgment on Mirah's modest hopes for a singing career, and this contrast between Mirah and Gwendolen extends to every level. Gwendolen's successes occur in various country seats; Mirah's under Lady Mallinger's auspices in London. Gwendolen and her mother depend financially on Grandcourt to maintain their social position; Mirah and the Meyricks, who work for a living and do not belong in fashionable society, depend for friendship and moral sustenance on Deronda; Gwendolen's treatment of an affectionate mother contrasts with Mirah's of an unscrupulous father. Even Grandcourt's secret, his relation with Mrs. Glasher, which is the means of Gwendolen's moral destruction, is balanced by Deronda's secret, the identity of his Jewish mother, the discovery of which not only destroys Gwendolen's illusions about him and initiates her into the moral experience of 'self-humiliation', but also unites him more completely with Mirah. Thus the division of the novel into two main stories, interweaving and touching, but never blending together, is reflected not simply in the attraction-repulsion feelings that exist between the two main characters, but in the two supporting groups of characters, each more or less dominated by opposed values: the one symbolized in its extreme form by Grandcourt, and deeply attractive to Gwendolen; the other by Mordecai, and vitally necessary to Deronda.

So much is familiar ground,[18] and my point in recounting these details is to ask how far this series of contrasts, achieved by the most skilful deployment of novelistic techniques, leads to a confrontation between Gwendolen's and Deronda's worlds? Where does the world of Deronda's extensive aspirations offer a strong, imaginative challenge to the one he has to leave? The answer surely is that it never does. Underlying all the links and parallels which draw the two stories into significant relationship there is a more powerful imaginative logic drawing them apart. There are a number of reasons for this. The outsider-critics (Deronda, Mordecai) are not only Jews, but European Jews, who look elsewhere than England for their origins, while Deronda's discovery of his race transforms him from a critical presence within English society into an expatriate who has decided to go home. There is also Deronda's shadowiness of character, which, many critics have argued, constitutes the novel's greatest weakness, but there is a sense in which the original premise of his character entails it. Unlike anybody else in his world, he is a man in search of his identity. Withdrawn, meditative, without any of the settled purposes or desires which make the basis of predominantly 'social' characterization, Deronda is a wanderer, a man in the making, whose energies only crystallize at the very end of the novel. This means that his characteristic relation with English society is one of withdrawal, e.g., his reaction to Gwendolen is always tinged with uneasiness about being caught up in a responsibility that has little to do with his deepest purposes. Then there is the choice of Zionism for the historical cause which will give Deronda his fulfilment. George Eliot's explanation of this choice belongs clearly enough within the context established so far. Noting the growth of 'a spirit of arrogance and contemptuous dictatorialness (towards the Jews and all oriental peoples) which has become a national disgrace to us', noting, that is, the transformation of national insularity into imperialist racial contempt, she goes on:

> There is nothing I should care more to do, if it were possible, than to rouse the imagination of men and women to a vision of human claims in those races of their fellow-men who most differ from them in customs and beliefs. But towards the Hebrews we western people who have been reared in Christianity, have a peculiar debt and, whether we acknowledge it or not, a peculiar thoroughness of fellowship in religious and moral sentiment. Can anything be more disgusting than to hear people called 'educated' making small jokes about eating ham, and showing themselves empty of any real knowledge as to the relation of their own social and religious life to the history of the people they think themselves witty in insulting? They hardly know that Christ was a Jew. And I find men, educated at Rugby, supposing that Christ spoke Greek. To my feeling, this deadness to the history which has prepared half our world for us, this inability to find interest in any form of life that is not clad in the same coat-tails and flounces as our own lies very close to the worst kind of irreligion. The best that can be said of it is, that it is a sign of the intellectual narrowness – in plain English, the stupidity, which is still the average mark of our culture.[14]

It is with this honourable goal in mind that we have to understand the rôle of Mordecai (John the Baptist to Deronda's Christ), and the didactic pressure that works so strongly in the Deronda half of the novel. But the fact remains that it is because of this choice that the novel proceeds without any substantial conflict between Deronda's world and Gwendolen's. George Eliot's letter argues for the cultural and historical relevance of Judaism to Christian England, but there is no sign of this theme in the novel. And the political cause to which Deronda dedicated his life has no evident bearing on English life. Henry James makes a perceptive contrast between Deronda and Turgenev's Insarov which brings this out.[15] His public cause is directly connected with Russian history, and with the contemporary debates about Panslavism, but Deronda's has not even the shadowy connection with English history of Felix Holt's vague future. His personal withdrawal from intimate relations with Gwendolen's world culminates in his physical departure from England on a mission that fulfils his ideals as thoroughly as it is unlikely ever to allow him to return. Finally, there is the fact that the 'Deronda' group of characters who prefigure his departure from England, in being already outside established English society, are not much more than extensions of Deronda himself. Except in the contrived delays intervening between his rescue of Mirah and discovery of her brother, what is there to test the authenticity of his impulses, or his determination to follow where they lead? The Meyricks, Cohens, and London working men contribute little more than an opportunity for Deronda to display that goodwilling, earnest seriousness of purpose which sets him off from the fashionable world. Their function is too clearly dependent on Deronda's search to make a separate impact.

In one of the early articles on *Daniel Deronda*, Edward Dowden contrasted it with *Middlemarch*,[16] proposing that where the earlier novel showed the failure of large and heroic aspiration, the later showed its success both in Deronda's future and in his having rescued Gwendolen from her trivial life. I am arguing for the opposite conclusion. The choice of Zionism has the effect of removing the ideal aspirations associated with Deronda from any effective engagement with the English scene. It will be remembered that Gwendolen's final encounter with Deronda is represented as an awakening to history, but this history is wholly located outside England. Concealed within this lies the assumption that English life has become unhistorical, its public character represented by the performance of a Mr. Bult or the traditions of Sir Hugo, and only capable of high drama in the personal crises of Gwendolen. This completes the withdrawal from a significant English politics, argued for in *Felix Holt* and confirmed in *Middlemarch*, and repeats even more emphatically than either of them the distinction between social and political reform. The shadowy confrontation between these of the earlier novels persists within Deronda's critical attitude towards English life, but the structural attempt to apply in this more detail is nullified by the steady movement away from English society. We may see in this combination both George Eliot's attempt to bring Deronda's idealism to bear on the life of his time and the working out of assumptions which make this impossible. Deronda's mission, that is, represents a final example of that abstracting idealism which characterized George Eliot's response to the events of 1848.

NOTES

1. Karl Marx and Frederick Engels, *Selected Works* (Foreign Languages Publishing House, Moscow, 1951), ii. p. 366. For a modern example of 'religious alienation', see the account of working-class life in Northamptonshire in Jeremy Leabrook, *The Underprivileged*, (1967), p. 28.

2. *ibid.*, p. 365.

3. Feuerbach's Preface to Vol. I of *Sämmtliche Werke* (1846), cited in *Ninetenth Century Studies*, p. 231.

4. Marx and Engels, *op. cit.*, p. 367.

5. *Nineteenth Century Studies*, p. 237.

6. *The Sad Fortunes of the Rev. Amos Barton*, ch. 5.

7. *The Art of George Eliot.*

8. *op. cit.*, p. 367.

9. *Letters*, i. 267

10. *Culture and Society*, p. 108. The point is made during a discussion of *Felix Holt*, to which I am a good deal indebted, both in my own comments on the novel and in a more general way.

11. *Letters*, i. 253–4.

12. See, for example, the account of the 1830s in G. D. H. Cole and Raymond Postgate, *The British Common People 1746–1936* (Methuen, 1939), pp. 253 foll.

13. *The Novels of George Eliot*, Barbara Hardy, pp. 111–14.

14. *Letters*, vi. 301–2.

15. 'Daniel Deronda: A Conversation' in *A Century of George Eliot Criticism*, ed. Gordon S. Haight (Houghton Mifflin Co., 1965), p. 104.

16. '*Middlemarch* and *Daniel Deronda*', *op. cit.*, pp. 113–16.

IX

IDEA AND IMAGE IN THE
NOVELS OF GEORGE ELIOT[1]
W. J. Harvey

I

IN HIS *Religious Humanism and the Victorian Novel*[2] Professor U. C. Knoepflmacher pays tribute to recent critics of George Eliot, but maintains that:

> They have somehow perpetrated the illusion that George Eliot's art and ideology are best examined in separation, that two divorced 'principles' govern her novels, and that these principles, the one artistic and the other intellectual, must remain irrevocably apart.

We must certainly agree that it is vital to understand how George Eliot blends art and ideology; we may also agree that this is likely to prove a difficult and delicate task. Just how difficult and delicate Professor Knoepflmacher illustrates in one of the appendices to his study; if I seem to turn his evidence against him this must be understood as an oblique tribute to his largely pioneering endeavours. In this appendix he writes of *Middlemarch*:

> The metamorphosis of Rosamond and of Lydgate himself is presented through a kind of evolution in reverse which shows the extent of George Eliot's scientific preparation. In 1864 T. H. Huxley had proved conclusively 'that many extinct reptiles had bird characteristics and many extinct birds, reptilian characteristics' and had argued that consequently both species should be classified as 'sauroids' (William Irvine, *Apes, Angels and Victorians* (Jordan, 1955) p. 240). In *Middlemarch*, where the archiac 'Dodo' Brooke triumphs over the 'scientific phoenix

151

Lydgate', a 'creature who had talons, but Reason too, George Eliot turns Huxley's biological insight on Lydgate through a gradual metaphoric alteration of his wife.

He then goes on to analyse Rosamond in terms of the bird-like and reptilian images that characterize her. In doing so he exemplified, I think, two dangers inherent in any discussion of the way art blends with ideology. The first danger is aesthetic; that of over-ingenuity, of reading too much into too little. We may well feel that he rides his evidence too hard. The evidence itself is striking but *very* slender. Even in the passage I have quoted we may feel that he is dragooning with too cavalier a spirit Dorothea's nickname 'Dodo' into the service of his argument. Can we really make the jump from a nickname to an extinct bird and thence to a contrast with a fabulous creature, the phoenix, in order to delineate the contrast between the two characters? Do we *need* to? Phoenixes, certainly, are hardly to be brought within the terms of any biological theory! And can we really, in any sense that rings true to the novel, speak of Dorothea triumphing over Lydgate? Moreover, in the whole appendix, Professor Knoepflmacher is very selective in his choice of images; the reference to birds and reptiles must surely be taken in the context of George Eliot's total use of animal imagery in *Middlemarch*.

The second danger is much more likely to be encountered by the historian of ideas rather than by the critic. This is the assertion of too narrow, too specific a relationship between intellectual cause and aesthetic effect. Certainly T. H. Huxley's temperament and philosophic outlook has many striking *general* resemblances to that of George Eliot. There is no good reason to suppose, however, that this proof of 1864[3] was the specific source of this kind of imagery and idea in *Middlemarch*. For what Huxley does is to adduce evidence reinforcing a more general idea, something that was almost commonplace in Victorian biological thought and which was, therefore, *generally* accessible to George Eliot. It is just barely possible, I suppose, that Huxley may have led George Eliot to put a slightly heavier stress on birds and reptiles, but this is a far cry from showing 'the extent of George Eliot's scientific preparation' or from proving that George Eliot in any conscious way 'turns Huxley's biological insight on Lydgate'. It is just possible, but I doubt in fact whether there is anything in her terms to suggest a particular debt to Huxley. I would maintain, on the contrary, that, in order to appreciate the aesthetic expression of ideology, we need to operate on the level of the general commonplace rather than on the level of specific example, to state the controlling idea in as broad and as inclusive a fashion as possible. Stated in this broad, commonplace way, the idea is that we are the sum of our origins and development. If we desire a more closely biological statement of this idea, then we can conveniently cite Haeckel's formulation in 1866 of his fundamental law of biogenesis:

> The organized individual repeats during the rapid course of his own development the more important phases through which its ancestors passed in the course of their long palaeontological evolution.

Or, more briefly, in the dictum that Freud transferred from biology to psychology, 'Ontogeny recapitulates phylogeny'.

Stated in this general way, the idea gives a resonance, not merely to particular images, but also to some of George Eliot's most deeply felt convictions; to her statement in *Adam Bede*, for example, that:

> A certain consciousness of our entire past and our imagined future blends itself with all our moments of keen sensibility.... The secret of our emotions never lies in the bare object, but in its subtle relations to our own past.

> (ch. 18)

This conviction is part of the tap-root of George Eliot's 'ideology'; it reverberates throughout all her novels; it colours her whole vision of human nature. It is at this level rather than at the level of particular images that the recapitulation theory is likely to have stirred her consciousness.

The recapitulation theory was already well formed before Haeckel's classic formulation of it in 1866, and I believe that we could find distorted echoes of it in Victorian authors before George Eliot began to write. There seems no need to establish a precise causal relation between her and Huxley. Indeed, we may in general ask what are the conditions which have to be fulfilled before we can assert such a specific causal relationship between idea and artistic expression. Leaving aside the possibility of the author's explicit acknowledgement of indebtedness, we must surely have *as a minimum*, one of the following conditions.

(*a*) The idea must not be a commonplace, but must be an odd, exceptional, or particularly striking idea. Or it must be an odd, exceptional, or striking collocation and structure of commonplace ideas.

(b) The idea, if not exceptional, must be illustrated by striking and particular examples, which are then repeated by the artist.

(c) There must be extremely close verbal similarities in the formulation of the idea.

Let me take an example which illustrates chiefly the first two of these conditions. Consider the idea formulated in the passage from *Adam Bede* that I quoted earlier; or, better, consider this more detailed formulation from *The Mill on the Floss*:

> The wood I walk in on this mild May day, with the young yellow-brown foliage of the oaks between me and the blue sky, the white star-flowers and the blue-eyed speedwell and the ground ivy at my feet – what grove of tropic palms, what strange ferns or splendid broad-petalled blossoms, could ever thrill such deep and delicate fibres within me as this home-scene? These familiar flowers, these well-remembered bird-notes, this sky, with its fitful brightness, these furrowed and grassy fields, each with a sort of personality given to it by the capricious hedgerows – such things as these are the mother tongue of our imagination, the language that is laden with all the subtle inextricable associations the fleeting hours of our childhood left behind them. Our delight in the sunshine on the deep-bladed grass to-day, might be no more than the faint perception of wearied souls, if it were not for the sunshine and the grass in the far-off years which still live in us, and transform our perception into love.
>
> (I. 5)

Set beside this a passage from Herbert Spencer's *Principles of Psychology*:

> The cawing of rooks usually produces pleasurable feelings – feelings which many suppose to result from the quantity of the sound itself. Only the few who are given to self-analysis are aware that the cawing of rooks is agreeable to them because it has been connected with countless of their greatest gratifications – with the gathering of wild flowers in childhood; with Saturday-afternoon excursions in schoolboy days; with midsummer holidays in the country, when books were thrown aside and lessons were replaced by games and adventures in the field; with fresh, sunny mornings in after-years, when a walking excursion was an immense relief from toil. As it is, this sound, though not caus-

ally related to all these multitudinous and varied past delights, but only often associated with them, rouses a dim consciousness of these delights; just as the voice of an old friend unexpectedly coming into the house, suddenly raises a wave of that feeling which has resulted from the pleasures of past companionship.

Let us suppose, as I indeed do, that Herbert Spencer was a powerful influence on that ideology which George Eliot transmuted into art. None of us I trust, would wish to assert that the passage I have just quoted was, in any sense, the *source* of the passage from *The Mill on the Floss*. Both are responding independently, though in somewhat similar terms, to the same commonplace. Let us suppose that we could find – as I think we could – scores of such vaguely parallel passages in Spencer and in George Eliot. All that we would then have established is a sympathy between their two minds, a similarity of tone and feeling in their responses, such as to suggest a possible predisposition on the part of George Eliot to be influenced by Spencer. We should still have to be extremely cautious in going from the general to the particular, in asserting a specific causal relationship between idea and artistic expression. Let me illustrate by an absurdity. Professor Knoepflmacher, in his advocacy of Huxley, cites as one of his supporting ideas that fact that Lydgate 'begins to flinch from his wife's "torpedo contact"'. (The actual phrase in *Middlemarch* is: 'The very resolution to which he had wrought himself by dint of logic and honourable pride was beginning to relax under her torpedo contact.') Suppose, then, that I adduced as a source for this sentence the following passage from Spencer's *Principles of Psychology*:

> But for the accidental observation of Galvani, the suspicion that the nerve-force is electric or quasi-electric, would probably never have been entertained; and it should have been abandoned as soon as it was found that the other disturbing agents, physical and chemical, work just the same effects. The conception has, indeed, been kept alive by the discovery that electricity is generated by certain fishes. But the supposed support is wholly imaginary. It, because the Torpedo evolves electricity by the help of nerves ramifying through its electric organ, is inferred that the nerve-force is sensible motion, because it generates sensible motion in the muscles.

I should, I hope, be hooted out of court; in Spencer's own words, 'the supposed support is wholly imaginary'. My intellectual history would be just as absurd as Spencer's science in the passage I have just quoted. But, I fear, equal absurdities are often to be found when the historian of ideas attempts to explain the transmutation of ideology into art.

We have moved, so far, from a few particular images to the more general notion that 'ontogeny recapitulates phylogeny'. This idea, I have suggested, may be widely applied to areas of experience remote from embryology and can be varyingly expressed. 'The child is father to the man' is, for example, one formulation of such an idea.

If, then, it is difficult to trace a causal relationship between so relatively precise an idea and the fiction which may embody it, how much more difficult must it be delineate the impact on George Eliot of the whole of evolutionary theory of which this idea is just one part. Consider, first, the evidence we have concerning George Eliot's relation to Darwin and the *Origin of Species*.

The first mention of it that we have comes in George Eliot's journal for 23 November 1859:

> We began reading Darwin's work on 'The Origin of Species' tonight. It seems not to be well-written: though full of interesting matter, it is not impressive for want of luminous and orderly presentation.

Two days later she mentions it in a letter to Charles Bray – just one odd paragraph in a letter full of other matters:

> We are reading Darwin's Book on Species, just come out, after long expectation. It is an elaborate exposition of the evidence in favour of the Development Theory, and so, makes an epoch.
>
> (*Letters*, iii. 214)

This is expanded in a letter to Barbara Bodichon, written on 5 December:

> We have been reading Darwin's Book on the 'Origin of Species' just now: it makes an epoch, as the expression of his thorough adhesion, after long years of study, to the Doctrine of Development – and not the adhesion of an anonym like the author of the 'Vestiges', but of a long-celebrated naturalist. The book is ill-written and sadly wanting in illustrative facts – of which he has collected a vast number, but reserves them for a future book of which this smaller one is the avant-courier. This will prevent the book from becoming popular, as the 'Vestiges' did, but it will have a great effect in the scientific world, causing a thorough and open discussion of a question about which people have hitherto felt timid. So the world gets on step by step towards brave

clearness and honesty! But to me the Development Theory and all other explanations of processes by which things came to be, produce a feeble impression compared with the mystery that lies under the processes.

(Letters, iii. 227)

While George Eliot recognizes the importance of Darwin's work ('it makes an epoch'), this evidence surely points to a fairly cool and unsurprised reaction on her part. It is not that, for her, Darwin is saying anything strikingly new; his importance rather is that he will promote franker discussion of issues she already takes for granted. If *The Origin of Species* had by itself any effect on her creative imagination, it cannot have been much greater than that of the recapitulation theory – the effect of sharpening and pointing a few specific images. This happens most in *The Mill on the Floss,* and Professor Haight has summarized the evidence very judiciously in the Introduction to his edition of that novel; further we cannot safely go. For the fact is that we cannot clearly separate *The Origin of Species* from all the other formulations of what George Eliot calls the Development Theory; all together formed part of her intellectual climate. Part of this climate filtered through to her via the biological interests of G. H. Lewes. Again we must take into account the popularization of such theories in *The Vestiges of Creation* (1844); George Eliot knew its author Robert Chambers, very well. Above all, there is the possible impact of an even closer friend, Herbert Spencer. Spencer had published his 'Development Hypothesis' in *The Leader* and his 'Theory of Population' in *The Westminster Review.* With both journals, of course, George Eliot was intimately connected. Her letters are full of enthusiastic references to his *First Principles* and his *Principles of Psychology.* There is evidence that George Eliot must have discussed with him the ideas contained in some of these works. All the external evidence, in fact, points to Spencer rather than to Darwin as the prime intellectual influence concerning ideas on Evolution.

Spencer's claims to scientific seriousness are now completely exploded. He is remembered, if at all, as the subject of a gibe by Huxley – 'Spencer's idea of a tragedy was a deduction killed by a fact' – and as the man who first linked the development of the species with the phrase, 'the survival of the fittest'. Yet it is precisely because of his shortcomings as a scientist that his general ideological influence may have been more attractive to an artistic mind. For Spencer is one of the great intellectual eclectics and synthesizers, always dodging from one field of knowledge to another, always creating often dubious analogies between different areas of experience. In other words, his intellectual processes are intrinsically closer to the novelist's activity; these analogies, though scientifically absurd, are far more imaginatively suggestive than what George Eliot felt to be Darwin's 'want of luminous and orderly presentation'.

Spencer's general definition of evolution in his *First Principles* is not very promising if we are thinking of its possible effects on the creative imagination:

> Evolution is an integration of matter and concomitant dissipation of motion; during which the matter passes from an indefinite, incoherent homogeneity to a definite, coherent heterogeneity; and during which the retained motion undergoes a parallel transformation.

What is remarkable, however, is the fertility of his illustrations. I will instance just one section of his argument, the chapter in which he discusses evolution as a progression from incoherence to coherence, the whole process being the combination and interaction of many different parts. He draws his examples from astronomy, geology, biology, botany, sociology, Bushmen, feudal society, European federation, class structure, industry, transport, the trade unions, philology, the history of science, the industrial arts and the pure arts – painting, music, and literature. On this very last point his account of the development of narrative is – no doubt entirely by accident – a precise description of George Eliot's kind of fiction. Whereas primitive stories

> are made up of successive occurrences, mostly unnatural, that have no natural connections ... in a good modern work of imagination, the events are the proper products of the characters living under given conditions; and cannot at will be changed in their order or kind, without injuring or destroying its general effect. Further, the characters themselves, which in early fiction play their respective parts without showing how their minds are modified by one another or by the events, are now presented to us as held together by complex moral relations, and as acting and reacting on one another's natures.

I suggest no causal connection, but it must surely be true that the cast of mind revealed here would find a sympathetic response in George Eliot. Moreover the list of examples, the constant building of intellectual and imaginative bridges between one world and another, must have made this exposition of evolution more attractive to her than that of Darwin. What is a weakness in scientific discourse – this constant analogical interplay between different areas of experience – is a strength in the world of art.

Nevertheless, I do not wish to maintain that one can find in Spencer, any more than in Darwin or Huxley, a specific source of George Eliot's ideas. Intellectual influences do not work in this way. For one thing, George Eliot had a powerful and independent mind and she was just as likely to have influenced Spencer as he her – indeed, at one point in his *Principles of Psychology* he acknowledges his indebtedness to her. Secondly, the ideas in Spencer are already largely commonplace; thus it would be difficult to sort out in any detail the different effects on her of his theories of social and intellectual evolution as compared with those of Auguste Comte. Again, it would be easy to excerpt passages from his *Principles of Psychology* – the chapters, for example, on memory or on altruism and egotism – which are strikingly close in substance and tone to passages in George Eliot's novels. Yet it is much more likely that her doctrine of sympathy – if it was borrowed at all – was more directed by her translation of Feuerbach than by her knowledge of Spencer.

Surely a truer account of the relation of artist to intellectual climate than the hunt for specific sources and influences will allow us has been given by Hugh Kenner in his discussion of the connections between the poetry of T. S. Eliot and the philosophy of F. H. Bradley:

> He was uniquely equipped to exert that sort of tonal influence on a disciple; he is not the sort of philosopher who can be tied, rhetorically, to a cause. It is as a colouring, not as a body of doctrine that he stays in the mind. . . . Bradley has an attractive mind, though he has perhaps nothing to tell us. He is an experience, like the taste of nectarines or the style of Henry James; to bethink him is to recall with labour a landscape once seen in a dream; he is like a vivid dream in that, as Eliot said, he modifies the sensibility.

If I may stretch Mr. Kenner's metaphor even a little further, then we arrive, surely, at something like this: George Eliot's art reveals a particular intellectual coloration which is part of her general sensibility. This is the result of the blending together of a number of primary colours (i.e. her intellectual sources), the particular chemistry of the blending being determined by her own mind and temperament. By analysis we can be reasonably sure that this or that primary colour must have been an ingredient in the process, but in what proportions and with what reactions to other ingredients we cannot pretend to say with any accuracy. It is a dispiritingly negative conclusion, but surely a safer and more accurate account than any attempt to decompose her mind into an intellectual spectrum with individual colours labelled Comte, Feuerbach, Spencer, Lewes, Darwin, Huxley, etc. If we rest here, then we are, after all, only observing George Eliot's cautionary statement in a letter to Sara Hennell:

> Surely it is a part of human piety we should all cultivate, not to form conclusions, on slight and dubious evidence, as to other people's 'tone of mind'.
>
> (*Letters*, iii. 338)

II

I return now to that nexus of ideas summed up in the formula, 'ontogeny recapitulates phylogeny'. What we have to discuss are the ways in which this idea works *within* George Eliot's fiction, just how and to what ends ideology is transmuted into art. I intend to treat this idea in a truly Spencerian manner, to let it run wild, branching off into analogies and attracting to itself very diverse areas of experience. While this method has obvious dangers, it also has for me the overriding virtue of corresponding more closely to the complicated mesh of ideas and feelings that we do actually encounter in the novels. As George Eliot herself observed, 'for getting a strong impression that a skein is tangled, there is nothing like snatching hastily at a single thread'. Indeed, the great danger for the intellectual historian – concerned as he is with the lucid unravelling of his tangled subject – is that he will tend to 'snatch hastily at a single thread', will tend to treat a particular idea in an unnatural isolation. But when an idea enters George Eliot's work, it is immediately modified by being placed into relation with other ideas; it takes a colour from thoughts and emotions which may be quite disparate in origin and direction. The 'tangled skein' is in fact part of the nature of life as George Eliot sees it and evokes a corresponding quality in her fiction. We must allow our formula to flourish, therefore, even at the risk of getting tangled in its luxuriance.

Let us ask, therefore, in what sense can we say that as adult human beings we recapitulate our origins and growth. There are, surely, three chief possible answers:

1. The adult contains within him his individual childhood.
2. The individual, as part of society, contains within him the historical past of his culture.
3. The individual, as biological product, contains within him, not only his particular hereditary endowment, but also the whole of the evolutionary past. He is a very special kind of animal, but still rooted in a common Nature.

I propose to work from the general to the particular and will, therefore, treat these three categories in reverse order. Let us always remember that they *are* categories, that they do not adequately re-create the intermingled nature of George Eliot's fiction. The 'tangled skein' with which we are dealing is, so to speak, made up of three-ply threads.

III

Man and Nature

The novel in which our hereditary nature is most important is *The Mill on the Floss*. But George Eliot knows that we are shaped by a tremendous number of determining forces, many of which conflict and cancel each other out. In that conflict lies our freedom; the main reason why we do not think of George Eliot as crudely deterministic is her reluctance to trace effects back to a single cause. Thus even in *The Mill on the Floss* heredity is only one of the natural forces that play upon us; in general, George Eliot puts much greater stress upon environment. Eppie in *Silas Marner*, for example, owes nothing to hereditary nature, but everything to nurture, while Adam Bede has his 'inborn inalienable nature' (ch. 50). The paragraph that contains this phrase also stresses how much he has been changed by circumstance and experience. Mr. Tulliver is wiser than he knows when he says of his children, 'That's the warst on't wi' the crossing o' breeds; you can never calkilate what'll come on't' (ch. 2). *Like father, like son* has a grain of truth in it, but is really too simple a formula; Mr. Tulliver is definitely wrong when he says of Philip Waken, 'Don't you be getting too thick with him – he's got his father's blood in him too. Ay, ay, the grey colt may chance to kick like his black sire' (II. 6). Part of our common human tragedy is the gap that separates us from those to whom we are by nature bound:

> Family likeness has often a deep sadness in it. Nature, that great tragic dramatist, knits us together by bone and muscle, and divides us by the subtler web of our brains; blends yearning and repulsion; ties us by our heart-strings to the beings that jar us at every movement.... The father to whom we owe our best heritage – the mechanical instinct, the keen sensibility to harmony, the unconscious skill of the modelling hand – galls us, and puts us to shame by his daily errors.
>
> *(Adam Bede*, ch. 4)

Our genetic code, then, gives us the vocabulary of our being, but whether we make prose or poetry of it depends on ourselves and on Nature in a much wider sense.

That George Eliot's imagery embodies her conception of the way human beings are rooted in nature is so obvious as to need no demonstration. Since most of her novels take place in rural surroundings, it is natural enough that her characters should be defined in these terms. But we should distinguish between those occasions when such images form part of the natural flavour of a character's speech (as in examples of Mr. Tulliver quoted above), and those when they form part of the author's commentary or analysis. In this latter case they are nearly always mocking or ironic, pointing either to similarities between the human and the animal creation of which the characters themselves are unconscious, or to discrepancies which are not entirely to man's advantage. In one of her letters, discussing the readers of the *Cornhill Magazine*, she wrote: 'Natural selection is not always good, and depends (see Darwin) on many caprices of very foolish animals' (*Letters*, iv. 377). That man is a foolish animal and that the evolutionary highest is not always the best are amply exemplified in her fiction; consider these few random examples:

> (*a*) Tom, terrorizing the farmyard animals, indicates, thus early, that desire for mastery over the inferior animals, wild and domestic, including cockchafers, neighbour's dogs, and small sisters, which in all ages has been an attribute of much promise for the fortunes of our race. Now, Mr. Pullet never rode anything taller than a low pony, and was the least predatory of men ...' (I. 9).

One notices the carefully casual inclusion in the catalogue of 'small sisters' and the way in which the first sentence spills over into 'predatory' of the second. The human world has its predators, too; later we learn that Mr. Tulliver is a 'roach' to Wakem's 'pike'.

(b) But all this while Mrs. Tulliver was brooding over a scheme by which she, and no one else, would avert the result most to be dreaded, and prevent Wakem from entertaining the purpose of bidding for the mill. Imagine a truly respectable and amiable hen, by some portentous anomaly, taking to reflection and inventing combinations by which she might prevail on Hodge not to wring her neck, or send her and her chicks to market; the result could hardly be other than much cackling and fluttering (III. 7).

One notices again how the image reflects back on the statement, so that 'brooding' almost becomes 'broody'. Mrs. Tulliver's hen-like stupidity (one may justly think of a pecking-order as the social principle of the Dodson and Tulliver clan) produces, of course, the reverse of what she intends; it is a fine example of a general moral theme which runs throughout George Eliot's work and which, in *Middlemarch*, is characterized in evolutionary terms:

We know what a masquerade all development is, and what effective shapes may be disguised in helpless embryos. In fact, the world is full of hopeful analogies and handsome dubious eggs called possibilities.

(ch. 10)

(c) Perhaps it was because teaching came naturally to Mr. Stelling, that he set about it with that uniformity of method and independence of circumstances, which distinguish the actions of animals understood to be under the immediate teaching of nature.

(II. 1)

He is then compared to a beaver: 'with the same unerring instinct Mr. Stelling set to work' – an image which is perhaps mutated later in *The Mill on the Floss*:

Besides, how should Mr. Stelling be expected to know that education was a delicate and difficult business? any more than an animal endowed with a power of boring a hole through a rock should be expected to have wide views of excavation.

(II. 4)

(d) And lastly, from *Middlemarch*:

When the animals entered the Ark in pairs, one may imagine that allied species made much private remark on each other, and were tempted to think that so many forms feeding on the same store of fodder were eminently superfluous, as tending to diminish the rations. (I fear that the part played by the vultures on that occasion would be too painful for art to represent, those birds being disadvantageously naked about the gullet, and apparently without rites and ceremonies.)

The same sort of temptation befell the Christian Carnivora who formed Peter Featherston's funeral procession ... (ch. 35).

The analogy is perhaps a little heavily facetious, but nevertheless a just comment on the 'vultures' who have come for the reading of the will and who are outdone by the 'frog-faced' Joshua Rigg. And there are other kinds of 'Christian Carnivora' in the novel; thus Farebrother can say of Bulstrode:

'I don't like the set he belongs to: they are a narrow ignorant set, and do more to make their neighbours uncomfortable than to make them better. Their system is a sort of worldly-spirited cliqueism: they really look on the rest of mankind as *a doomed carcass which is to nourish them for heaven.*'

(ch. 17. Italics mine)

Many more examples could be cited, but even from the few I have quoted it should be clear that George Eliot is using this analogy for more than merely comic or ironic purposes; it can also give a wider perspective and a greater weight to her moral judgments. For the analogy is more than a mere analogy; it is also for her a literal truth, part of her vision of that unbroken continuum between man and Nature. Human and animal are subsumed in the same universal process. Thus the spiritual growth or decay of an individual may become a microcosm of those limited successes or painful failures that George Eliot saw as implicit in the Development Theory and which led her to a cautious meliorism tinged with stoical resignation. One of the few examples of a direct debt to Darwin that Professor Haight detected in *The Mill on the Floss* is this touch of descriptive detail:

She was calmly enjoying the free air, while she looked up at the old fir trees, and thought that broken ends of branches were the records of past storms, which had only made the red stems soar higher.

(V. 1)

We are surely meant to feel this detail when, a few pages later, Philip thinks of Maggie:

Then – the pity of it, that a mind like hers should be withering in its very youth, like a young forest-tree, for want of the light and space it was formed to flourish in.

As with the individual so with society; thus St. Oggs may be viewed as part of the biological continuum, bearing within itself the evidence of its own history:

> It is one of those old, old towns which impress one as a continuation and outgrowth of nature, as much as the nests of the bower-birds or the winding galleries of the white ants: a town which carries the traces of its long growth and history like a millennial tree. . . .
>
> (I. 12)

In the famous comparison of this society to the Rhone villages, George Eliot again invokes the universal evolutionary process:

> I have a cruel conviction that the lives these ruins are the traces of were part of a gross sum of obscure vitality that will be swept into the same oblivion with the generations of ants and beavers.
>
> (IV. 1)

Beavers we have already met in the description of Mr. Stelling, while the Dodsons and the Tullivers are almost immediately characterized as 'emmet-like'.

Against this bleak prospect George Eliot can only pose a carefully limited faith 'that [young natures] in the onward tendency of human things have risen above the mental level of the generation before them, to which they have been nevertheless tied by the strongest fibres of their hearts' (*The Mill on the Floss*, IV. 1). Human development is slow, faltering and painful. George Eliot is always careful to discriminate and to strike a balance. Human beings are both like and unlike animals; they, too, are controlled by their environment, but, unlike the rest of Nature, they can also exert a reciprocal influence upon their surroundings. Hence she can use the same imagery to assert antithetical moral judgments. Animal imagery may characterize the charm of young children; they are like animals in their innocence:

> We learn to restrain ourselves as we get older. We keep apart when we have quarrelled, express ourselves in well-bred phrases, and in this way preserve a dignified alienation, showing much firmness on one side, and swallowing much grief on the other. We no longer approximate in our behaviour to the mere impulsiveness of the lower animals, but conduct ourselves in every respect like members of a highly civilized society. Maggie and Tom were still very much like young animals, and

so she could rub her cheek against his, and kiss his ear in a random, sobbing way, and there were tender fibres in the lad that had been used to answer Maggie's fondling. . . .

(*The Mill on the Floss*, I. 5)

The spontaneity and tenderness of children is here a judgment on the repression and restraint of adult life. But George Eliot also knows that what is charmingly appropriate in children may be damagingly immature in a grown-up. Most of her egoists are characterized in part by animal imagery; what may seem attractive about them (their 'kittenish' or 'puppyish' characteristics) can so easily turn into an index of their moral inadequacy; the clearest example of this is, I suppose, Hetty Sorrel, who in prison is 'at first like an animal that gazes, and gazes, and keeps aloof'. But it is a constant thread in George Eliot's moral pattern.

The same doubleness of vision, the same awareness that what seems good in some circumstances may turn into its opposite, also characterizes George Eliot's largest and most inclusive subsumption of man to Nature. Occasionally in her work the word *Nature* (like Destiny or Providence) is used as a sign which sums up her total sense of 'the way things are', of the multifarious and mysterious complex of forces and processes which constitute reality. Man's attitude to Nature in this sense may again be twofold, may work for good or ill. At its simplest, it may be no more than the fatalistic resignation of the countryman responding to the way things turn out, as Mrs. Poyser responds to natural circumstance: 'As for the weather, there's One above makes it, and we must put up wi't; it's nothing of a plague to what the wenches are' (*Adam Bede*, ch. 18). At its best it may reflect the wisdom of those who feel the great pressure of the general course of things and who see their freedom is the recognition of this necessity, but without abrogating their duty to strive nevertheless for the right. It comes out in Adam Bede's 'The nature o' things doesn't change, though it seems as if one's own life was nothing but change' (ch. 11), as in his brother's declaration that we must 'do our duty, and leave the rest to God's will'. Most explicitly it comes out in the native wisdom and goodness of Dolly Winthrop:

'Ah,' said Dolly with soothing gravity, 'it's like the night and the morning, and the sleeping and the waking, and the rain and the harvest — one goes and the other comes, and we know nothing how or where. We may strive and scrat and fend, but it's little we can do arter all – the big things come and go wi' no striving o' ow'n – they do, that they do. . . .'

(Silas Marner, ch. 14)

and later:

'That's all as ever I can be sure on, and everything else is a big puzzle to me when I think on it. For there was the fever come and took off them as were full-growed, and left the helpless children; and there's the breaking o' limbs; and them as 'ud do right and be sober have to suffer by them as are contrairy – eh, there's trouble i' this world, and there's things as we can niver make out the rights on. And all as we've got to do is to trusten, Master Marner – to do the right thing as far as we know, and to trusten.'

(Silas Marner, ch. 16)

The sense of Nature here can easily slide into the sense of God; the rustic characters, in their simplicity, make little distinction between the two. For that reason they are better mouthpieces of this aspect of George Eliot's vision of the world than more sophisticated characters, like Dorothea, whose religious intensities must suffer from a lack of theological definition. For what these characters are expressing is not a Christian viewpoint, but rather that resigned acceptance of one's relation to the general course of things which is so ingrained a part of George Eliot's sensibility and which is summed up by that most stoical of dramatists, George Chapman:

> A man to join himself with th' Universe
> In his main sway, and make (in all things fit)
> One with that All, and go on round as it;
> Not plucking from the whole his wretched part,
> And into straits, or into nought revet,
> Wishing the complete Universe might be
> Subject to such a rag of it as he;
> But to consider great Necessity
> All things as well refact as voluntary
> Reduceth to the prime celestial cause . . .
> (Revenge of Bussy d'Ambois, IV. 1)

In this sense, then, acquiescence in Nature is the mark of the wise man. But just as animal imagery may characterize both innocence and evil, so this acquiescence may be perverted into a belief in God, Providence, Luck, or Necessity as a way of absolving oneself from moral responsibility. This again is a distinguishing feature

167

of George Eliot's egoists; one remembers Bulstrode with his belief in a special Providence; one remembers Stephen Guest justifying his passion by an appeal to 'natural law' (*The Mill on the Floss*, VI, 14); one remembers Arthur Donnithorne:

> There was a sort of implicit confidence in him that he was really such a good fellow at bottom, Providence would not treat him harshly.
>
> (*Adam Bede*, ch. 29)

There is, then, no simple or schematic 'message' to be elicited from man's varying relations to Nature; the same imagery may carry very different significances; apparently similar attitudes may conceal profound opposites, innocence and ignorance, good and evil, insight and blindness. As George Eliot says:

> For if it be true that Nature at certain moments seems charged with a presentiment of one individual lot, must it not also be true that she seems unmindful, unconscious of another? There is no hour that has not its births of gladness and despair, no morning brightness that does not bring sickness to desolation as well as new forces to genius and love. There are so many of us, and our lots are so different; what wonder that Nature's mood is often in harsh contrast with the great crisis of our lives?
>
> (*Adam Bede*, ch. 27)

George Eliot has earned the right to talk of *Nature* in this way; it is no convenient abstraction, but rather the icon of that mysterious complexity of things which she enacts so concretely in the body of her fiction.

IV

Man and Society

Just as human nature contains animal nature, so the progress of Society is not uniform, but contains vestiges of its more primitive stages of development. The present is built upon historical strata, and these sometimes push through the surface – outcrops reminding us of our past. Moreover, the present is not uniform, but contains more or less sophisticated societies, coexisting at the same time. Some of these irregularities are charming, some ridiculous or pernicious; but in every case they remind us of that basic continuity of human life, that strict connection of present to past which is

implicit everywhere in George Eliot's fiction and which she celebrates most explicitly in the Proem to *Romola*:

> The great river-courses which have shaped the lines of men have hardly
> changed; and those other streams, the life-currents that ebb and flow
> in human hearts, pulsate to the same great needs, the same great loves
> and terrors. As our thought follows close in the slow wake of the dawn,
> we are impressed with the broad sameness of the human lot, which
> never alters in the main headings of its history – hunger and labour,
> seed-time and harvest, love and death.

One notices here the three-ply nature of our ideological thread; the
appropriateness of celebrating historical continuity in natural
terms, in metaphors of rivers, of tides, and of dawn yielding to day.
Romola is one of those many Victorian works which use history
as a mirror to show us our true selves; the spiritual crises of
fifteenth-century Florence are strikingly similar to those of Victorian
England. Whether the past society is mythically remote, as in the
Idylls of the King, or relatively close in time, as in *Middlemarch*,
the perspective of history is used to stress human continuity, sameness beneath change.

But often the historical mirror is slightly distorted in order to
focus our historical self-awareness in a particular way. We may
take Browning's 'Cleon' as an example. This poem, you will
remember, is a letter written by a man who sums up in himself
the whole of Hellenic culture, noble but decadent, almost rotten
in his ripeness. At the very end, almost as a postscript, the writer
of this epistle alludes to the writer of much more famous epistles:

> And for the rest
> I cannot tell thy messenger aright
> Where to deliver what he bears of thine
> To one called Paulus – we have heard his fame
> Indeed, if Christus be not one with him –
> I know not, nor am troubled much to know.

And he concludes:

> Their doctrines could be held by no sane man.

Now surely we would be wrong to take the irony of the work as
directed simply at Cleon; that would be to cheapen the poem. We
can enjoy the irony afforded us by historical hindsight, but surely
we ought also to recognize that the irony is directed by Browning

at himself and at his readers. Cleon, he says, is historically limited and blind to the great events of his epoch – but then so are we all. Who knows but that at this minute some modern equivalent of Paul is preaching apparently ludicrous doctrines in provincial obscurity? (And history may well tell us that there was such a one in Browning's England, his name being Karl Marx). 'Cleon', then, is a poem which implicitly contains the question later posed by Yeats:

> And what rough beast, its hour come round at last,
> Slouches towards Bethlehem to be born?

It is this kind of irony that informs a great deal of George Eliot's fiction: 'Consider, dear reader,' she seems to say, 'what atavisms your superior modernity conceals. When you declare my characters quaint, consider how quaint your descendants will think you. For "primitive fetish" read "status-symbol" and you will see how time gains its revenge. Your present, which seems so satisfyingly solid, is as evanescent as any society you glimpse in my novel. And you are more like these characters than you imagine; beneath your contemporary veneer there still lives a good deal that is ludicrously savage.' What seems to be a rather clumsy disquisition in *Middlemarch* makes this more explicit:

And here I am naturally led to reflect on the means of elevating a low subject. Historical parallels are remarkably efficient in this way. The chief objection to them is, that the diligent narrator may lack space or (what is often the same thing) may not be able to think of them with any degree of particularity, though he may have a philosophical confidence that if known they would be illustrative. It seems an easier and shorter way to dignity, to observe that – since there never was a true story which could not be told in parables where you might put a monkey for a margrave, and *vice-versa* – whatever has been or is to be narrated by me about low people, may be ennobled by being considered a parable; so that if any bad habits and ugly consequences are brought into view, the reader may have the relief of regarding them as not more than figuratively ungenteel, and may feel himself virtually in company with persons of some style. Thus while I tell the truth about loobies, my reader's imagination need not be entirely excluded from an occupation with lords; and the petty sums which any bankrupt of high standing would be sorry to retire upon, may be lifted to the level of high commercial transactions by the inexpensive addition of proportional ciphers.

As to any provincial history in which the agents are all of high moral rank, that must be of a date long posterior to the first Reform Bill, and Peter Featherstone, you perceive, was dead and buried some months before Lord Grey came into office.

(*Middlemarch*, ch. 35)

This may look clumsy because it *is* so explicit; yet the nature of the irony and the means of its control are rather more complicated than may at first sight appear. At first sight it appears that the author has withdrawn from her narrative and is inviting us to share with her the superiority of a distant and omniscient view. But it becomes clear, especially in the final sentence, that this is a confidence trick, that we have been betrayed into superiority only to have our share in common human foolishness brought home the more sharply to us. And if, with this realization, we look back at the passage we see that George Eliot is, in fact, laughing not just at us but also at herself — or rather, at the pompous kind of omniscient narration she is commonly but erroneously supposed to indulge in. From this point of view, the passage links up with those other self-deprecating comments on the author's rôle and privilege that are to be found throughout *Middlemarch*. (See, for example, the openings of Chapters 15, 41 and 59.) It is because of this that we feel no unfairness in the author's betrayal of our confidence, no sense that we are being merely manipulated by her. She admits that she, too, is involved in common human foolishness, in feeling complacent about the superiority of the present and its comfortable pretensions to historical hindsight. Thus this local passage enacts in miniature something which is basic to her view of the past: the idea that the present is equally vulnerable to time and change, that the beliefs and tastes of today may all too easily become the superstitions and grotesqueries of tomorrow. That the human species is not necessarily the culmination of the evolutionary process was not an uncommon idea in the nineteenth century, and nowhere could the truth of this be seen more clearly than in the speeded-up version of evolution that we call 'social change'.

The uncomfortable ironies of this historical self-awareness are most apparent in those aspects of life where change is most rapid — for instance, in the world of fashion. Thus Dorothea is described:

She would perhaps be hardly characterized enough if it were omitted that she wore her brown hair flatly braided and coiled behind so as to expose the outline of her head in a daring manner at a time when public feeling required the meagreness of Nature to be dissimulated by tall barricades of frizzed curls and bows, never surpassed by any great race except the Feejeean.

(Middlemarch, ch. 3)

Or, again, Mrs. Pullet (a roughly contemporaneous character):

It is a pathetic sight and a striking example of the complexity introduced into the emotions by a high state of civilization – the sight of a fashionably drest female in grief. From the sorrow of a Hottentot to that of a woman in large buckram sleeves, with several bracelets on each arm, an architectural bonnet, and delicate ribbon-strings – what a long series of graduations.

(The Mill on the Floss, I. 7)

But in no case is the joke merely at the expense of an earlier generation; it also includes a glance at George Eliot's readers, whether in the 1860s or the 1960s. We are all particular examples of the same human weakness and there is nothing new under the sun:

Mr. Tulliver was speaking to his wife, a blonde comely woman in a fan-shaped cap (I am afraid to think how long it is since fan-shaped caps were worn – they must be so near coming in again).

(The Mill on the Floss, I. 2)

In a more serious vein, George Eliot demonstrates how akin our most serious beliefs may be to the passions of our primitive ancestors. Religion, for example, may be only a highly rationalized form of superstition; as she says of Bulstrode, 'religion can only change when the emotions which fill it are changed; and the religion of personal fear remains nearly at the level of the savage' (*Middlemarch,* ch. 41). Like a faith in Providence, superstition may be a sign of moral corruption. But just as a blind trust in Fortune must be distinguished from a wise acceptance of Nature, so superstition is the obverse of something that is valuable, a primitive reverence that may be stultified by a more sophisticated culture. One recalls her comment on Darwinism:

To me the Development Theory and all other explanations of processes by which things came to be, produce a feeble impression compared with the mystery that lies under the processes.

(Letters, iii. 227)

A response to the mystery of things, together with the sense of awe and wonder that it produces, is one of the great human sanctities for George Eliot. As a man may be both wise and foolish, so he can also be shrewd, superstitious, and reverent; just how closely these qualities are intermingled, George Eliot demonstrates in her characterization of Adam Bede:

> Adam was not a man to be gratuitously superstitious; but he had the blood of the peasant in him as well as of the artisan, and a peasant can no more help believing in a traditional superstition than a horse can help trembling when he sees a camel. Besides, he had that mental combination which is at once humble in the region of mystery, and keen in the region of knowledge; it was the depth of his reverence quite as much as his hard common sense which gave him his disinclination to doctrinal religion, and he often checked Seth's argumentative spiritualism by saying, 'Eh, it's a big mystery; thee know'st but little about it.' And so it happened that Adam was at once penetrating and credulous. If a new building had fallen down and he had been told that this was a divine judgement, he would have said, 'Maybe: but the bearing o' the roof and walls wasn't right, else it wouldn't ha' come down'; yet he believed in dreams and prognostics, and to his dying day he bated his breath a little when he told the story of the stroke with the willow wand. I tell it as he told it, not attempting to reduce it to its natural elements: in our eagerness to explain impressions, we often lose our hold of the sympathy that comprehends them.
>
> (*Adam Bede*, ch. 4)

There is much that could be stressed here: the dig at doctrinal religion, the related fear that explanation may involve explaining away, the link between a reverence open to mystery and an understanding sympathy. But notice also the three-ply nature of our ideological thread, how what is valuably primitive in man is linked, by the analogy with horse and camel, to that idea of humanity as part of a natural continuum which we explored in a previous section.

Somewhere in her letters George Eliot wrote:

> I am reading about savages and semi-savages and think that our religious oracles would do well to study savage ideas by a method of comparison with our own.

This is much more than a plea for the study of comparative religion. It betrays, too, an awareness of how much modern society owes, both for good and for ill, to its primitive origins; an awareness that is everywhere implicit in the fabric of her fiction.

V

Man and Childhood

Since analysis must work through artificial categories, I have been at pains to stress what I called the three-ply nature of our ideological thread. We have already seen several instances where the imagery links the civilized and the primitive, the historical and the natural, as part of the same evolutionary continuum. The wise acceptance of Nature is one with the reverent sense of the mysterious; the superstition of the savage is one with the blind faith in an absolving Providence. Such images connect the moral to the natural life, and yet make the necessary discriminations:

> The theory that unusual virtue spring by a direct consequence out of personal disadvantages, as animals get thicker wool in severe climates, is perhaps a little overstressed.
>
> (*The Mill on the Floss*, V.3)

And such imagery also characterizes the society as well as the individual; it is no accident that St. Oggs should be described thus:

> And the present time was like the broad plain where men lose their belief in volcanoes and earthquakes, thinking tomorrow will be as yesterday and the giant forces that used to shake the earth are for ever laid to sleep.
>
> (I. 12)

It is because of the spiritual torpor of this society that George Eliot can characterize their religion; although 'that belief in the Unseen, so far as it manifests itself at all, seems to be rather of a pagan kind', yet 'a vigorous superstition, that lashes its gods or its own back, seems to be more congruous with the mystery of the human lot than the mental condition of these emmet-like Dodsons and Tullivers' (IV. 1).

Human and natural, moral and animal, civilized and primitive are all interwoven in such images. So it is not surprising that the sense in which the adult recapitulates the child should also be linked with the ideas of the natural and the primitive. The notion that children are young animals/savages is not, after all, an uncommon point of view.

So we have young Maggie with her Fetish doll (I. 4): unlike St. Oggs, she lashes her gods and later – metaphorically – lashes her own back in the ardour of her renunciation. Or again:

> Yap . . . had also been looking on while the eatables vanished, with an agitation of his ears and feelings which could hardly have been without bitterness. Yet the excellent dog accepted Tom's attention with as much alacrity as if he had been treated quite generously.
>
> But Maggie, gifted with that superior power of misery which distinguishes the human being and places him at a proud distance from the most melancholy chimpanzee, sat still on her bough, and gave herself up to the keen sense of unmerited reproach.
>
> (I. 6)

Yet her tears flow for only 'the next ten minutes'; in the brevity of her ecstasies and agonies she is only slightly distinguished in degree from Yap. It is in more than mere appearance that George Eliot can describe her several times as a young puppy, 'a Skye terrier', 'a rough, overgrown puppy' to Lucy's 'kitten' nature.

But it is the persistence of childhood into adult life that must concern us here. We know that, as we grow up, maturity is not something we arrive at, a fixed destination. Maturity is not an even, undivided front, but a shifting process, broken by great salients where we may advance or regress. We know that we are mixed creatures: at some points mature, at other points adolescent, at yet other points simply childish. Most of us, I imagine, would agree that this is a matter of both gain and loss, consolation and regret, strength and weakness. George Eliot mirrors this in her fiction; one of her great strengths as a novelist is her sense of how we all carry our childhood within us. And she knows that, like the other two strands of the thread we have so far unravelled, this recapitulation of childhood can bear opposing moral significances. By using it she can point both similitude and difference, can simultaneously correct and discriminate.

If we decompose the notion of *childhood* we see that it contains related components that we may call *childlike* and *childish*. On the one side it signals innocence, intensity, generosity, spontaneity. Because it borders helplessness, it can command compassion. But on the other side it signals ignorance, selfishness, temper, unreflecting egoism. In a child it is natural and tolerable, partly because the child's emotional life is characterized by brevity – the tantrum doesn't last. But if these childish qualities are combined with the

175

persistence of the adult, then the results may be terrifying. We don't need William Golding's *Lord of the Flies* to tell us that.

We have only to think of Hetty Sorrel to see how George Eliot combined these two sets of qualities and mingled the two kinds of response that they evoke. Maggie Tulliver is a slightly more complicated case. I am not thinking so much of the description of her literal childhood, which foreshadows so much that is to come. It is partly because her early life is so solidly created that the subsequent references to childhood gain such a resonance. And these allusions work both ways; her relation to Stephen Guest is consistently characterized in terms of childishness. The examples are individually so slight, but cumulatively so frequent as not to need quotation here; but, taken together, they bear out Philip Wakem's warning to her:

> 'You will be thrown into the world some day, and then every rational satisfaction of your nature that you deny now, will assault you like a savage appetite.'
>
> (V. 3)

But if *childish* characterizes the Maggie-Stephen relationship, then *childlike* has already characterized the Maggie-Philip relationship, and this note is resumed at the very end of the book in the reconciliation of Maggie and Tom. We are told that –

> There had arisen in Tom a repulsion towards Maggie that derived its very intensity from their early childish love in the time when they had clasped their tiny fingers together.
>
> (VII. 3)

But what separates them also unites them; the sentence I have just quoted is surely answered by the moment when they drown,

> living through again in one supreme moment the days when they had clasped their little hands in love, and roamed the daisied fields together.
>
> (VII. 5)

The echo could hardly be clearer; at whatever risk of sentimentality, *childlike* has met and conquered *childish*. Yet for all its fine inevitability, and for all the cunning, aesthetic means by which it has been contrived, do we not feel a question hovering over the end of *The Mill on the Floss*? Is there not some evasion here, some regression on George Eliot's part from the problems of adult life? Does she, after all, manage to control the conflicting impulses of the two senses of childhood? The question recurs when we consider the relation of Dorothea Brooke to Will Ladislaw in *Middlemarch*. Most critics have felt that this is one of the weakest parts of the novel. While there is no single cause for George Eliot's failure here, one contributory reason may be that she failed to control the two streams of meaning that diverge from the word *childhood*, that some of the negative implications of the word (i.e. *childish*) infect some of the positive associations (i.e. *childlike*).

The Will-Dorothea relationship must, of course, be seen in conjunction with two very powerful portraits of the way in which the childish ego can persist into adult life. The first, and less damaging, case is that of Fred Vincy; he is redeemed partly by the quasi-paternal figures of Galeb Garth and Mr. Farebrother, but mainly by Mary Garth, of whom we are told:

> There is often something maternal even in a girlish love, and Mary's hard experience had wrought her nature of an impressibility very different from that hard slight thing which we call girlishness.
>
> (ch. 25)

In this Mary contrasts with the Dorothea of the novel's outset; but mainly she contrasts with Rosamond Vincy. For where Fred is malleable, his sister is cast in a fixed mould of selfish indifference, of cold neutrality, of moral triviality. It is interesting that when Rosamond rises from her habitual egoism into moments of naturalness or generosity, these are also conveyed by drawing on the associations of childhood. The first of these – innocently destructive in its results – is the moment of disappointment which leads to her engagement to Lydgate:

> At this moment she was as natural as she had ever been when she was five years old; she felt that her tears had risen, and that it was no use to try to do anything else than let them stay like water on a blue flower or let them fall over her cheeks, even as they would.
>
> (ch. 31)

Balancing this, in strikingly similar terms, is the moment when she tells Dorothea the truth about Will's feelings for her:

> Her eyes met Dorothea's as helplessly as if they had been blue flowers. What was the use of thinking about behaviour after this crying? And Dorothea looked almost childish, with the neglected trace of a silent tear.
>
> (ch. 81)

But Rosamond cannot sustain this; she lapses almost at once to the childish 'he cannot reproach me any more', and we are left with Lydgate's vision of his future with her:

> He had chosen this fragile creature, and had taken the burthen of her life upon his arms. He must walk as he could, carrying that burthen pitifully.
>
> (ch. 81)

But Lydgate's image of a parent cradling a child is wrong; we know how indestructibly tough this 'fragile creature' really is.

Only a few *childlike* associations, then, offset the mass of negative *childish* associations clustering around Rosamond. With Dorothea the process is reversed, but at the outset *childish* associations cling to her too, reinforcing her ardent, theoretic nature, turning innocence into ignorance. At the outset she repeats the fatal flaw in the Lydgate-Rosamond marriage; she 'retained very childlike ideas about marriage . . . the really delightful marriage must be that where your husband was a sort of father' (ch. 1). Casaubon 'was being unconsciously wrought upon by the charms of a nature which was entirely without hidden calculations either for immediate effects or for remoter ends. It was this which made Dorothea so childlike and, according to some judges, so stupid, with all her reputed cleverness' (ch. 5). When her marriage to Casaubon goes wrong, it is for Dorothea in terms that recall for us Maggie Tulliver's passion for her Fetish doll: 'if she could have fed her affections with those childlike caresses which are the bent of every sweet woman, who has begun by showering kisses on the hard pate of her bald doll' (ch. 20). In these two last examples I think we can sense George Eliot beginning to feel uneasy about her control over the *childish* associations clustering around Dorothea. The first example is as much a limiting judgment on those who think Dorothea stupid as on Dorothea herself, while the second smuggles in a generalizing clause, 'which are the bent of every sweet woman'. She has good cause to feel worried, for in switching from Dorothea-Casaubon to Dorothea-Will she has to switch from negative to positive, from *childish* to *childlike*. Thus we find Dorothea and Will 'looking at each other like two fond children who were talking confidentially of birds' (ch. 39). And later, at the crisis of their love:

> Dorothea darted instantaneously from the window; Will followed her,

seizing her hand with a spasmodic movement; and so they stood, with their hands clasped, like two children, looking out on the storm.

(ch. 83)

It is not enough to write this off as mere sentimentality. The problem is this: Dorothea is shown as maturing through the painful education of her marriage to Casaubon. She is shown as growing out of her initial childishness. Consequently, however hard George Eliot tries to switch from *childish* to *childlike*, Dorothea's subsequent love for Will must be felt as a regression from her hard-won maturity. A similar possible regression at the end of *The Mill on the Floss* is abruptly checked by the fact of death; but here there is no check, no death. We are left with a gesture towards a childlike wonder and innocence; but the childlike has already been so contaminated by the negative implications of the childish that George Eliot can only, via Will Ladislaw, take refuge in a totally inaequate and unreal image of that archetypal childhood state, Paradise:

All their vision, all their thought of each other, had been as in a world apart, where the sunshine fell on tall white lilies, where no evil lurked, and no other soul entered. But now – would Dorothea meet him in that world again?

(ch. 82)

Alas, they meet in that world again all too easily. Dorothea has experienced her fall from innocence to experience, has lost her Paradise in her marriage to Casaubon. She is allowed much too comfortably her Paradise Regained.

We have been beguiled into criticism. But the main purpose of this essay has been descriptive, not evaluative – to see how one idea ramifies and diversifies throughout George Eliot's fiction. It has been an attempt to follow just one contour in her imaginative terrain. In doing so we have allowed one particular biological idea to branch and grow, by metaphor and analogy, into very diverse areas of experience. This, I would plead, is a better way of getting to know the shape and feel of George Eliot's world than the precise cause-and-effect relationship desired by the strict intellectual historian. It allows us to see, for example, how George Eliot can discriminate complex and overlapping moral states, how each mutation of the idea carries within it both positive and negative charges. Above all, it helps us to respond to that sense of the interconnectedness of things of which George Eliot wrote in *The Mill on the Floss*:

The suffering, whether of martyr or victim, which belongs to every historical advance of mankind, is represented in this way in every town, and by hundreds of obscure hearths; and we need not shrink from this comparison of small things with great; for does not science tell us that its highest striving is after ascertainment of a unity which shall bind the smallest things with the greatest? In natural science, I have understood, there is nothing petty to the mind that has a large vision of relations, and to which every single object suggests a vast sum of conditions. It is surely the same with the observation of human life.

(IV. 1)

VI

So far we have followed just one thread in the 'tangled skein'. I have been concerned to stress what I called its 'three-ply' nature; I have tried to show that it stretches through very diverse areas of experience, and I have argued that it leads us to understand the interconnectedness of George Eliot's world, her sense of 'the mysterious complexity of things'. But in what ways, precisely, does it do this? How can we infer the whole 'tangled skein' from one single thread? What are the modes of connection? The rest of this essay will explore two possible answers to these questions.

One reason why we may sense the tangled skein in the single thread is because the idea – that man is what was, summing up in his present his threefold past – and its accompanying imagery may figure in the background of our minds when we are responding to other, apparently quite disparate themes in the novels. Earlier in this essay I said that, stated generally, the idea gives a resonance to some of George Eliot's most deeply felt convictions; to her statement in *Adam Bede*, for example, that:

> A certain consciousness of our entire past and our imagined future blends itself with all our moments of keen sensibility . . . the secret of our emotions never lies in the bare object, but in its subtle relations to our past.

Certainly one of George Eliot's central themes is the dependence of our moral natures upon our sense of time, our present deeds and feelings stretching out into the past and the future, into the worlds of cause and consequence. But what is meant when I say that the idea and imagery of recapitulation 'gives a resonance' to this theme? In trying to answer this question, I shall concentrate mainly on one novel, *The Mill on the Floss*.

The theme is clearly central to the novel, with an especial stress on the importance of childhood:

> Every one of those keen moments has left its trace, and lives in us still, but such traces have blent themselves irrecoverably with the firmer texture of our youth and manhood.
>
> (I. 7)

> There is no sense of ease like the ease we felt in those scenes where we were born, where objects became due to us before we had known the labour of choice, and where the outer world seemed only an extension of our own personality: we accepted and loved it as we accepted our own sense of existence and our own limbs. Very commonplace, even ugly, that furniture of our early home might look if it were put up to auction; an improved taste in upholstery scorns it; and is it not the striving after something better and better in our surroundings, the grand characteristic that distinguishes man from the brute – or, to satisfy a scrupulous accuracy of definition, that distinguishes the British man from the foreign brute? But heaven knows where that striving might lead us, if our affections had not a trick of twining round those old inferior things – if the loves and sanctities of our life had no deep immovable roots in memory.
>
> (II. 1)

There is a good deal that is by now familiar about these passages: the relation of past to present, the mocking glance *via* British insularity at the animal bases of human nature, the natural metaphors of *twining* and *roots*. The latter especially is a key-word; 'Things out o' natur niver thrive,' says Luke, and one remembers Hetty Sorrel, who puts herself beyond Nature:

> There are some plants that have hardly any roots; you may tear them from their native nook of rock or wall, and just lay them over your ornamental flower-pot, and they blossom none the worse. Hetty could have cast all her past life behind her, and never cared to be reminded of it again.
>
> (*Adam Bede*, ch. 15)

To lose one's roots is to lose that sense of oneself as part of the continuum of things, to blind oneself to that sense of looking before and after which is so necessary for maturity. It is part of the mysterious complexity of things that George Eliot sees our adult selves as rooted in the essentially pre-moral world of childhood, 'before we had known the labour of choice'. Continuity is vital; for Maggie 'to have no cloud between herself and Tom was still a perpetual yearning in her, that had its root deeper than change' (VI. 12). For out of childhood comes that unreflecting sense of unity and interconnectedness which the reflective adult must see as altruism or sympathy, a principle to be consciously striven for. Yet continuity is not sameness; merely to extend the pre-moral life of childhood into the adult world is disastrous. For the child is also a simple ego, with little sense of cause or consequence. Like an animal, like a savage, his moods and passions are intense but fugitive, lacking that necessary sense of time before and time after. Both these sides of childhood the paradoxical blend – of strength and weakness – are beautifully poised in the one phrase, 'where the world seemed only an extension of our own personality'.

The child, then, sees and feels only the present; when George Eliot stresses this as a characteristic of adult life, it nearly always betokens a moral disaster. It may affect an individual or a society; at his breakdown, Mr. Tulliver loses all sense of time; St. Ogg's, because it is narrow, provincial and sluggish, 'did not look extensively before or after. It inherited a long past without thinking of it, and had no eyes for the spirits that walked its streets' (II. 12). But, of course, the crucial case is Maggie, particularly in her relationship with Stephen Guest.

Maggie, even as a child, is a special case. Although she shares the transient intensities of childhood, there is more to her than that:

> Maggie rushed to her deeds with passionate impulse, and then saw not only their consequences, but what would have happened if they had not been done, with all the detail and exaggerated circumstance of an active imagination.
>
> (I. 7)

It is largely this intensity, this impetuousness combined with imagination, that differentiates her from Tom, who exemplifies the strength and limitations of a willed narrowness:

> A character at unity with itself – that performs what it intends, subdues every counteracting impulse, and has no visions beyond the distinctly possible – is strong by its very negations.
>
> (V. 2)

Impetuousness in childhood will lead to nothing worse than pushing Lucy into the mud or cropping one's hair; imagination will lead to nothing worse than a romantic notion of oneself as Queen of the Gipsies. But, unchecked in adult life, they lead to disaster. Imagination, in particular, is an equivocal faculty. On the one side it may become the great moral agent, leading to that sympathetic extension of ourselves in which we transcend egoism. Thus Maggie is able to respond to Thomas à Kempis and to see herself as part of a larger continuum:

> For the first time she saw the possibility of shifting the position from which she looked at the gratification of her own desires, of taking her stand out of herself, and looking at her own life as an insignificant part of a divinely-guided whole . . . it remains to all time a lasting reward of human needs and human consolations; the voice of a brother who, ages ago, felt and suffered and renounced – in the cloister, perhaps, with serge gown and tonsured head, with much chanting and long fasts, and with a fashion of speech different from ours – but under the same silent far-off heavens, and with the same passionate desires, the same strivings, the same failures, the same weariness.
>
> (IV. 3)

Maggie recapitulates history; yet at the same time we know that there is something factitious in her response to Thomas à Kempis. Imagination may be a source of weakness as well as of strength; it may seem to consider future consequences only in fact to warp them to present desires:

> If we only look far enough off for the consequences of our actions, we can always find some point in the combination of results by which those actions can be justified; by adopting the point of a view of a Providence who arranges results, or of a philosopher who traces them, we shall find it possible to obtain perfect complacency in choosing to do what is most agreeable to us in the present moment.
>
> (V. 3)

This is written of Philip Wakem, but it is surely equally true of the temptation presented to Maggie by Stephen Guest. If one can rationalize one's passions, if one can see them as providential and appeal like Stephen to 'a law of nature', then one can easily abandon oneself to drifting down the stream, to being 'borne along by the tide'. I said earlier that the Maggie-Stephen Guest relationship is characterized by a resurgence of childhood imagery. It is also characterized by the childhood impulse to 'live in the present':

> She was absorbed in the direct, immediate experience, without any energy left for taking account of it, and reasoning about it.
>
> (VI. 6)

> Thought did not belong to that enchanted haze in which they were enveloped – it belonged to the past and the future that lay outside the haze.
>
> (VI. 13)

And, of course, it is in these terms that Maggie's moral recovery is characterized. It is part of the argument with which she counters Stephen's temptation:

> 'If the past is not to bind us, where can duty lie? We should have no law but the inclination of the moment . . . we can only choose whether we will indulge ourselves in the present, or whether we will renounce that, for the sake of obeying the divine voice within us – for the sake of being true to the motives that sanctify our lives.'
>
> (VI. 14)

The lesson is generalized by the moral spokesman of the novel, Dr. Kenn; she has escaped from something that he sees as part of the world around him:

> 'At present everything seems tending towards the relaxation of ties – towards the substitution of wayward choice for the adherence to obligation, which has its roots in the past.'
>
> (VII. 2)

As we have seen the resurgence of the childish (Maggie-Stephen) is finally answered by the resurgence of childlike reunion (Maggie-Tom). Maturity is a mingled affair; it recapitulates both aspects of childhood experience. But as we grow up we emerge from the child's 'strangely perspectiveless conception of life' (I. 7), and one of the main perspectives by which our moral life shapes itself for us is the awareness of ourselves in time, as creatures caught in the tangled web of past and future, cause and consequence.

VII

I hope I have shown how our initial three-ply thread (the idea of recapitulation in its widest sense) connects with another strand (the temporal nature of our moral life) in the whole 'tangled skein' of George Eliot's fiction. (In doing so we have touched on yet other strands – the nature of imagination, for example – to which I will return.) But these two ideas, though distinct, are after all closely related. If George Eliot's vision of the world is unified in her novels, then ideally it should be possible to start with a totally different idea and its associated imagery, and to show how it entwines itself, both ideologically and linguistically, with the imaginative patterns we have already unravelled. This I shall now attempt to do.

One of the great, commonplace images by which man has explored his sense of himself and his rôle in the world is best expressed in the speech beginning 'All the world's a stage' from *As You Like It*. Though simple, the famous speech is part of a fairly complicated dramatic situation; we have Jacques, a character within the play, commenting on life in terms of an extended analogy between the real world and the theatre. It is as though he has turned the tables on the normal relation between actor and audience. 'You sitting out there in the theatre,' he is implicitly saying, 'you think you are merely watching a play. But what if you, too, are characters in some great drama of life; if you, like me, are acting out you rôle? If this is so, then you and I are brothers and what you are enjoying as a fiction is really a true image of your own condition.'

This notion – that the world *is* a stage and that we are all acting out our parts in the great drama of life – has a very long history; it can be traced as least as far back as the Stoic philosophers of ancient Greece. Jacques is in fact a mouthpiece – part serious, part comic – of Stoicism. Just as a dramatist creates his play, the argument runs, so God creates the world and allots to all of us our respective rôles. (Or for God, read Evolution or Historical Necessity.) This would be a very pessimistic notion – it implies that our parts are predetermined, written for us. Indeed, this speech of Jacques is filled with a profound melancholy, though his character as a whole is subjected to comedy. But the point of this notion is primarily a moral one – even if our parts are written for us, then how well we play them will depend on us alone. The analogy preserves man's moral dignity and significance; we can still tell a good actor from a bad actor, a good man from a bad man.

The image of the stage can also bear a metaphysical significance; Plato saw the empirical world as the shadow or imperfect imitation of the real, divine world of eternal Ideas and Forms. In these terms, just as the play is an imitation of our lives, so our lives in turn are the reflection of some further reality. This speculation lies perhaps behind Prospero's great speech in *The Tempest*:

> Our revels now are ended. These our actors,
> As I foretold you, were all spirits and
> Are melted into air, into thin air;
> And, like the baseless fabric of this vision,
> The cloud-capp'd towers, the gorgeous palaces,
> The solemn temples, the great globe itself,
> Yea, all which it inherit, shall dissolve
> And, like this insubstantial pageant faded,
> Leave not a rack behind.

Not unnaturally, these ideas and their associated images entered the novel as it developed. It would take far too long to trace their history, and I mention the point only to stress that they would have been commonplace by the time George Eliot came to write. But I would like to glance briefly at their use by one of her immediate predecessors, Thackeray. Most reviewers compared the two novelists, particularly in their handling of the omniscient mode of narration. In both cases the notion of life as drama plays an important part. The *persona* of the omniscient author was a part-real, part-dramatic creation, standing in much the same relation to the novels as Jacques does to *As You Like It*. Jacques, not Shakespeare; for where the dramatist is totally invisible behind his creation, the novelist sets the scene, self-consciously comments on the plot, and expatiates on his characters.

Many critics, Victorian and modern, have felt this intrusive commentary to be a flaw, yet Thackeray – like George Eliot – can sometimes triumphantly turn it to advantage. For, as Professor Tillotson in his study, *Thackeray the Novelist*, points out: 'Thackeray is an author who writes for the common reader. The common reader does not find it difficult to stay inside the novels which include . . . the showman on the edge of his stage.'

Professor Tillotson is, of course, alluding to the prologue to *Vanity Fair*, called 'Before the curtain', an extreme instance of Thackeray's deliberate intrusion into his work. The novel begins:

> As the Manager of the Performance sits before the curtain on the boards, and looks into the Fair, a feeling of profound melancholy comes over him in his survey of the bustling place. There is a great

quantity of eating and drinking, making love and jilting, laughing
and the contrary, smoking, cheating, fighting, dancing, and fiddling:
there are bullies pushing about, bucks ogling the women, knaves
picking pockets, policemen on the look-out, quacks (*other* quacks,
plague take them!) bawling in front of their booths, and yokels looking up at the tinselled dancers and poor old rouged tumblers, while
the light-fingered folk are operating upon their pockets behind. Yes,
this is VANITY FAIR; not a moral place certainly; nor a merry one,
though very noisy. Look at the faces of the actors and buffoons when
they come off from their business; and Tom Fool washing the paint
off his cheeks before he sits down to dinner with his wife and the
little Jack Puddings behind the canvas. The curtain will be up pre-
sently, and he will be turning over head and heels, and crying 'How
are you?'

This prologue, with its melancholy, is echoed in the famous conclusion of the novel:

Ah! *Vanitas Vanitatum!* Which of us is happy in this world? Which
of us has his desire? or, having it, is satisfied? – Come children, let
us shut up the box and the puppets, for our play is played out.

The effect here is surely akin to Prospero's speech; 'Our revels
now are ended' – the same note is struck. But when in *The Tempest*
this note may sound a metaphysical theme, in *Vanity Fair*, as we
might expect, it is the moral note as struck by Jacques which predominates. For the novel deals primarily with moral issues, with the
nature of man in society, and only rarely concerns itself with
metaphysical speculation. Certainly one of the unavoidable themes
of fiction if that of appearance and reality – but reality here refers
not to Platonic Forms but to the essentially human reality which is
disguised by the various masks man adopts in society. Man plays
many rôles on this great stage of life, the novelist says, but let us
strip off his grease paint and see him as he really is. But seeing him
as he really is involves the perceiver as well; the narrator must be
present as 'the showman on the edge of his stage', just as Jacques is
both character and commentator. It is through this deliberately self-
conscious, self-involving kind of fiction that Thackeray also impli-
cates the reader in the moral life of his characters. I take as typical
an example from *The Newcomes*. The narrator, nominally Arthur
Pendennis, is dilating on the truism that our status in life determines the view that other people take of us. He is speculating on the
motives behind Miss Honeyman's kindness to her nephew, Clive

Newcome, and extends this to take in the treatment of Clive by his other aunt, Mrs. Newcome:

> Is it gratitude for past favours? is it desire for more? is it vanity of relationship? is it love for the dead sister, or tender regard for her offspring, which makes Miss Martha Honeyman so fond of her nephew? I would never count how many causes went to produce any given effect or action in a person's life, and have been for my part many a time quite misled by my own case, fancying some grand, some magnanimous, some virtuous reason, for an act of which I was proud, when lo, some pert little satirical monitor springs up inwardly, upsetting the fond humbug which I was cherishing. . . . In a word, Aunt Honeyman was a kind soul, and such was the splendour of Clive's father . . . that the lad really did appear a young duke to her. And Mrs. Newcome was not unkind; and if Clive had really been a young duke, I am sure he would have had the best bedroom at Marble Head, and not one of the far-off little rooms in the boys' wing; I am sure he would have had jellies . . . instead of mere broth . . . and when he was gone . . . I am sure Mrs. Newcome would have written a letter to Her Grace the Duchess Dowager, his mamma, full of praise of the dear child, his graciousness, his beauty and his wit, and declaring that she must love him henceforth and forever as a son of her own. You toss down the page with scorn, and say, 'It is not true. Human nature is not so bad as this cynic would have it to be. *You* make no difference between the rich and the poor.' Be it so. *You* would not. But own that your next-door neighbour would. Nor is this, dear madam, addressed to you; no, no, we are not so rude as to talk about you to your face; but if we may not speak of the lady who has just left the room, what is to become of conversation and society?

The point I wish to stress about this apparent digression in the novel is the way in which the narrator's commentary extends out in a steady radiation. At first he simply comments on the mixed motives of Miss Honeyman; then he broadens his perspective to include himself, 'the showman of the edge of his stage', and to analyse his own mixed motives and lack of self-knowledge. Next he returns to Clive's other aunt, Mrs. Newcome, and lays bare the hypocrisy which derives from *her* lack of self-knowledge. Finally, he addresses the reader directly and involves him in the same moral question: Does the reader know himself any better than the narrator or the characters know themselves? '*Hypocrite lecteur, mon semblable, mon frère!*' — it is in this way that the self-conscious work of art may act upon the reader. Thackeray's novel says in effect, 'You read me as mere fiction. But look in your own hearts and if you are honest you will have to admit, dear reader, that you are no better and no worse than the characters I contain.' If all the world is a stage, then actors and audience are united in the community of human virtues and failings. Thus, far from being an intrusive flaw, Thackeray's performance as stage manager is necessary for the success of his art and of his moral purpose. By his deliberate, self-regarding showmanship he does directly what Shakespeare does obliquely through a character like Jacques; he opens the frontiers between the worlds of literature and life so that actor and audience, character and reader, may more easily communicate and interact.

I have discussed Thackeray's use of omniscient narration at some length, partly because I did not wish to repeat what I have said elsewhere about this aspect of George Eliot, partly because I wished to stress that there was a tradition of narration which she inherited and modified, a tradition which had already made use of the anlogy between life and drama. Surely we can say that her use of the convention is strikingly like that of Thackeray? In both cases, like the speech of Jacques, it expands, radiates, involves both author and reader in the fiction world. Thackeray envied Henry Fielding for his freedom and George Eliot echoes that envy in an image drawn from the life of the theatre. Fielding, she says:

> glories in his copious remarks and digressions as the least imitable parts of his work, and especially in those initial chapters to the successive books of his history, where he seems to bring his arm-chair to the proscenium.
>
> (*Middlemarch*, ch. 15)

It is the 'showman at the edge of his stage' all over again. Moreover, the stoicism and the melancholy inherent in the life-stage analogy would accord naturally with George Eliot's temperament. The rôle of the actor contained within the play of life would adapt very well to George Eliot's vision of man as both free and yet determined. To this point I will return later.

We must, first of all, deal with the more obvious and local ways in which the life-drama analogy manifests itself in George Eliot's fiction. For, like Thackeray's, her novels are full of imagery and other linguistic patterns which depend on the basic idea, 'All the world's a stage'. These linguistic patterns naturally vary a great deal in importance and function. At one end of the scale they may become part of the literal narrative, enacting what images can only suggest, just as the conclusion of *The Mill on the Floss* enacts the proleptic images of flood and natural catastrophe. The most important example of this is perhaps Lydgate's youthful infatuation with the actress, Madame Laure. They may take the form of allusion, in which the sense of similitude or disparity, or a mixture of both, may be the important factor. Thus Mr. Tulliver is linked with Hotspur; Maggie with Sir Andrew Aguecheek; Dorothea with Antigone and Imogen. They may take the form of fully developed images (and here, I think, we must allow in as a reinforcing-thread images which refer to other areas of the imaginative life – to life seen as romantic fiction, for example). And, finally, they may reside in very quiet, neutral words – words like *scene* or *theatre* or *tragic* – which in themselves have no great analogical potential, but which may gain a quasi-metaphoric charge from being put into relation with cognate but more sophisticated linguistic patterns.

One need hardly do more than cite a representative example of what I have called neutral words. They generally indicate one of three things – the perturbations of the mind, the liveliness of the imagination, or the implication of the characters in the great general course of human nature and society. Thus, of the first, 'Maggie was . . . intensely conscious of some drama going forward in her father's mind' (*The Mill on the Floss*, III. 9); of the second, 'Hetty, her cheeks flushed and her eyes glistening from her imaginary drama' (*Adam Bede*, ch. 15); of the third, 'the tragedy of human life' (*Adam Bede*, ch. 33, but a frequently-repeated phrase) or 'War, like other dramatic spectacles might possibly cease for want of a public' (*The Mill on the Floss*, II. 4). Such instances as these have a double function: as we shall see, they may serve to extend the life-drama analogy to even more neutral terms – words that, taken in isolation, might be thought to have nothing to do with the analogy. And they also provide a base from which George Eliot can slide unobtrusively into rather more developed images illustrating the same point. Thus: 'the stranger who had been interested in the course of her sermon, as if it had been the development of a drama – for there is this sort of fascination in all sincere unpremeditated eloquence, which opens to one the inward drama of the speaker's emotions' (*Adam Bede*, ch. 2); 'There were passions at war in Maggie at that moment to have made a tragedy, if tragedy were made by passion only, but the essential τι μέγεθος which was present in the passion was wanting in the action' (*The Mill on the Floss*, I. 10); ' his mind seemed as passive as a spectator at a diorama; scenes of the sad past, and probably sad future, floating before him' (*Adam Bede*, ch. 4); 'inartistic figures crowding the canvas of life without adequate effect . . . play no small part in the tragedy of life' (*Adam Bede*, ch. 5); 'plotting covetousness and deliberate contrivance, in order to compass a selfish end, are nowhere abundant but in the world of the dramatist; they demand too intense a mental action for many of our fellow-parishioners to be guilty of them' (*The Mill on the Floss*, I. 3). It will be obvious from this last example that I consider the life-drama analogy works in terms of distinctions as well as similitude. George Eliot is careful to point out the ways in which all the world is *not* a stage. This is important in several ways – for example, some of her characters come to grief because they think of life wrongly in terms of this analogy. But when she points out the ways in which life is not a stage, she brings to our minds those points where the analogy is valid and, because of her careful discrimination, convinces us the more easily of their validity.

In isolation, such images as these would be of little significance. But, like Thackeray, George Eliot uses the life-drama analogy to point one of her main moral themes. Appearance and reality is a well-nigh universal tension in fiction, but George Eliot is particularly concerned to point out the dangers in the self-dramatizing, narcissistic nature of her egoists. These characters see life as conforming to their own wishes and imagine themselves at the centre of the stage. The novel in which this plays least part is *Silas Marner*; the most important instance – which I have analysed elsewhere – is the rôle of Gwendolen Harleth in *Daniel Deronda*. But the idea and its associated imagery are fairly consistent throughout George Eliot's fiction. One remembers Hetty Sorrel spinning her romantic dreams; she finds a fit partner in Arthur Donnithorne:

'It's a little drama I've got up in honour of my friend Adam. He's a fine fellow and I like the opportunity of letting people know that I think so.'
'A drama in which friend Arthur piques himself on having a pretty part to play,' said Mr Irwine, smiling.

(*Adam Bede*, ch. 22)

Throughout the novel Arthur is 'too much preoccupied with the part he was playing' (*Adam Bede*, ch. 27). Again, one remembers that even in the ardour of Maggie's renunciation 'her own life was still a drama for her, in which she demanded that her part should be played with intensity' (*The Mill on the Floss*, IV. 3). Or one thinks of that 'charming stage Ariadne', Rosamond Vincy: 'she even acted her own character, and so well, that she did not know it to be precisely her own' (*Middlemarch*, ch. 12). In this one may perhaps link her with Madame Laure, in whose murder of her husband intention is not to be distinguished from theatrical performance. (If Madame Laure murders her husband quickly, then Rosamond's marriage to Lydgate is a slow-motion murder, as Lydgate comes close to recognizing in Chapter 81). The distinguishing feature of this analogy as it is used in *Middlemarch* is that it is applied impartially to all the characters. Thus Casaubon is uneasily aware of the 'cold, shadowy, unapplausive audience of his life' (ch. 20) and much the same thing – though the effects are opposite – applies to Fred Vincy:

> Even much stronger mortals than Fred Vincy hold half their rectitude in the mind of the being they love best. 'The theatre of all my action is fallen,' said an antique personage when his chief friend was dead; and they are fortunate who get a theatre where the audience demands their best.
>
> (ch. 24)

The analogy is even used to check any idealization of hero and heroine. There is more than a grain of truth in Mrs. Cadwallader's remark about Dorothea's propensity for martyrdom, 'playing tragedy queen and taking things sublimely' (ch. 54). As for Will Ladislaw, he is one of those 'characters which are continually creating collisions and modes for themselves in dramas which nobody is prepared to act with them' (ch. 19). He is 'without any neutral region of indifference in his nature, ready to turn everything that befell him into the collisions of a passionate drama' (ch. 82).

It is here that the life-drama analogy begins to tangle with the thread of Nature in George Eliot's fiction. For if characters dramatize themselves then, as we saw earlier, Nature is 'that great tragic dramatist' (*Adam Bede*, ch. 4). And if characters, because of their impulse to dramatize, deceive both themselves and others, so

Nature may deceptively blend appearance and reality. When the stranger at Dinah's sermons thinks 'nature never meant her for a preacher', George Eliot comments:

> Perhaps he was one of those who think that Nature has theatrical properties, and, with the considerate view of facilitating art and psychology, 'makes up' her characters, so that there may be no mistake about them.
>
> *(Adam Bede*, ch. 4)

Something like a pun is operating here. Nature does, in one sense, make us up, endow us with hereditary attributes, compound what we really are. But the reality of our natural make-up is not to be confused with mere appearance, with 'make-up' in the theatrical, grease-paint sense of the phrase. George Eliot's novels are full of similar warnings about the deceptions of the surface:

> Every man under such circumstances is conscious of being a great physiognomist. Nature, he knows, has a language of her own, which she uses with strict veracity, and he considers himself an adept in the language. . . . Nature has her language, and she is not unveracious; but we don't know all the intricacies of her syntax just yet, and in a hasty reading we may happen to extract the very opposite of her real meaning.
>
> *(Adam Bede*, ch. 15)

When I discussed earlier this sense of Nature in George Eliot's novels, I asserted that 'it is no convenient abstraction but rather the icon of that mysterious complexity of things which she enacts so concretely in the body of her fiction'. One way in which she 'enacts concretely' is by linking the thread of Nature with other threads (e.g. the life-drama analogy) in her 'tangled skein'. But clearly, her use of apparent abstractions demands further justification. The problem is obviously sharpened when we meet a cognate example like this:

> Destiny stands by sarcastic with our *dramatis personae* folded in her hand.
>
> *(Middlemarch*, ch. 11)

The problem in a case like this is that the abstraction may be felt to be philosophically intrusive, blatantly suggesting a crude determinism. One answer to this might seem to be in Hardy's terms: he constantly protested that the readers of his novels took literally what was meant figuratively, that they mistook rhetorical tropes for assertions of belief:

> I should have to remind him . . . of the vast difference between the expression of fancy and the expression of belief. My imagination may have often run away with me; but all the same, my sober opinion – so far as I have any definite one – of the Cause of Things, has been defined in scores of places, and is that of a great many ordinary thinkers; that the said Cause is neither moral nor immoral, but *un*moral.... I have of course called this Power all sorts of names – never supposing that they would be taken for more than fancies. I have even in prefaces warned readers to take them as such – as mere impressions of the moment, exclamations in fact. But it has always been my misfortune to presuppose a too intelligent reading public, and no doubt people will go on thinking that I really believe the Prime Mover to be a malignant old gentleman, a sort of King of Dahomey – an idea which, so far from my holding it, is to me irresistibly comic.[4]

Hardy's answer sounds convincing, but it is hardly sufficient. If we feel uneasy about George Eliot's introduction of a sarcastic Destiny, we surely feel even more uneasy about a similar trope by Hardy – this, for example, from *The Mayor of Casterbridge*:

> The ingenious machinery contrived by the gods for reducing human possibilities of amelioration to a minimum – which arranges that wisdom to do shall come *pari passu* with the departure of zest for doing – stood in the way of all that. He had no wish to make an arena a second time of a world that had become a mere painted scene for him.
>
> (ch. 44)

The case is thus: both George Eliot and Hardy make frequent use of the life-drama analogy; both push this analogy beyond the pointing of a moral theme into the area of metaphysical speculation; both use it to suggest those aspects of man's life in which he figures as a determined creature. Why, then, should the nature and expression of George Eliot's determinism be felt to be more acceptable than Hardy's? On a local level it is partly a matter of tact in expression. In its context we respond to George Eliot's remark about destiny as a trope, whereas Hardy's takes on the assertive force of a statement, seeming to command our assent or disbelief. On a larger scale, it is partly a matter of plot and structure. George Eliot disperses her Determinism over a wide range of characters – we do not feel that any one of them is singled out. But in *The*

Mayor of Casterbridge every twist and turn of the narrative leads us back to a single figure, Henchard, so that he seems a doomed and predestined man. But ultimately – despite Hardy's protestations – I believe it is a matter of philosophy, of the way the life-drama analogy is informed by the author's controlling vision of the world. We may figure the difference between the two novelists in this way; Hardy is content simply to write:

> But most probably luck had little to do with it. Character is Fate, said Novalis, and Farfrae's character was just the reverse of Henchard's, who might not inaptly be described as Faust has been described – as a vehement gloomy being who had quitted the ways of vulgar men without light to guide him on a better way.

Contrast this with George Eliot's formulation and the differences are obvious:

> But you have known Maggie a long while, and need to be told, not her characteristics, but her history, which is a thing hardly to be predicted even from the completest knowledge of characteristics. For the tragedy of our lives is not created entirely from within. 'Character,' says Novalis in one of his questionable aphorisms – 'character is destiny.' But not the whole of our destiny. Hamlet, Prince of Desmark, was speculative and irresolute, and we have a great tragedy in consequence. But if his father had lived to a good old age, and his uncle had died an early death, we can conceive Hamlet's having married Ophelia, and got through life with a reputation of sanity notwithstanding many soliloquies, and some moody sarcasms towards the fair daughter of Polonius, to say nothing of the frankest incivility to his father-in-law.
>
> *(The Mill on the Floss, VI. 6)*

It is not enough to say that where Hardy merely accepts Novalis, George Eliot questions his dictum. The point is that *The Mayor of Casterbridge* as a whole contradicts Hardy's acceptance of Novalis. Granted that a great deal depends upon the character of Henchard, nevertheless the twists and turns of the plot, with its manifold coincidences, suggest some external Fate or Destiny working upon him. George Eliot is much more careful to allow for the reciprocal action of character and circumstance. 'Our deeds determine us as much as we determine our deeds' (*Adam Bede*, ch. 29). As much, but no more; the very syntax suggests how scrupulously the balance of forces is preserved. Throughout her novels she stresses the intermeshing of the human will with all those forces she sometimes sums up as Nature or Destiny:

> 'Our life is determined for us – and it makes the mind very free when we give up wishing, and only think of bearing what is laid upon us, and doing what is given us to do.'
> 'But I can't give up wishing,' said Philip impatiently. 'It seems to me we can never give up longing and wishing while we are thoroughly alive.'
>
> (*The Mill on the Floss*, V. 1)

One reason why George Eliot can successfully exploit the life-drama analogy to suggest the nature of man's conditional freedom is that this analogy is not isolated, but is linked up with all those other images of natural process which we analysed earlier. We are thus brought back to the way in which at a linguistic level her images and ideas intersect and interact; we see how the different threads are woven together into her 'tangled skein'. The intersection may be at the level of those neutral terms, so casual and brief that we never notice them at their cumulative work. Thus the one word *scene* may point in two directions, towards the natural scene and towards the stage. 'Marty and Tommy, who saw a perpetual drama going on in the hedgerows' (*Adam Bede*, ch. 18); 'the drama that was going on was almost as familiar as the scene' (*Adam Bede*, ch. 21); 'a green hollow almost surrounded by an amphitheatre of the pale pink dog-roses' (*The Mill on the Floss*, V. 1); 'he did not live in the scenery of such an event' (*Middlemarch*, ch. 4) – such phrases are literal or have the barest metaphorical charge. But they form the unobtrusive background to rather more developed images of the same thing. Thus we can move gradually from neutrality to something like this:

> Scenes which make vital changes in our neighbours' lots are but the background of our own, yet like a particular aspect of the fields and trees, they become associated for us with the epochs of our own natural history, and make a part of that unity which lies in the selection of our keenest consciousness.
>
> (*Middlemarch*, ch. 34)

Here *scene* gains a quasi-dramatic force from its context; the gentry are looking down on the tableau-like procession at Featherstone's funeral: 'the country gentry of old time lived in a rarefied social air: dotted apart on their stations up the mountain they looked down with imperfect discrimination on the belts of thicker life below'.

We move from this to something slightly more developed. George Eliot describes St. Oggs society in terms I have already quoted; comparing them with deserted Rhône villages, she says:

> I have a cruel conception that these lives those ruins are the traces of were part of a gross sum of obscure vitality that will be swept into the same oblivion with the generations of ants and beavers.
>
> (*The Mill on the Floss*, IV. 1)

And immediately she applies this to the Dodsons and the Tullivers, switching from the imagery of recapitulation to the image of the stage; 'this old-fashioned family life on the banks of the Floss, which even in sorrow hardly suffices to life above the level of the tragi-comic'.

This linking of Nature and stage can be far more emphatic; thus within one paragraph Mr. Tulliver is described in these terms:

> And Mr. Tulliver, you perceive, though nothing more than a superior miller and maltster, was as proud and obstinate as if he had been a very lofty personage, in whom such dispositions might be a source of that conspicuous, far-echoing tragedy, which sweeps the stage in regal robes, and makes the dullest chronicler sublime. . . . There are certain animals to which tenacity of position is a law of life – they can never flourish again after a single wrench; and there are certain human beings to whom predominance is a law of life. . . .
>
> (*The Mill on the Floss*, III. 1)

The rest of this paragraph, which modulates between these two views of Tulliver as tragedy king and as tenacious animal, states a very common theme in George Eliot's novels:

> The pride and obstinacy of millers, and other insignificant people, whom you pass unnoticingly on the road every day, have their tragedy too; but it is of that unwept, hidden sort, that goes on from generation to generation, and leaves no record. . . .

This is one of George Eliot's main emphases – that tragedy is to be found not merely in high-life romance or in extreme situations, but in homely and monotonous existence, in the great, ordinary course of everyday human life. *All* the world is a stage; George Eliot frequently uses the life-drama analogy to generalize her theme, to implicate her readers, to appeal to common human nature. Thus she speaks, for example, of 'that partial, divided action of our nature which makes the tragedy of the human lot' (*The Mill on the Floss*, VII. 3); such appeals are common in her fiction. And she can involve us in her vision of humdrum tragedy by linking the life-drama analogy with imagery drawn from Nature:

> Some discouragement, some faintness of heart at the new real future which replaces the imaginary, is not unusual, and we do not expect people to be deeply moved by what is not unusual. That element of tragedy which lies in the very fact of frequency, has not yet wrought itself into the coarse emotion of mankind; and perhaps our frames could hardly bear much of it. If we had a keen vision and feeling of all ordinary human life, it would be like hearing the grass grow and the squirrel's heart beat and we should die of that roar which lies on the other side of silence. As it is, the quickest of us walk about well wadded with stupidity.
>
> (Middlemarch, ch. 20)

It is *natural* that life should be tragic; to have said that calmly, without undue emphasis, to have given this recognition its proper place and proportions within our total awareness of life, in all its mysterious complexity – this is one of George Eliot's greatest achievements. It is part of the moral nature of her fiction; she strips away a little of our 'wadded stupidity' and enables us a little better to bear the burden of human reality. And she does more than merely *say* this – she enacts it, incarnates it in the structure of her stories, the nature of her characters and, ultimately, in the complex patterns of her language. Her words reverberate, her ideas expand and mutate, her images intersect and interact; all combining in one 'tangled skein' which is the very stuff of life itself. The few threads I have unravelled in this essay are, indeed, a representative 'sample of an even web'.

NOTES

1. Had he lived, W. J. Harvey would have revised and shortened this essay. [Editor's note.]

2. U. C. Knoepflmacher, *Religious Humanism and the Victorian Novel* (Princeton University Press, 1965).

3. In fact, Knoepflmacher has made a mistake here – due to depending on secondary sources: Huxley's relevant essays date from 1868 not 1864 (i.e. two years *after* Haeckel).

4. F. E. Hardy, *The Later Years of Thomas Hardy, 1892–1928* (Macmillan, 1930), ch. XVII, pp. 216–18.

X

THE PASTORAL OF INTELLECT
John Bayley

———————————————

GEORGE ELIOT's genius as a novelist lies, it seems to me, in the ways in which she explored and individualized that peculiarly nineteenth-century fictional form which might be called historic pastoral. She did not of course invent it. Balzac, whom she admired, and who – though with all the differences in the French tradition – comes closest to her, had already consciously set himself to do for the present what Scott had done for the past. The scope and grandeur of the enterprise consists not only in creating and characterizing the present as if it were the past, but of framing the one in terms of the other; and by insulating a prospect or a retrospect to establish a continuum in which the novelist's process can cope with the largest issues and the most diverse scenes and people; can distinguish and contemplate them so as to produce a panorama of social process, of case, type, and idea.

Behind George Eliot's own development of this creative method there are two important premises. One is that immensely serious and conscious search for the meaning of history and for an understanding of its process which we associate with the nineteenth-century heirs of Vico, with Hegel, Proudhon, and Marx. The other, closely intertwined with it, is the search for a moral system based on idea, which shall replace the received historic truths of religion. The fact of Jesus and his divinity is dubious or exploded: the idea of Jesus is timelessly valuable. Writing to Miss Sara Hennell in 1863, George Eliot remarks that Renan's *Life of Jesus* 'has so much artistic merit that it will do a great deal towards the culture of ordinary minds, by giving them a sense of unity between that far-off past and our present'. That shows very clearly the two connected premises behind her method; and shows us, too, how history becomes for her kind of creative intelligence a timeless present, the source and inspiration of culture and morals that would otherwise have to be built on vacancy.

The paradox is that when history is so consciously felt as idea, it is in one sense abolished as fact. The past is always with us, and not only reassures our present consciousness, but is identified with it. This explains the remarkable confidence with which George Eliot and other novelists embarked on historical subjects, a confidence which reminds us of Matthew Arnold's contention that ' the future of poetry is immense' because it immortalizes ideas, so that such a line as *La sua Voluntade e nostra pace* expresses for us, and will express for future generations, not something specific about Dante's God and Dante's sense of God, but something which we feel as part of the culture which bequeaths us our moral consciousness. The achievement of *Romola* is erected on the same premise.

What is potentially embarrassing about the dissolution of the fact in the all-embracing idea is that the actuality of other beings and other worlds, as separate and distinct from our own today, can become unrecognized or unimportant. And this is a danger that George Eliot, as we might expect, is fully aware of. She must therefore strive for exactitude, for detail, for distinction. 'The psychological causes', she writes to R. H. Hutton, 'which prompted me to give such details of Florentine life and history as I have given, are precisely the same as those which determined me in giving the details of English village life in *Silas Marner*, or the "Dodson" life, out of which were developed the destinies of poor Tom and Maggie.' And she indicates in the same letter what those causes were: 'It is the habit of my imagination to strive after as full a vision of the medium in which a character moves as of the character itself.' With this comment we are at the centre of the most weighty theoretical preoccupation of historic pastoral. It is clear, and it is also immensely impressive, that George Eliot did not see any need to distinguish between the process by which she hoped to actualize Romola, Guido, and Baldassarre and the process she brought to bear on the young Tullivers, Adam Bede, Silas Marner, or Dorothea.

What that process entailed was 'the severe effort of trying to make certain ideas thoroughly incarnate, as if they had revealed them-

selves to me first in the flesh and not in the spirit'. In the same letter
she also writes of her excitement over her 'attempt at a drama' –
The Spanish Gypsy – and how it is still 'in that stage of creation in
which the idea of the characters predominates over the incarnation'.[1]
We do not, it may be, find this emphasis wholly reassuring, not because it implies too abstract and intellectual a tendency, but because, on the contrary, the need to clothe her projections in the flesh,
to give them a local habitation and a name, strikes us as *too*
devotional, *too* loving. This over-insistence is the Nemesis of the
pastoral process of the great nineteenth-century realists, of Balzac
as of George Eliot. It is a process, above all, of making things and
people lovingly characteristic of themselves, but the very minuteness
and care in the externalization reveals all too clearly its origins in
the pictured world of historical idea, of pondered subject. It is for
this reason that Dr. Leavis was less than fair to Professor Elton's
comment that 'in exhaustively describing life, George Eliot is apt to
miss the spirit of life itself'. 'For anyone whose critical education
has begun', fumed Dr. Leavis, 'this must be breathtaking in its
absurdity.'

Not necessarily. Professor Elton's only fault was not to have gone
on to say what he meant here by 'life'. What he had in mind, I
would guess, is that George Eliot's comprehension of life cannot
allow for the contingent, the incongruous, the unframed, the in-
definitely questioned and receding aspects of experience, which are
not only what we have round us all the time, but which writers as
various as Jane Austen, Shakespeare, and Tolstoy are able without
apparent effort to represent in and through the artificiality of their
forms. It is not artifice that threatens 'life' in this sense, but the
pastoral attempt to secure too characteristic and comprehensive a
picture of it.

In making its ideas 'thoroughly incarnate' the intellect makes a
picture. George Eliot herself courts the pictorial analogy, as if
it afforded a proof of successful incarnation, emphasizing the
'Flemish' realism she strove for, in the scenes at the Rainbow Inn
in *Silas Marner*, and more studiously still in the Poysers and the
Dodsons. Perhaps a closer resemblance, however, is with the Victorian *genre* painters, with Bastien-Lepage and Leibl, Rossiter and
Holman Hunt, even with the historical *Weltgeschichtliche Bilder*
of Kaulbach, though she did not admire them. Flemish *genre* in
fact makes an impression very different from hers, an impression

in which objects and people appear to have been left over, as if by accident, in the created area of isolation and tranquillity. Be that as it may, it is the pictorial art of her own time, and not that of any earlier period, which lays such emphasis on what is characteristic for its own sake. (Martineau's picture, *Kit's Reading Lesson*, could well illustrate *The Mill on the Floss*. Hans Meyrick's projected picture in *Daniel Deronda*, of Titus sending away Berenice, *invitus invitam*, would have belonged to a rather grander form of the same *genre*. It is clearly intended to point to the Gwendolen-Deronda relation, a reference to history as meaningful as the references to Greek tragedy in *Adam Bede* and *Felix Holt*.) And, like that art, she uses our image of what was typical in the past to body forth her more contemporary incarnations. *Quattrocento* man casts his shadow over Stephen Guest:

> He might have been sitting for his portrait, which would have re-presented a rather striking young man of five-and-twenty, with a square forehead, short dark-brown hair standing erect, with a slight wave at the end, like a thick crop of corn, and a half-ardent, half-sarcastic glance from under his well-marked horizontal eyebrows.
>
> *(The Mill on the Floss, VI. 5)*

And even more emphatically over the Grandcourts as they appear before their fatal boating expedition:

> This handsome, fair-skinned English couple manifesting the usual eccentricity of their nation, both of them proud, pale and calm, without a smile on their faces, moving like creatures who were ful-filling a supernatural destiny – it was a thing to go out and see, a thing to paint. The husband's chest, back, and arms showed very well in his close-fitting dress, and the wife was declared to be like a statue.
>
> *(Daniel Deronda, VII. 54)*

Of course her groupings and dialogues, even when executed with what she called 'the subdued colouring, the half-tints, of real life', are always richly animated: to borrow the distinction of Lukacs, they are realistic, not naturalistic; in the spirit of Balzac and not that of Flaubert and Zola. Yet the devotional insistence on these incarna-tions leaves them no room not to be typical of what she had in mind; her love for them is inevitably a total possessiveness.

This possessiveness is most obvious when she is surveying the character who has no formed consciousness:

Hetty had never read a novel; if she had ever seen one I think the words would have been too hard for her; how then could she find a shape for her expectations?

(Adam Bede, ch. 13)

One must be found for her, and the 'finding of a shape' under these conditions exactly illustrates the technique of intellectual pastoral. This appeal to it makes Hetty seen more completely in her frame, as a character in a novel, precisely because it is claimed she cannot feel herself as one. And when possessiveness veers towards knowingness – the knowingness, that is, which comes from the author's assuming an absence of any self-knowledge in the character – the result can be not so far from Kipling's knowing emphasis on the framing environment to which the individual owes his recognizable self. Indeed, Kipling's pictorial analogies for his creative process – the 'overlaid tints and textures', etc. – are oddly reminiscent of George Eliot's, and may make us wonder whether this kind of picture vocabulary goes with a kind of art in which the individual is carefully 'shaped by the wider public life', though in such a comparison every advantage in scope and feeling, of calmness and generosity of temper, is of course, on George Eliot's side. One can compare, too, a certain kind of dialogue, heard as unmistakably in the carpenter's shop at the beginning of *Adam Bede* as among the officials in one of Kipling's best stories, *Without Benefit of Clergy,* and designed to instruct us in an environmental set-up at the expense of any actual and individual probability. Carpenters do not chat so as to reveal the workings of their calling to one another, and neither do civil servants.

I observed that George Eliot's confidence in recreating and re-feeling history as a part of her own mental life is something she shares with the other serious novelists of her age who make use of history. But there are some important exceptions. Flaubert worked as laboriously on the setting of Carthage for *Salammbo* as George Eliot did on that of Florence for *Romola,* and it is instructive to compare them: both, I think, are undervalued now after being overpraised in their own day. Flaubert may be said to have succeeded, ingeniously, in turning the very weakness of Naturalism – its appearance of unfeeling objectivity – into a historical truth. His Carthaginians are too remote in their meticulously barbaric world for us to understand them or feel anything for them (though as Saint-Beuve pointed out, this alienation is compromised by the palpably romantic *amour fatal* of the heroine). None the less, Flaubert's treatment implies a kind of truth that most of us today would accept. History can be reconstructed, after a fashion, but not *re-felt*: whereas George Eliot's history is coterminous with her own culture and her own being. Like her contemporaries, she admired the insipid *Esmond*, while ignoring Thackeray's much better first novel, *Barry Lyndon*, which was a deliberate attempt to debunk the sentimentalization of the past and to reconstruct an eighteenth-century hero in a literary *genre* of that time.

War and Peace is closer to her vision, for Tolstoy takes over his epoch as completely as she does hers – indeed, he insists on the essential sameness of human life throughout history. But Tolstoy totally rejects any labour on the characteristic. An extraordinary feature of *War and Peace* is the absence throughout its great length of any local colour, any account of houses, clothes, places, features, any striving for 'as full a vision of the medium in which a character moves as of the character himself'. Tolstoy goes further, and specifically disclaims any interest in many aspects of his apparently enormous world, in anything that is 'incomprehensible and strange' to him. Such an admission could only be made by a writer with immense experience and immense natural privileges, although – bizarrely enough – its tone reminds us of Jane Austen's mock-modest disinclination to leave her small world for the adventurous undertaking of a historical novel on the Saxe-Coburg family. The fact is that Tolstoy knew his world as Jane Austen knew hers, and not by anything approaching the process by which George Eliot united her childhood with her re-creation of the past and her vision of the future. A confidence in not knowing would have been impossible to her. Her details so laboriously acquired, so lovingly collected, must be all harmonized and shaped together. By contrast, Tolstoy's innumerable details all distinguish and disunite; they are, as it were, details of finger and hand, of voice and gesture, details that are not characteristic of the setting but contingent in the person. Though *War and Peace* and *Middlemarch* share a sense of the past that is also the present, a majestic grasp of a culture that is in both cases the summation of a sense of history, Tolstoy succeeds in abolishing history as pastoral where George Eliot confirms it.

I should perhaps make clear at this point, since the last comparison may seem particularly invidious, that I have nothing but admiration for the way in which George Eliot employs what I would call 'pastoral' as her chosen and yet inevitable form, the form in which – in G. K. Chesterton's words – 'culture becomes entirely conscious'. It is the form which preferably embodies both her intellect and her power of love, her scientific analysis and her devotional piety. It suits her, it *is* her, in the same way that Lawrence's most characteristic form (seen at its best in the 'bitty' elementals of *Kangaroo*) most surely and superbly conveys his essentiality. Indeed, we can concur wholeheartedly with Dr. Leavis's assumption of the affinity between the two. Both are intensely conscious of the traditions of their literature and race, but both are cut off, by that consciousness, from the involuntary participation in those things which produces another kind of art.

Dr. Leavis's comparison of George Eliot's sense of rural life with Shakespeare and Hardy is surely quite misleading, for this reason: Nothing could be less like Shakespearian dialogue than that rustic perfection of the Poysers, in which every confirming touch rings just too typical to be true. By contrast, the speech of Shallow, Dogberry, or Bottom, of Doll Tearsheet and Mistress Overdone shoots off into peculiarity and contingency: it continually suggests the presence of a world elsewhere, of an uninsulated oddity that is outside the immediate scope of artful presentation. This is surely an aspect of what we mean by the power of primary creation, and we are doing George Eliot no disservice in emphasizing that she does not and cannot exhibit it.

Hardy's is a different case, for he admired George Eliot and was influenced by her; and no less than she he was an intellectual, with all that the word implies. But he was also, as a novelist, something else, and we can see what it is if we compare the way he makes use of Tess with George Eliot's handling of Hetty Sorrel. Tess eludes Hardy's proclaimed vision of her. Her figure implies a more ambivalent and a more genial awareness than does Hardy's overt presentation of her story. Similarly, Hardy's rustics escape from their immediate and sometimes ponderously ironic typicality into a world of being that seems less specified and more instinctive. '*I never cared for life: life cared for me*' – his poem well illustrates the saving contradiction in Hardy's process. Life does indeed care for his creations, while George Eliot cares for hers too much for life – the larger and less congruous totality – to be given the same chance.

We learn another lesson about her mode, and the kind of

appreciation it requires, if we compare her didacticism with Tolstoy's. The clue to our acceptance of Tolstoy's purely didactic interludes in his great novels – if we do accept them, and I think most of his readers come to do so – is our growing sense that their kind of assertion is modified and even contradicted by the totality of the work, a totality which they help to expand and with which they ultimately harmonize. Tolstoyan contradiction simply enlarges: it neither muddles nor contracts. Events, families, the story, individuals such as Stiva and the old Prince Bolkonsky counterpoise the pressure of Tolstoy's views on history and family life: they embody the objections and exceptions and complete the whole. George Eliot's didacticism invariably echoes her story and is an aspect of it, so that if a rift occurs, as in *Middlemarch*, between what she asserts and what certain implications of the tale suggest, the upshot can only be weakening and diminishing. When she shows us over a consciousness – her comment reinforcing and echoing what plot and 'incarnation' have already arranged and destined – the thing succeeds in relation to her confidence and authority, and our assent to them. In other words, the more she 'uses' a character the more impressive her performance can be.

This is again an aspect of historic pastoral – the inner life of her most effective beings framed and typified as she frames her *genre* scenes. The inner life is seen, accumulated, and reconstructed like the interior of Silas Marner's cottage or the streets and houses of medieval Florence. It is precisely her strength that she can do this, but we are not to consider her folk as living among the contingencies of the non-pastoral world any more than we are to consider their minds not being open, like those streets and houses, to an accurate and painstaking scrutiny. Human motivation, like human history, is a matter of laborious but essentially feasible reconstruction.

All the more remarkable that her structuring of mind has a warmth and illumination, an understanding brooded in something like the medium of poetry. The *clou* that establishes Silas as particularly moving, showing, as it does, all the author's power of sympathetic reconstruction of a social phenomenon in the past now silted over by others of a different kind:

> Such colloquies have occupied many a pair of pale-faced weavers whose unnurtured souls have been like young winged things, fluttering forsaken in the twilight.
>
> (*Silas Marner*, I. 1)

We see here the best kind of use of historical imagination combined with the author's personal sense of identification with the weavers' mode of being, and with their sterile preoccupation about election and 'assurance of salvation', in a cramped solitude which has neither the wholesome thoughtlessness of rural routine nor the intellectually fructifying atmosphere of scepticism and analysis. She knew it herself; and by knowing it she can render it in a historical setting. *Romola*, though far more 'deeply studied and elaborately justified', rests on the same foundation. One of the best things in it, and already implicit in her first conception, is the killing power of highmindedness and penetration (George Eliot's own qualities) on the accommodating man whose virtues depend on an equivalent accommodation in others. With an uninsistent but very conscious justice, she shows how Romola destroyed Tito where Tessa would have preserved him:

> Poor Romola, with all her self-sacrificing effort, was really helping to harden Tito's nature by chilling it with a positive dislike which had beforehand seemed impossible in him; but Tessa kept open the fountains of kindness.
>
> (*Romola*, III. 50)

Tito is as much at home in Tessa's placidity as James's Gilbert Osmond is in Madam Merle's worldliness. Both are undone by the supposition that their wives will acquiesce in the limits which enable them to be good to themselves and to others.[2]

I should argue that it is the pure historic-pastoral artifice in which Tito is enclosed which makes him a more successful character – in terms of George Eliot's kind of genius – than is Lydgate in *Middlemarch*. We, and George Eliot, know where we are with Tito. The sticky end to which he comes is perfectly proper, and the coincidences necessary to push him toward it are equally acceptable in terms of her pastoral form. But she does not quite possess Lydgate. He is, or should be, too complex a figure, too involved in contemporary uncertainties to be made a pastoral case and held in the frame of her studious intentness. As a case history of a nineteenth-century gentleman-surgeon he is superb: as an accepted being he barely exists. The young enjoy Lydgate, as they enjoy *Middlemarch* as a novel, because the psychology of his case both instructs and flatters their inexperience: he gives them a valued sense of grasping the development of a life in literary terms, and hence of exercising a certain prognostic power over their own future and that of their friends. But at each re-reading Lydgate surely becomes less and less responsive and suggestive. He shares with Dorothea and with Ladislaw the prime defect of an unmanageable pastoral conception – the possibilities of life in him seem actually inimical to the kind of life that George Eliot can compass and create.

What I have in mind here can perhaps be demonstrated best by reference to the kind of character who seems to owe its success to precisely those elements which in George Eliot's treatment constitute failure. Of this order of being, I think, are Dolokhov in *War and Peace* and Jane Fairfax in *Emma*. Both are characters whose authors seem uncertain about what they have done, and who fall back – perhaps for that reason – on seeing them through the eyes of characters with whom they feel more at home and in whom they have a more instinctive confidence: Emma in the case of Jane Austen, and the Rostov family in that of Tolstoy. None the less, the pair unmistakably endorse their creator's gift in that they are both immensely and harmoniously suggestive: they offer themselves to the reader's own powers of query and exploration. Nor do we, as readers, feel that our exploration is inhibited or made superfluous by the author's intention: we feel, in fact, our contribution as an allowed aspect of the novel's scope.

But in *Middlemarch* this is not the case. Separately and in their relation to one another, Dorothea and Lydgate promote a muddle out of which the reader can do nothing to help the author. Even Rosamond Vincy is disconcertingly unframed by her author's unadmitted animosity towards her. Such an animosity can be a positive asset to Jane Austen, as we can see in her superb admission – *via* Emma – of her feelings toward the sort of paragon who is talked about as Jane Fairfax is talked about. Generous – solicitously generous – as she is, George Eliot tries to *make amends* for her feelings about Rosamond, a very different thing. Just how different we can see from the sybilline emphasis with which she assured a correspondent that her pen seemed to take on its own life when she described the confrontation of Rosamond and Dorothea, and that she wrote the scene straight out in a state of intense emotional excitement. This suggests something too near the intimacies of the unconscious for her method to master and make clear, and indeed I think we feel on re-readings that the famous scene is without true psychological justness and resonance; that it is a *scène à faire*, stopping short – in our reception of it – at a superficially dramatic and sentimental level.

The emotional working of amends and animosities, and the muddle it makes, is very different here from that analysis which is so engaging in the portrait of Maggie; so coolly perceptive in the relations of Romola and Tito; and so initially promising in the dialogues of Dorothea and Celia. George Eliot drew on her elder sister for Celia, as she had drawn on her own youthful self for Maggie, and this may be why *Middlemarch* opens with a more sophisticated version of the confidence sustained throughout *The Mill on the Floss*. But *Middlemarch* goes on to break the pastoral mould, and though in doing so it becomes George Eliot's most diverse and ambitious novel, it also incurs weaknesses which reveal how much that mould suited her kind of creative intelligence.

George Eliot could put herself into her fictional form with triumphant ease – Maggie shows that. But Dorothea shows that she cannot afford to be disingenuous about it. *Middlemarch* contains her most moving moments – Dorothea and Casaubon walking hand in hand in their mutual disillusionment down the bleak corridor is one of many such. They are much more memorable than the safe, pastoral themes: the Bulstrodes, Mrs. Bulstrode's forgiveness. They are things we associate with the best in another kind of novelist, Trollope or Dickens, who appear to compose on the same level as their creations and who are not dependent, as George Eliot is, on total possession from above. But George Eliot cannot achieve such moments without a corresponding loss of control. Her relation to Dorothea, and through Dorothea to Casaubon, is very close. Herbert Spencer and Lewes himself are on the threshold, and she must draw back: honesty and amplitude of demonstration are no longer possible. There is something much more intimate here than anything in the legend of Mark Pattison – it is as if she seized on what is tellingly characteristic in the make-up of the male scholar in order to protect herself from actualities to which she could not come closer. But in this case even the characteristic lands her in the area of the unmanageable. If we leave Mark Pattison out of it, there remains at the back of the Casaubon theme something more complex and incongruous than George Eliot can allow for; an unexplored dimension which threatens her balance and meaning, instead of enhancing the total effect of the work as I have suggested it can do in Tolstoy or Jane Austen. While if we let Mark Pattison in, we must admit, I think, that the motivation of his marriage and the complexity of his nature is much more interesting in itself, and in what it might offer another kind of novelist, than it becomes in George Eliot's treatment. Her handling of the *clou* here is thus the reverse of how Henry James thought its process should go. Art is not refining and completing the voiceless complications and full-stops of life, but schematizing and suppressing them, even as it claims to give them a faithful and meticulous recording.

Almost as if she had sensed that there were elements in *Middlemarch* that were too intractable for her natural mode, George Eliot returned in *Daniel Deronda* to the historic pastoral. Like *Felix Holt*, it presents a human drama coupled with an historical vision, and Zionism is peculiarly well fitted to George Eliot's pastoral in that it unites past with future in one embracing ideal.[3] The relations of Deronda and Gwendolen are similarly felicitous, as those of Lydgate and Dorothea are not, for both are characters completely insulated in a device for emotional and cultural inquiry, undisturbed by the disconcerting personal echoes heard in *Middlemarch*. The accepted view that the novel divides in two, and that the Gwendolen part is good, the Deronda part bad, seems to me to ignore the homogeneity of the themes here, and their successful harmonization – *Middlemarch* is much more radically divided. The coming to awareness of Gwendolen – the universe pressing in upon her – parallels Deronda's discovery of his historic fate and duty: both are equally cut off from any perspective of individuality; both exemplify their author's preoccupation with the development of social and cultural consciousness. The process is set off by the absolute unreality, in ordinary fictional terms, of Grandcourt, which makes him as effective in the rôle required of him as is the Mephistopheles of Goethe's *Faust*. And yet *Daniel Deronda*, unlike *Middlemarch*, is surely a novel which increases in intellectual interest when we re-read it and measure it against the growth of our own awareness of historical and cultural developments; showing us, as it does, a graphic model of typically modern kinds of sexual and national emancipation. These two themes are united by the mode in which both are drawn, the personal case – as in all good pastoral fiction – becoming one with the cultural. The more we understand George Eliot's method and mind, the less we feel that one half of the book is somehow 'real' and the other half not.

The same, with some reservation, might be said about *Felix Holt*, in which the Aeschylean tragedy of the Transomes is very much a part of George Eliot's cultural dream, emerging out of that solitary and immensely impressive self-education of hers, even more evident in the borrowed Greek motif in the story of Arthur Donnithorne. The Transome story may strike us as more effective than the idealization of the young Radical, but there is no doubt that both have the same kind of inspiration and represent the same order of imaginative construction. Though he emphasizes the influence on the Transome side of her reading of Greek tragedy, Dr. Leavis is surely misleading when he goes on to suggest that Felix himself shows the same traces of an over-indulgent handling that disturbs us in Dorothea. The two cases are very different. Felix is right in his place and according to the formula of the book: he is an adequately incarnated ideal. And though his speech and the language of his mind are as much made up as those of Tito Melema in *Romola*, they are equally unsentimentalized, executed with that rigour of perception which is not only built into the author's method, but is the most interesting aspect of her contemplative powers. Felix is purely a creature of her imagination, but for that very reason he can be seen with its corresponding clarity – that clarity that traces his relation to Esther (for example, his determination to let her know, however much more miserable it may make her, what it costs *him* to give her up). With Dorothea, on the other hand, George Eliot is divided between her *clou* of a 'later-born Teresa' (who might in practice be something like a Florence Nightingale) and her more confusingly autobiographical and intimate claim for a womanly woman: a muddle fatally accentuated by the solution of Ladislaw. It is true that she effectively wishes the division on to the character ('these blundering lives') but the real blunder is further back – in the author.

Clarity and certainty are the virtues of characterization in the pastoral mode, and the final proof of George Eliot's superiority in this mode is surely given by Maggie Tulliver. For obvious reasons, Maggie is the most completely *known* of all George Eliot's characters, a triumph of 'the contemporary culture and emancipation becoming conscious of itself'. She is perfect, and her perfection means, among other things, that the book resolves her potentiality completely in its form. Like the death of Tito and the marriage of Felix and Esther, her drowning is a perfectly satisfactory *dénouement*, because it is wholly in keeping with the mode that determines her presentation. Such a character cannot be allowed to escape into the merely suppositious, the possibilities of continued existence: the fact that Dorothea is allowed to escape in this way shows that her author is not so wholly in control of her, and for George Eliot this can only be a weakness. Because of Casaubon, she cannot quite bring herself to face what constitutes the attractiveness of Ladislaw; and the true outline she draws of her men is blurred in the consequence; but Stephen Guest is the perfect foil for Maggie. Their physical attrac-tion for each other is rendered with intensity and complete assur-ance, because it is far enough back in George Eliot's life to be recollected in honesty; and the same assurance disposes of them. Her letters show her sensitive about her endings, and the arbitrary bounds to her subjects which they assert. But though they are the endings of popular and traditional fiction they are also, at a deeper level, in complete harmony with the more intellectual part of her process. Because she made such good use of her characters she had to finish them off. Her high intelligence is always on the best terms with humble fictional device.

To say this is not a depreciation – on the contrary. George Eliot's novels are about the coming of the kind of consciousness which Freud hoped for the human race. 'Where Id was shall Ego be.' And therefore we have no subterranean connection with her or with her characters, except the ones we have noticed in *Middlemarch*, which are, as it were, an embarrassment to all parties. We feel instead about her art, as Mrs. Carlyle did when she read *Scenes from Clerical Life*, that 'it makes us *feel friends* at once and always with the man or woman who wrote it'. Yet with other great authors we wish to have the connections that are other than friendly, and to have experience with them in modes of being which George Eliot could not analyse or approve:

> Don't you agree with me that much superfluous stuff is written on all sides about purpose in art? A nasty mind makes nasty art, whether for art or any other sake; and a meagre mind will bring forth what is meagre. And some effect in determining other minds there must be, according to the degree of nobleness or meanness in the selection made by the artist's soul.
>
> (Letter to Edward Burne-Jones, March 1873.)

That puts the matter, as she saw it, very trenchantly. However much we rejoice to concur in the principle, we none the less have to admit – with however many complex qualifications – that it is the 'nasty mind' of Dickens and Dostoevsky, of Proust and Henry James.

even of Tolstoy, that we respond to in their creations. The contradictions in their natures are not only a prime source of creative energy, but also of their many-sidedness, their 'negative capability'. And it is the glory of George Eliot that all her capabilities are positive ones.

NOTES

1. Extracts from these letters are taken from *George Eliot's Life as Narrated in Her Letters and Journals*, edited by J. W. Cross, pp. 372, 366 and 402.

2. It is usually taken for granted that James's *Portrait of a Lady* owes much to the *Middlemarch* situation, but in fact it possibly owes even more to the triangular pattern of *Romola*, with Tessa oddly but very effectively transmuted into Madame Merle.

3. She was a great admirer of Lessing's *Nathan der Weise* – 'dear Lessing whose great spirit lives immortally in this crowning work of his' (*Berlin Recollections*).

INDEX

Adam Bede, viii, x, 19–41, 60, 81, 83, 84, 153, 154, 161ff., 166, 168, 173, 180, 190ff., 195, 196, 202, 203
Aeschylus, 210
alienation, 27ff., 37ff., 60, 133
altruism, *see* sympathy, doctrine of
American Civil War, 142
Anglicanism, 21
Arkwright, Richard, 36
Armstrong, Isobel, viii, 116 (essay)
Arnold, Matthew, 100, 114, 200; *Culture and Anarchy*, 99, 113
Austen, Jane, 79, 120, 201, 204; *Emma*, 208

Bagehot, Walter, 64, 122; *English Constitution*, 99
Balzac, Honoré de, 199, 201, 202
Barth, Karl, 11
Bastien-Lepage, Jules, 201
Bayley, John, vii, ixff., 199 (essay)
Belinsky, 36
Bennett, Joan, 45, 62, 78, 79
Blackwood, John, 2, 8, 13, 59, 60, 66
Blake, William, 6
Blanc, Louis, 139
Bodichon, Barbara, 156
Bradley, F. H., 159
Bray, Cara, 5
Bray, Charles, 3, 156
Brontë, Charlotte, 120; *Jane Eyre*, 43ff., 48, 50–1
Browning, Robert, 62, 169
Bunyan, John, 58
Burke, Edmund, 137
Burne-Jones, Edward, 212

Carlyle, Mrs, 212
Carlyle, Thomas, 17, 35, 145; *Past and Present*, 21, 34

Chambers, Robert, *The Vestiges of Creation*, 156, 157
Chapman, George, *Revenge of Bussy d'Ambois*, 167
Chapman, John, 4
Chartism, 110ff., 139–40
Chaucer, Geoffrey, 62
Chesterton, G. K., 205
children, 65, 69ff., 165–6, 174ff., 181ff.
Clough, Arthur Hugh, 66
Coleridge, S. T., 44; *The Ancient Mariner*, 24
Comte, Auguste, 37, 160
Conrad, Joseph, viii
convention, social, 23, 34, 37, 40, 51; *see also* natural law
Coveney, Peter, 65, 70
Crabbe, George, 62, 66
Craik, Mrs, *John Halifax, Gentleman*, 10
Cross, John, 46

Dallas, E. S., 52
Daniel Deronda, x, 37, 81, 89, 91ff., 96, 133–50, 191, 202, 210
Dante Alighieri, 200
Darwin, Charles, 53, 156ff., 164, 172; *Origin of Species*, 156, 157
determinism, social, 49, 91, 116, 137, 158, 160ff., 185, 194; *see also* evolution
development theory, *see* determinism
dialogue, use of, 63ff.
Dickens, Charles, viii, 114, 209, 212; *Bleak House*, 107; *David Copperfield*, 43ff.
didacticism, 20, 116ff., 149, 206
Disraeli, Benjamin, 103
Dostoevsky, Feodor, 212
Dowden, Edward, 149

duty, 48, 55, 89, 145, 184

education, 139
egoism, *see* personality
Eliot, T. S., 159
Elton, Professor Oliver, 201
Evangelicalism, 5, 8, 17, 48
Evans, Isaac, 46
Evans, Marian (real name of George Eliot), 5
evolution, 22, 28, 33, 36, 153, 156ff., 171, 185; *see also* determinism

fantasy, 42ff., *see also* imagination
Felix Holt the Radical, x, 94, 99–115, 136, 137, 139ff., 150, 202, 210, 211
Feuerbach, Ludwig, ix, 2ff., 7ff., 11, 17, 32, 37, 38, 48, 133ff., 138, 159, 160; *Essence of Christianity*, 2, 134
Fielding, Henry, 116, 189; *Tom Jones*, 24
Flaubert, Gustave, 139, 202ff.
Forster, E. M., 8
Franklin, Benjamin, *Poor Richard's Almanack*, 36
Freud, Sigmund, 153, 212
Frye, Northrop, 87

Gaskell, Mrs, x, 37; *Mary Barton*, 108 110; *Ruth*, 10, 29; *Sylvia's Lovers*, 34
Goethe, J. W., von, *Faust*, 210
Golding, William, *Lord of the Flies*, 176
Gombrich, E. H., 22
Goode, John, viii, x, 19 (essay)
Gregor, Ian, 19, 34

Haddakin, Lilian, viii, 59 (essay)
Haeckel, Ernst Heinrich, 153
Haight, Gordon, 48, 157, 164
Hardy, Barbara, vii (introduction), 12, 39, 42 (essay), 79, 82; *The Novels of George Eliot*, 103
Hardy, Thomas, 100, 193, 205; *Far from the Madding Crowd*, 28, 47; *The Mayor of Casterbridge*, 194–5; *The Return of the Native*, 47
Harrison, Frederic, 107, 111
Harvey, W. J., viiff., 65, 104, 108, 117, 118, 151 (essay)
Hazlitt, William, 1
Hegel, G. W. F., 199
Hennell, Sara, 82, 85, 160, 199

history, x, xi, 17, 20, 21, 37, 79, 99ff., 142, 148ff., 168ff., 185, 199ff.
Holloway, John, *The Victorian Sage*, 74, 75
humanism, 2, 5, 7, 9, 14, 36, 51, 69, 76, 134ff., 199
humour, 16, 52, 65, 144; *see also* irony
Hunt, Holman, 201
Hutton, R. H., 80, 95, 200; *Studies in Parliament*, 99
Huxley, T. H., 151, 152, 155, 157, 160

Ibsen, Henrik, *Ghosts*, 107
idealism, 136ff., 147ff.
imagery, 151–98; animal, 12, 22, 28, 151–2, 162ff., 173ff.; birds and reptiles, 12, 151, 152; blindness, 43–4, 83; child, 65, 69ff. (*see also* children); cross, 87, 89; death's head, 89; drama, 189ff.; gold, 65, 72–3; ring, 84ff.; river, 46, 47, 134, 169; skein, mesh or web, 137, 160, 180, 193; tabernacle, 87, 88; trees, 164, 165
imagination, 44, 49, 154, 182, 183, 185, 190ff.
Industrial Revolution, 100
irony, 162ff., 169ff.

James, Henry, viii, 45, 46, 78, 81, 85, 93, 119, 149, 159, 207, 210, 212; *Portrait of a Lady*, 47, 50, 126, 213n.
Janet's Repentance, see *Scenes of Clerical Life*
Jews, 142, 144, 147ff.

Kaulbach, 201
Keats, John, 44, 118
Kenner, Hugh, 159
Kettle, Arnold, x, 99 (essay)
Kingsley, Charles, *Alton Locke*, 110
Kipling, Rudyard, *Without Benefit of Clergy*, 203
Knoepflmacher, U. C., 155; *Religious Humanism and the Victorian Novel*, 151, 152

Lamartine, Alfonse de, 138
Lawrence, D. H., xi; *Kangaroo*, 205; *The Rainbow*, 100; *Sons and Lovers*, 56
Leavis, F. R., 45, 52, 109, 201, 205, 211; *The Great Tradition*, vii
Leibl, 201

Lerner, Laurence, *The Truthtellers*, 49
Levine, George, xi, 78 (essay)
Lewes, G. H., 2, 5, 10, 13, 51, 62, 79, 157, 160, 209
liberalism, middle-class, 112–14, 138
love, 4, 9, 32, 52, 66–7, 134
Lowe, Robert, 100
Lukacs, 202
Lyrical Ballads, 1, 24; *see also* Coleridge, S. T.; Wordsworth, William

Main, Alexander, 116
Martin, Graham, x, 133 (essay)
Martineau, Harriet, 202
Marx, Karl, 38, 133, 135, 136, 138, 170, 199; *Theses on Feuerbach*, 38, 133, 135
materialism, 35–6, 135–6
memory, personal integration and, 67, 153, 180ff., 199–200
Methodism, 19, 21, 23, 25, 35, 37, 39
Middlemarch, viii, xi, 13, 37, 55, 60, 81, 83, 85, 89, 91ff., 95, 116–32, 136, 140, 141, 149ff., 163, 169ff., 177, 192, 193, 198, 204, 206ff.
Mill on the Floss, The, xiff., 42–58, 60, 79, 81, 154, 155, 157, 161, 163ff., 168, 172, 173ff., 179ff., 190ff., 195ff., 202, 209, 211
Miller, Hillis, viii
mob, fear of, 113, 139
Mr. Gilfil's Love-Story, see *Scenes of Clerical Life*

narrator, intrusion of, 12–13, 32, 171, 186ff; *see also* sayings
natural law, 23, 27, 29, 34, 37, 40
Nature, 68, 69, 166ff., 174, 181, 183, 192ff.

Oldfield, Derek and Sybil, ix, 1 (essay)
organicism, x, 16–17, 20ff.; *see also* determinism

pastoral, 19ff., 199–213
Pattison, Mark, 209
Paul, St, 169, 170
personality, whole, 7; egoism, 141ff., 175, 177, 183; memory and integration, 67, 153; outward symbols, 84ff.; search for identity, 148
Plato, 185, 187
Pope, Alexander, *Essay on Man*, 24
Preyer, Robert, 116

Protestantism, 21
Proudhon, Pierre Joseph, 199
Proust, Marcel, 212
Providence, 45, 47, 49, 172, 174, 183

Quaker Girl, 109

radicalism, x, 17, 101ff., 137ff.
reader, attitude to, 120ff., 185ff.
realism, problem of, xi, 10, 18ff., 50, 79; characters defined empirically, 52; humour and, 62; ideological shaping of, 26, 29, 34, 36ff.
Reform Bill, (1832) 99, 110, 140; (1867) 100, 140
religion, 38–9, 47ff., 52, 53, 71–2, 75, 133, 172, 199
Renan, Ernest, *Life of Jesus*, 199
Revolution, French, 1848, 137ff., 150
Riehl, Wilhelm Heinrich, *The Natural History of German Life*, 20
Ritchie, Lady, *Blackstick Papers*, 53
Robinson, H. Crabb, 5
Romola, xi, 51, 60, 78–98, 169, 200, 203, 207, 211
Rossiter, Thomas Pritchard, 201
Rutherford, Mark, 109

Sad Fortunes of Amos Barton, see *Scenes of Clerical Life*
Sainte-Beuve, C. A., 203
sayings, 116ff., 171
Scenes of Clerical Life, ix, 1–18, 212; *Janet's Repentance*, 5, 8–9, 11, 12, 15, 94; *Mr. Gilfil's Love-Story*, 7–8, 11ff.; *Sad Fortunes of Amos Barton*, 1ff., 10, 11, 13, 15, 135
Scott, Walter, 17, 54, 55, 199
secularism, *see* humanism, idealism, religion
self-denial, 48ff.; *see also* sympathy
sexual choice, 46, 50, 51
Shakespeare, William, 44, 201, 205; *As You Like It*, 185; *King Lear*, 5; *The Tempest*, 186, 187
Sibree, John, 137
Silas Marner, viii, xi, 52, 56, 59–77, 79ff., 161, 167, 191, 200, 201, 206
sociology, 16–17, 23ff., 29, 33, 34, 37, 102, 109ff., 145
Spanish Gypsy, The, 201
Spencer, Herbert, 26, 36, 37, 155, 157ff., 209; *First Principles*, 157ff.;

Spencer, Herbert (*cont.*)
  Principles of Psychology, 154, 155,
  157
Steiner, George, 117
Stephen, Leslie, 107
Stoicism, 167, 185, 189
suffrage, 99, 100, 111, 139
Svaglic, Martin J., 47, 48
sympathy, doctrine of, 1, 8–9, 29, 30,
  134, 146, 159, 182, 183

Tennyson, Alfred Lord, *Idylls of the
  King*, 169
Thackeray, W. M., 121ff., 131, 186ff.;
  Barry Lyndon, 204; *Esmond*, 204;
  The Newcomes, 187; *Vanity Fair*,
  186–7
Thomas à Kempis, 48, 54, 55, 183
Tillotson, Geoffrey, 121; *Thackeray
  the Novelist*, 186
Tolstoy, Leo, 201, 206, 213; *War and
  Peace*, 204, 208
Trollope, Anthony, 209
Turgenev, Ivan, 149

Utilitarians, 26

Vermeer, Jan, 22
verse, use of, 62ff.
Vico, 199

Willey, Basil, 6, 134
Williams, Raymond, 113, 137
Wilson, Edmund, viii
Wise, Witty and Tender Sayings,
  116
wish-fulfilment, *see* fantasy
Wordsworth, William, 44, 62, 66, 67,
  69ff.; 'Michael', 62, 65; 'Old Cumberland Beggar', 66; *The Thorn*, 24

Yeats, W. B., 170
Yonge, Charlotte, *The Heir of Red-
  clyffe*, 10
Young, Arthur, 24

Zionism, 142, 148, 149, 210
Zola, Émile, 202